Understanding
and Teaching
the ICT National
Curriculum

1E

Also available:

Information and Communication Technology in Primary Schools: Children or Computers in Control?
Richard Ager (1-84312-042-9)

Science and ICT in the Primary School: A Creative Approach to Big Ideas
John Meadows (1-84312-120-4)

Understanding and Teaching the ICT National Curriculum

Franc Potter and Carol Darbyshire

 David Fulton Publishers

David Fulton Publishers Ltd
The Chiswick Centre, 414 Chiswick High Road, London W4 5TF

www.fultonpublishers.co.uk

First published in Great Britain in 2005 by David Fulton Publishers

David Fulton Publishers is a division of Granada Learning Limited, part of ITV plc.

10 9 8 7 6 5 4 3 2 1

Note: The right of Franc Potter and Carol Darbyshire to be identified as the authors of their work has been asserted by them in accordance with the Copyright, Designs and Patents Act 1988.

British Library Cataloguing in Publication Data
A catalogue record for this book is available from the British Library.

ISBN 1-84312-133-6

Typeset by FiSH Books, London
Printed and bound in Great Britain

Contents

Preface

We have found that students training to be primary teachers, and indeed many teachers, find it difficult to make sense of the ICT National Curriculum and how to teach it. They therefore have a tendency to fall back on the QCA Scheme of Work for Key Stages 1 and 2, and to deliver that without really understanding the main objectives underlying that scheme. In addition, the emergence of computer suites in primary schools has sometimes led to an emphasis on teaching ICT skills rather than ICT capability, and a decontextualisation of ICT from other subjects.

We have also found it difficult to refer trainee teachers and teachers to any books or articles that might help them. While there is an abundance of literature about using ICT to enhance other subjects, there is very little to help students and teachers understand the ICT National Curriculum. We have therefore written this book to fill that gap, and we think it will prove useful to teachers as well as students training to be teachers.

We would recommend reading Chapters 1 and 2 before reading Chapters 3, 4, 5 or 6. Some readers may find they can skim-read Chapter 1. We would also recommend reading Chapters 3 to 7 before reading Chapter 9.

Acknowledgements

We would like to thank Andrew Brookes for his helpful comments on earlier drafts of this book and for stimulating discussions.

We are also grateful to the following publishers for permission to include screenshots etc:

Bourneville database activity
Cadbury's History Learning Zone
http://www.cadburylearningzone.co.uk/history/

Flowol 2
Keep IT Easy
www.flowol.com
Available from: Data Harvest Group Ltd, 1 Eden Court, Leighton Buzzard, LU7 4FY
http://www.data-harvest.co.uk/index.html

'How to make peppermint creams' – a multimedia recipe
Priory Woods School, Tothill Avenue, Netherfields, Middlesbrough, TS3 0RH
http://www.priorywoods.middlesbrough.sch.uk/index.htm

Information Workshop and Black Cat Designer
Granada Learning, Granada Television, Quay Street, Manchester, M60 9EA
http://www.granada-learning.com

My World **(Dress Teddy and Find Ted)**
Dial Solutions, PO Box 84, Leeds, LS15 8UZ
http://www.dialsolutions.com/welcome.html

RM Colour Magic
RM plc, New Mill House, Milton Park, Abingdon, OX14 4SE
http://www.rm.com/

Textease
Softease Ltd, Market Place, Ashbourne, Derbyshire, DE6 1ES
http://www.softease.com/

The Big Bus
7 Dukes Court, Chichester, PO19 8FX
www.thebigbus.com

The Model Shop
Sherston Publishing Group, Angel House, Sherston, Malmesbury, Wiltshire, SN16 0LH
http://www.sherston.com/

1

The nature and purpose of the ICT National Curriculum

Objectives

- To understand what the ICT National Curriculum is all about – its fundamental nature and purpose
- To understand the essence of each aspect of the ICT National Curriculum and to understand how the Programmes of Study relate to the uses of ICT in the wider world
- To be able to relate the Programmes of Study to your own experiences of ICT

Consider two scenarios, both relating to Year 6 children:

Scenario 1: Some children are using a computer to take part in an interactive maths activity in which they have to type in the correct answer to a multiplication question. If their answer is correct they move on to the next problem; if it is incorrect they are given another go.

Scenario 2: Some children are trying to find out, using a spreadsheet, how to construct a sheep pen, with the maximum area, from a fixed amount of fencing and a brick wall, and to create a graph to demonstrate their solution.

While both are relevant to the mathematics National Curriculum, only the second is relevant to the ICT National Curriculum. In the first case, the ICT capability required of the pupils is negligible (all they have to know is how to use the keyboard to type in their answer); in the second, they have to know how to use a spreadsheet to solve a real problem, including entering formulae and creating a graph.

The first scenario shows how ICT can be used to enhance the learning and teaching of another subject (in this case mathematics), making negligible demands on the children's ICT capability. This use of ICT to help another subject has been referred to as 'ICT across the curriculum'; 'The use of ICT in subject teaching', and is now referred to as '*e-learning*'.

The second scenario is concerned with using ICT for a real purpose, but demands a certain degree of ICT capability, that of being able to use some of the functions of a spreadsheet. The ICT National Curriculum is concerned with ICT as a subject in its own right. It is also concerned with ICT capability, rather than just ICT skills, and so is always concerned with using ICT for a real purpose. It will therefore usually relate to another National Curriculum subject other than ICT.

ICT as a subject in its own right

The Programmes of Study of the ICT National Curriculum are composed of four 'aspects':

1. Finding things out
2. Developing ideas and making things happen
3. Exchanging and sharing information
4. Reviewing and modifying work as it progresses

and, in addition to the four aspects, the fifth Programme of Study is entitled 'Breadth of study'.

These Programmes of Study are statutory orders, that is what schools are legally required to teach. For Key Stage 2 they are defined as follows in the statutory orders (the differences between Key Stages 1 and 2 will be discussed in the chapter concerned with progression):

The Programmes of Study

Finding things out (the first aspect)

1. Pupils should be taught:
(a) to talk about what information they need and how they can find and use it [for example searching the internet or a CD-ROM; using printed material; asking people]
(b) how to prepare information for development using ICT, including selecting suitable sources, finding information, classifying it and checking it for accuracy [for example finding information from books or newspapers; creating a class database; classifying by characteristics and purposes; checking the spelling of names is consistent]
(c) to interpret information, to check it is relevant and reasonable and to think about what might happen if there were any errors or omissions.

Developing ideas and making things happen (the second aspect)

2. Pupils should be taught:
(a) how to develop and refine ideas by bringing together, organising and reorganising text, tables, images and sound as appropriate [for example desktop publishing; multimedia presentations]
(b) how to create, test, improve and refine sequences of instructions to make things happen and to monitor events and respond to them [for example monitoring changes in temperature; detecting light levels and turning on a light]
(c) to use simulations and explore models in order to answer 'What if ...?' questions, to investigate and evaluate the effect of changing values and to identify patterns and relationships [for example simulation software; spreadsheet models].

Exchanging and sharing information (the third aspect)

3. Pupils should be taught:

(a) how to share and exchange information in a variety of forms, including e-mail [for example displays; posters; animations; musical compositions]

(b) to be sensitive to the needs of the audience and to think carefully about the content and quality when communicating information [for example work for presentation to other pupils; writing for parents; publishing on the internet].

Reviewing, modifying and evaluating work as it progresses (the fourth aspect)

4. Pupils should be taught to:

(a) review what they and others have done to help them develop their ideas

(b) describe and talk about the effectiveness of their work with ICT, comparing it with other methods and considering the effect it has on others [for example the impact made by a desktop-published newsletter or poster]

(c) talk about how they could improve future work.

Breadth of study (the fifth and final Programme of Study)

5. During the key stage, pupils should be taught the Knowledge, skills and understanding through:

(a) working with a range of information to consider its characteristics and purposes [for example collecting factual data from the internet and a class survey to compare the findings]

(b) working with others to explore a variety of information sources and ICT tools [for example searching the internet for information about a different part of the world; designing textile patterns using graphics software; using ICT tools to capture and change sounds]

(c) investigating and comparing the uses of ICT inside and outside school.

The essence of the Programmes of Study

This section sets out to explain what the ICT National Curriculum is really about, its fundamental nature and purpose and the essence of the aspects. This includes examining what is different about ICT from other ways of doing the same activity.

To explain this we shall consider them in a slightly different order. First, we shall consider *Making things happen* (part of the second aspect), then *Exchanging and sharing information*, next *Finding things out*, and finally, *Developing ideas* (the other part of the second aspect). We shall then consider *Reviewing and modifying work as it progresses* and *Breadth of study*, and how these relate to the concept of ICT Capability.

First and foremost, it is necessary to bear in mind that the ICT National Curriculum is meant to relate to the uses of ICT in the wider world (we shall return to this later in the section on *Breadth of study*). Consequently, we need, even when considering the teaching of ICT at Key Stage 1, always to have one eye on where the ICT National Curriculum is leading.

Making things happen: using ICT to control devices

The essence of this aspect is control – using ICT to control devices. In the wider world, control goes hand-in-hand with sensing – with automated computer control the computer performs different tasks depending upon what it senses.

Key words

control
instructions
programs
repeats
procedures
sensing
input
output
control boxes
flow diagrams
programmable toys

When you walk into your favourite supermarket the likelihood is that the doors will open automatically. This is ICT 'making things happen' – a sensor is activated by your approach, and this, in turn, causes a device to be activated, which controls the opening of the door.

An intruder alarm works in the same way – it can be activated by an infra-red sensor, a pressure pad under the carpet, a magnetically operated switch that is tripped when you open the front door, etc.

The turning on and off of street lights is controlled by ICT – at dawn, light sensors detect the presence of light and switch the street lights off; at dusk, they detect the absence of light and switch them on.

Not all ICT-controlled devices involve sensors. For example, most microwave ovens are controlled by the operator who enters the temperature, cooking time etc. and then presses the start button.

In order for computers to be able to control devices they have to be programmed. Most, if not all, of this programming is done by someone other than the user. In the last example the user only enters the cooking time and temperature; the rest of the programming is built in by the manufacturer. *Making things happen* is all about children understanding what ICT can do in the wider world, which includes understanding something about how such devices are programmed, by actually writing simple programs themselves. The usual programming language that children learn at Key Stage 2 is LOGO and/or a program that represents a flow diagram such as Flowol.

Learning how to program a control system (such as an intruder alarm) is a quintessential example of ICT as a subject in its own right. It cannot be said to be unique, as there are examples of mechanical control systems (e.g. regulators in steam engines), but it is easy to see what counts as ICT subject knowledge in this case – at the core of it is computer programming.

The relation of *Making things happen* to *Developing ideas* is explained in the section 'Developing ideas' (see p. 12).

Expectations at the end of Key Stage 2

At the end of KS2 pupils are expected to know about computer control and sensing and to be able to write a program with repeats and procedures to control one or more devices, e.g. to turn lights on and off, to control a motor, etc. They are also expected to be able to use a data logging device to sense changes in the environment. In addition, they should be able to combine sense and control by programming a device to sense an input, and respond to this input with some sort of output – for example, responding to a change in light intensity by turning a light on or off (as with computer control of street lights).

Exchanging and sharing information: using ICT as a tool to help communicate ideas, feelings and emotions

The essence of this aspect is using ICT to enhance communication. In the wider world, ICT is used to enhance communication. For example, architects will use ICT to show what the final building will look like, and use this in a brochure, as part of their attempt to obtain the contract for the work.

Key words

communicating
conveying ideas, feelings, emotions etc. in a variety of media
painting programs
drawing programs
word processors
music programs
desktop publishing (dtp) applications
multimedia authoring programs
e-mail
hypertext
animations
virtual reality
video clips
sound clips
hypermedia
branching stories
hyperlinks

Whilst *Exchanging and sharing information* implies a two-way process, and should always be thought of as such, in the Programmes of Study the main thrust of this aspect is concerned with it from the perspective of the creator of the message, rather than the reader of the 'text' – what the 'transmitter' of 'information' is doing, rather than the 'receiver'.

The word 'information' in *Exchanging and sharing information* should not be thought of in its narrow connotation of merely factual information, but in its wider meaning, which could include feelings and emotions etc.

Hence a paint package may be used by an artist, or a music synthesiser by a musician, to help convey feelings and emotions, and, as such, that artist or musician will be using ICT to 'exchange and share information'. As the Programmes of Study at Key Stage 2 state, 'Pupils should be taught how to share and exchange information in a variety of forms, including e-mail [for example displays, posters, animations, musical compositions].'

So any kind of 'text' created with the help of ICT is subsumed under *Exchanging and sharing information*. The end-product may be electronic, or paper-based – so using a word processor to write a letter is also part of this aspect.

Just as at the core of *Making things happen* lies programming, so at the core of *Exchanging and sharing information* lies **hypermedia**, including **web authoring**.

Before we continue, it may help to define the kinds of programs used in this area. Strictly speaking,

- A text editor will allow the creation and editing of pure text files – files which contain characters that can be entered by pressing any of the keys on an ordinary (QWERTY) keyboard.

- A word processor will also allow the creation and editing of text files with formatting such as bold, underlining, different size fonts, etc.

- A DTP (desktop publishing) package will include all the functions of a word processor but will also allow the incorporation of images and text frames etc.

- A multimedia authoring program will include the functions of a DTP package but will also allow the inclusion of sound clips, animations, video clips and hyperlinks (links from a word or an object, such as an image, to another section of the 'text').

- A web authoring program is one example of a multimedia authoring program, which has as its end product the creation of a website.

Nowadays most word processors (such as Microsoft Word) have some of the functions of DTP packages and multimedia authoring programs. It is possible in Word to insert text boxes and images (DTP features), and sounds (a multimedia feature), and to create hyperlinks (a hyper-media feature). Hence the original distinctions between applications as defined above are being blurred.

Consider accessing the Web in order to purchase a book, video, CD, CD-ROM or DVD from Amazon.co.uk. When you enter the web address (or URL) you arrive at the home page of Amazon.co.uk, from which you can navigate by clicking on various hyperlinks to other pages (there is also a facility to search the site). The various books and CDs etc. are listed, often with an accompanying image. If you wish to buy an item, you click on a hyperlink to add the item to your shopping basket, and when you have finished selecting your purchases you click on another hyperlink, enter your name, address and credit card details and wait a day or two for your shopping to arrive by post.

Amazon have done most of the *Exchanging and sharing information* by setting up the website, and this is where the most ICT capability is needed. But you have entered your name, address and credit card details and sent them to them electronically. Hence there is a two-way communication.

Learning how to create a website, or some other hypermedia environment, is another quintessential example of ICT as a subject in its own right. The ability to combine different media and to make links, so that the 'text' can be read in a non-linear fashion, is what makes this aspect of ICT qualitatively different from other ways of communicating.

This unique aspect of ICT does not just affect the way we communicate; it is also likely that it will affect how we think. In this connection it is interesting to note the points Postman (1983: 30–1) makes concerning the effect of the introduction of printing:

> ...bookmakers could no longer use the scribal manuscript as their model of a book. By the mid-sixteenth century, printers began to experiment with new formats, among the most important innovation being the use of Arabic numerals to number pages. The first known example of such pagination is Johann Froben's first edition of Erasmus' *New Testament*, printed in 1516. Pagination led inevitably to more accurate indexing, annotation, and cross-referencing, which in turn led to, or was accompanied by, innovations in punctuation marks, section heads, paragraphing, title paging, and running heads. By the end of the sixteenth century the machine-made book already had a typographic form and a look – indeed, functions – comparable to books of today...
>
> Here it is recalling Harold Innis's principle that new communication technologies not only give us new things to think about but new things to think *with*. The form of the printed book created a new way of organizing content, and in so doing, it promoted a new way of organizing thought. The unyielding linearity of the printed book – the sequential nature of its sentence-by-sentence presentation, its paragraphing, its alphabetized indices, its standardized spelling and grammar – led to habits of thinking that James Joyce mockingly called ABCED-mindedness, meaning a structure of consciousness that closely parallels the structure of typography...even such a cautious scholar as Elizabeth Eisenstein believes that the emerging format of books, its particular way of codifying information, 'helped to reorder the thought of all readers, whatever their profession'.
>
> There can be little doubt that the organization of books into chapters and sections came to be the accepted way of organizing a subject: the form in which books presented material became the logic of the discipline.

It remains to be seen exactly how hypermedia will affect our way of re-ordering the way we think, reorganising subjects, and the logic of disciplines, but, rest assured, it will.

Expectations at the end of Key Stage 2

At the end of KS2 pupils are expected to be able to combine different media in a multimedia authoring program, and to make decisions about the most appropriate combination of media to communicate to a specific audience. For example, they might decide to record some of their text as speech for younger children who are still at the beginning stages of learning to read, and insert this into a multimedia authoring program.

Finding things out: using ICT as a tool to locate information, and to explore patterns and relationships in information in order to find things out

Key words

Is it true that…?
sort
search
boolean operators (AND, OR, NOT)
locating information
handling information
exploring patterns and relationships
display information as charts / graphs
databases
graphing programs

Consider someone accessing an information source such as a CD-ROM, or the internet, to find out specific information (for example, information about Brazil – what language is spoken there, its main exports etc.). The information may sometimes be found by doing a simple keyword search, but sometimes information may only be found quickly and easily by carrying out a more complex search. For example, to find out an ant's sense organs it is possible to enter the search term **ant** in a CD-ROM, and then to scan the article for the section containing the desired information. But it is far easier to enter the terms **ant** AND **sense organs**. You will then be taken straight to the desired section.

This is one way of finding things out with ICT – using information sources **to locate information**. ICT differs from more traditional sources, such as paper-based encyclopaedias etc., in that huge amounts of information can be searched rapidly, easily and accurately.

The largest information source is, of course, the internet, and by using appropriate searching techniques it is possible to locate information much more quickly and easily than from non-electronic sources. For example, a colleague of ours who worked in the library helped a student find the information she was looking for on the internet in the following manner:

> The request was for the full text of the lyrics of a song called 'Edith and the kingpin', which might or might not have been written by Joni Mitchell. The student could remember the title and some of the words in the text, but that was all. We tried various anthologies of contemporary verse under the title, but with no success. Because the student did not even know if Joni Mitchell had written the lyrics, we could not pursue the search easily through music anthologies.
>
> I did a www search and found the Joni Mitchell home pages, indexed by someone else. There is a section on lyrics which lists her albums in chronological order. The student had a vague idea of when she might have recorded the song, and I found the text of the lyrics under an album called *Shadows and Light* (I think that's right – it certainly has 'Shadows' in the title) – and there I found the lyrics.

Consider a company that wishes to find out more about the spending habits and preferences of its customers. Enter the loyalty card, which automatically records the purchases of individuals, and groups of individuals, and provides them with a database of information they can use to help them with stock control, advertising and special offers. With internet shopping, companies do not even need to offer a loyalty card – when you purchase one item from Amazon.co.uk you are given a list of other suggested purchases.

Customers who bought *Coupling: The Complete Third Series*, also bought:

- *Coupling* – Series 2
- *Book Group, The* – Complete first series (2002)
- *Coupling* – Series 1 – the complete series
- *Two Pints of Lager and a Packet of Crisps* – Series 1 and 2 (2001)
- *Teachers* – Series 2

Using ICT with databases such as these allows the user to find out patterns and relationships, as well as simply locating information.

To take a simpler example, a database of information about insects can be searched to locate information about a particular insect – e.g. the diet of a particular moth. But it can also be searched in order to find out about patterns and relationships, such as whether there is a relationship between length and wingspan etc.

Some useful and interesting databases are being made available on the internet. For example, the **Cadbury Learning Zone** site has census information about Bourneville a hundred years ago. This provides a meaningful opportunity for exploring patterns and relationships. For example, children might question the data to find out whether or not men and women were equally likely to have worked for Cadbury's.

Exploring patterns and relationships with large sets of data is something that it is not very practicable to do without ICT, although if the pay-off is big enough the will can be found to do it. So whereas, in the past, looking for patterns and relationships in, for example, large sets of census data may have been the preserve of someone researching for a PhD, with ICT this is now something that is within the reach of pupils in the upper end of the primary school.

These two different kinds of *Finding things out* – locating large information sources and exploring patterns and relationships – are not, in principle, unique to ICT. As we have said, keen PhD students would, in the past, have been motivated enough to wade through census data by hand. But it is the vast amount of information that can be accessed, quickly and easily, that, in practice, makes this aspect of ICT unique.

So whereas, in principle, this aspect of ICT may not be unique, in practice it is, in the same way that the electric drill and other power tools have made some projects possible for the DIY enthusiast that would otherwise have been impractical.

Expectations at the end of Key Stage 2

At the end of KS2 pupils are expected to be able to search for information in databases, on CD-ROMs and on the internet. They are also expected to be able to interpret their findings and to critically evaluate the information they have found. In addition, they are expected to be able to handle information in databases by looking for patterns and relationships.

Developing ideas: using ICT as a tool for thinking – *trying things out*

Key words

What would happen if…?
trying things out
solving problems
trial and error (trial and success)
experimenting
predicting
solving problems
models
simulations
creating a model for the purpose of understanding
selecting options
choices

The label 'Developing Ideas' for this aspect of the ICT National Curriculum does cause some confusion, and so it is helpful to think of it in terms of using ICT to *try things out*. In addition, we will need to distinguish between different kinds of 'developing ideas', as can be seen from the extract from the Programmes of Study below – 2(a), 2(b) and 2(c) need to be considered separately.

Extract from the Key Stage 2 Programme of Study:

Developing ideas and making things happen

2   Pupils should be taught:

(a) how to develop and refine ideas by bringing together, organising and reorganising text, tables, images and sound as appropriate [for example, desktop publishing, multimedia presentations]

(b) how to create, test, improve and refine sequences of instructions to make things happen and to monitor events and respond to them [for example, monitoring changes in temperature, detecting light levels and turning on a light]

(c) to use simulations and explore models in order to answer 'What if…?' questions, to investigate and evaluate the effect of changing values and to identify patterns and relationships [for example, simulation software, spreadsheet models].

Models and simulations

The Programme of Study 2(c) is all about simulations and models. While not unique to ICT, computer simulations and computer models are of a qualitative order to other kinds of simulations and models. What makes them so different is the ability to easily change the values and note the different effects. This allows the user to solve problems and explore patterns and relationships. It allows the user to **try things out**.

Computer models are very useful to help solve problems, to predict what might happen, and these models can also help develop our understanding of the world.

Solving problems

If you want a new kitchen, go to the showroom and see the actual units. But what is the best arrangement for your particular kitchen? Have your kitchen measured, enter this information into a computer program, and you can see different layouts and combinations of units before selecting the one that you prefer. Using such a computer model you are able to predict in advance what the different layouts will look like, and solve the problem as to which is the best for your circumstances.

Other examples are gardening simulations, where you can see what a particular arrangement of plants will look like throughout the year, or

- colour mixing simulations, e.g. on the Dulux website
- makeover simulations, e.g. on the Clairol website.

In the past, in order to test the aerodynamics of a new shape of car/aeroplane etc., a model of the car was created, and this was tested in a wind tunnel. Now such modelling is done with computers, effectively using 'virtual' wind tunnels. This is not only cheaper, but also different shapes can be tried out much more quickly and easily.

Short-term weather forecasting is very reliable these days, whereas 30 years ago it was very unreliable. The reliability is due to the use of computer simulation.

As was reported in the Radio 4 programme *Leading Edge* on 13 June 2003, work is well under way on a computer model of the human heart:

> Denis Noble, from Oxford University, has spent the last three decades trying to come up with a computer model of the heart, and we can expect, in the next year or two, that the first virtual heart will start beating in the middle of a supercomputer.
>
> One big advantage of such a model is that new drugs can be tested without resort to the use of animals. Indeed, some work has already been done with an American drug company to find out why treatment for high blood pressure was causing some unusual readings for some patients, and he was able to help that company satisfy American regulations. This does give a glimpse of the potential power of this new approach. And no animals were sacrificed in using the computer model.

These are all examples of using computer models or simulations in order to predict what would happen if...? to solve a problem.

Patterns and relationships

In addition to using an existing model to help solve a problem, we can also create a model for the purpose of furthering our understanding.

In order to predict the weather we need to have enough understanding of which variables affect the weather, and to be able to create a mathematical model of the weather. But as our knowledge is imperfect, we can of course create more than one mathematical model and test each forecast against the way the weather actually turns out. Testing out the mathematical models helps us test the underlying theories, and so advances our knowledge and understanding of the factors that influence the weather.

Computer modelling of this kind has been very influential in helping us to understand and predict human memory – Information Processing Psychology. Weizenbaum (1984: 160–5) outlines how psychologists used a computer model to increase our understanding of rote learning.

When we create computer models for the purpose of understanding we are essentially using ICT as a tool for thinking. As we shall be discussing in more detail in Chapter 6, for Papert (1980) Logo was essentially a *tool for thinking*, in the same way as other, more concrete models, were a tool for thinking. For him, gears served as a model for abstract mathematical ideas, and the equation $3x + 4y = 10$ immediately evoked the differential. In this case the gears were used to think about formal systems; they served as 'objects-to-think-with'. In the same manner, Logo can be 'a tool to think with'; it can serve as a model for abstract mathematical ideas. Papert conjectured that computers can help concretise (and personalise) the formal.

All the above examples relate to the cognitive domain – in other words, they all relate to thought. But there are, of course, other models and simulations which relate more to the psychomotor domain, one of the best-known being the flight simulator. It is, of course, invaluable – it is far better for learner pilots to make their mistakes in a flight simulator than with real planes.

The examples above are all concerned with simulations of the real-world environment, but there are models/simulations of imaginary situations – as with adventure game programs – and these are perhaps the earliest experiences that children have of simulations.

Developing ideas and its relation to *Making things happen*

We have already seen how ICT can be used to control devices. When programming the computer with the sequence of instructions to, say, control a set of traffic lights, essentially what we produce is a computer model. So this is one way in which *Making things happen* relates to *Developing ideas*.

More significantly, however, is the fact that in the process of producing these instructions it is most unusual to get the program right first time. What is more usual is that, once created, the instructions need to be tested and revised (improved and refined) to achieve the intended outcome. The person creating the program will *try them out*, and then revise them accordingly, until they get them to work correctly.

In both these senses, then, one can see how *Developing ideas* is related to *Making things happen*, and why they are both related in one aspect. We shall be discussing this in more detail in Chapter 6.

It is possible, with a simple program (simple, that is, relative to the ability of the programmer), to imagine the programmer making something happen without the need to try things out or develop their ideas, but usually the process does involve trial and error – it involves the user not only creating, but also *testing, improving* and *refining* sequences of instructions (see the Programme of Study reference 2(b) above).

How *Developing ideas* is related to *Exchanging and sharing information*

Developing ideas is also related to *Exchanging and sharing information* in a similar manner. The Programme of Study 2(b) states that pupils should be taught 'how to develop and refine ideas by bringing together, organising and reorganising text, tables, images and sound as appropriate [for example, desktop publishing, multimedia presentations]'

Take the use of a word processor to help communicate ideas, to help exchange and share information. Just as it is possible to create a simple text (simple, that is, relative to the writing ability of the author) without revising the text, so usually the process of writing involves some revision. Moreover, writing things down helps clarify our thinking. This is sometimes known as the 'heuristic' function of writing, and has been encapsulated by the saying 'How can I know what I think until I see what I write?' (attributed to a number of different authors, amongst them W.H. Auden and E.M. Forster).

Sometimes we write things down just to clarify our thinking, without intending to share it with others. So creating a text can serve to communicate with others, to clarify our thinking (develop our ideas), or both. Writing extended text, such as an undergraduate essay, to demonstrate understanding usually involves both, even if the only person the writer communicates with is their tutor.

The same is often true of creating other 'texts' – of images and sounds etc. The composer is usually concerned that his/her compositions are performed – that is, he/she is usually concerned to share his/her **products** with others. But in the **process** of composition, he/she will try out different ways of expressing himself/herself, and, in so doing, develop his/her musical ideas.

Similarly, a painter is usually concerned with sharing his/her products with others, but in the process of painting he/she will try out different ways of expressing himself/herself.

We can also think of a text as a model – a description of, say, a journey can be thought of as a simulation of that journey. We get engrossed in novels; they have the ability to conjure up a scene for us – and, with a really good one, it is 'just like being there'.

So just as there is a relationship between *Developing ideas* and *Making things happen*, so there is also a relationship between *Developing ideas* and *Exchanging and sharing information*.

Both relationships are reflected in the content of the Programmes of Study – namely 2(b) and 2(a), but only the connection between *Developing ideas* and *Making things happen* is reflected in the title of the aspects.

Further complexities of *Developing ideas* will also be highlighted when progression is discussed in Chapter 6.

Is *Developing ideas* related to *Finding things out*?

We saw, earlier, that computer models can not only help us solve problems, but also help us develop our understanding of the world.

When we solve a problem we find something out – for example, the best layout for our new kitchen. When we develop our understanding of the world we find something out. In both these senses the process of modelling – that of trying things out – helps us with the product –

which in this case is finding a solution to a problem, or helping us develop our thinking.

The relationship between *Developing ideas* and *Finding things out* will be explored in more detail when we examine progression in Chapter 6.

Exchanging and sharing information	Using ICT as a tool for communicating information
Finding things out	Using ICT as a tool for locating information and handling information
Making things happen	Using ICT as a tool for control (including systems which include devices for sensing)
Developing ideas	Using ICT to try things out; using ICT as a tool for thinking

ICT Capability

The fourth aspect of the Programmes of Study – *Reviewing, modifying and evaluating work as it progresses*, and the final section, *Breadth of study*, will be discussed in more detail in subsequent chapters. They are only discussed briefly here, in as much as they help introduce the notion of ICT capability, which itself will be discussed in much more detail in Chapter 2.

Reviewing, modifying and evaluating work as it progresses

The ICT National Curriculum is not about the learning and teaching of ICT skills (or techniques), but rather about ICT capability.

In brief, ICT capability is the knowledge, skills and understanding necessary to be able to make good use of ICT in a realistic, purposeful way.

This, of course, includes the skills/techniques necessary to make use of the relevant ICT applications, and to *apply* those skills/techniques, but it goes beyond this; it includes being able to select the best ICT tool for the job in question, and even whether or not to use ICT in the first place.

These two key features are reflected in the Programme of Study (KS2) as follows for *Reviewing, modifying and evaluating work as it progresses* (4a) which states that 'Pupils should be taught to describe and talk about the effectiveness of their work with ICT, comparing it with other methods and considering the effect it has on others [for example, the impact made by a desktop-published newsletter or poster]'.

In other words, pupils should be taught to appreciate that ICT is not being used simply because they are being told to by the teacher, but because ICT is more efficient and effective for some purposes and not for others. For example, ICT is better for writing extended text requiring some careful thought in how to express oneself (e.g. writing an essay), whereas leaving a note for the milkman is more appropriately done by scribbling a note on the back of an envelope with a pencil.

Breadth of study

The ICT National Curriculum is designed to work towards pupils learning how to choose the most appropriate ICT tools, and to be able to apply them for particular purposes in the wider world.

It is therefore most important that attention is drawn, whenever the ICT National Curriculum is being taught, to investigating and comparing the uses of ICT inside and outside school.

This is reflected in the Programmes of Study (KS2) as follows:

Breadth of study

5. During the key stage, pupils should be taught the Knowledge, skills and understanding through:
(c) investigating and comparing the uses of ICT inside and outside school.

The model below was developed within NCET (now Becta) as a way of representing the processes and concepts involved in the development of IT (now ICT) capability:

The links between the separate elements of *Reviewing, modifying and evaluating work as it progresses, Breadth of study*, and NCET's model of ICT capability are clear to see, and so underlines the importance of these two Programmes of Study. Nevertheless, we shall be describing a much more detailed analysis of ICT capability in the following chapter, as outlined by Kennewell *et al.* (2000). We consider their analysis provides a much clearer picture of what constitutes ICT capability, which in turn will help teachers ensure that pupils achieve ICT capability.

Activities

1. Within this chapter you will have read the short sections headed, 'Expectations at the end of KS2'. What is your opinion on the breadth and depth of the ICT curriculum? For example, were you surprised at the expected levels of achievement in primary school or would you have expected an eleven-year-old to have this level of knowledge and understanding in such a technological age?

2. We have indicated that the ICT National Curriculum relates to the uses of ICT in the wider world. How does the Programme of Study reflect your experience and use of ICT? Make notes on the following:

   - In what ways have you seen ICT used to make something happen?
   - In what ways have you used ICT to make something happen?

   - In what ways have you seen ICT used to exchange and share information?
   - In what ways have you used ICT to exchange and share information?

   - How many of the ICT tools listed on page 6 are you familiar with and how have you used them in your everyday life?

   - In what ways have you seen ICT used to find things out?
   - In what ways have you used ICT to find things out?

- In what ways have you seen ICT used to develop ideas?
- In what ways have you used ICT to develop ideas?

3. Within this chapter you will have read the section headed *Breadth of Study* and seen that *investigating and comparing the uses of ICT inside and outside of school* is part of the Programme of study. How might you incorporate this work into a lesson/series of lessons? Remind yourself of the essence of each aspect of the ICT curriculum and the expectations at the end of Key Stage 2. Choose one aspect and then outline how you could plan for pupils to investigate and compare the uses of ICT inside and outside of school, in relation to your chosen set of knowledge and understanding. What resources would you use? Which visitors might you invite into the classroom? What out-of-school experiences could you plan for? You may find the following headings useful when responding:

- An aspect of the ICT NC
- Investigating and comparing the uses of ICT inside and outside of school. Detail the knowledge and understanding relating to the chosen aspect of ICT
- Ideas for lessons/parts of a lesson. Resources to be used (including visitors), possible school trips

2

The nature of ICT capability

Objectives

- To understand the nature of ICT capability and, in particular, the notion proposed by Kennewell *et al.* (2000) that it comprises five components – routines, techniques, concepts, processes and higher-order skills;
- To understand each of Kennewell's five components of capability and be able to identify them within an ICT project. For example, identify each component in the production of a publication

At the end of Chapter 1 we described a simple and very general explanation of the notion of ICT capability, with reference to the model developed by NCET. Our experience, however, is that this raises more questions than it provides answers, and in this chapter we shall discuss the notion of ICT capability in more detail. To do this we shall lean heavily on the work of Kennewell *et al.* (2000). We have found this to be the most useful explication of ICT capability and we would urge the reader to read Chapter 2 of that book to supplement the account given here.

Kennewell *et al.* (2000) conclude that ICT capability comprises five components:

- routines (or basic skills)
- techniques
- concepts
- processes
- higher-order skills

Techniques and routines

A routine, or basic skill, is an operation that does not require conscious thought – it has been automatised. Kennewell *et al.* (2000) give as examples motor operations such as *moving the mouse* to point at a cell on the screen, dragging a file from one window to another, or *double-clicking* to open an application.

A technique is an operation which still requires a degree of conscious thought. So when a technique becomes automatised it can be said to have become a routine.

Learning to drive provides a good illustration of how techniques become automatic. In the process of learning to drive we first of all learn the individual techniques, such as steering, changing gear, and so on, but at first they require a great deal of conscious thought, and paying attention to some may interfere with others. Some learner drivers steer unintentionally to the left or right with their right hand when changing gear with their left. Some find it difficult to read road signs at the same time as concentrating on the process of driving. In contrast, most experienced drivers have had the experience of reaching their destination without having been aware of driving at all – the techniques needed to drive have become so automatic (including where and when to turn into different roads) that they have been carried out without any conscious effort at all. In other words the techniques have become routines or basic skills.

At this point it is worth mentioning the work of Fitts and Posner (1967) in relation to motor skills, who have identified three phases in the learning of motor skills:

1. The **cognitive** phase. The initial stages are concerned with trying to understand what the task or skill is all about. This is a stage where events and cues which demand much attention early on, go unnoticed later.

2. The **associative S-R learning** phase or intermediate phase. This is so called because it marks a period when old habits previously learned are tried out and are either consolidated if successful or else discarded. Gross errors are gradually eliminated. Actions are better-timed and smoother movement patterns emerge.

3. The **automaticity** phase. During the final stage of learning, skilled movements become increasingly autonomous, less subject to interference from other, ongoing activities and environmental distractions. Skills require less processing; i.e. they can be carried out while new learning is in progress or while the performer is engaged in other activities.

The associative learning phase corresponds to the learning of techniques, whereas the automaticity phase corresponds to those techniques becoming routines or basic skills.

Concepts

The cognitive phase emphasises the importance of conceptual understanding. Fitts and Posner state that the initial stages are concerned with trying to understand what the task or skill is all about. For example, understanding the difference between an *effect* and a *style* is essential to being able to learn the difference between them, and key to being able to use them appropriately. One advantage of using styles is that we can change, say, a heading in many ways with a couple of mouse clicks. If a style is defined as *Arial, size 16, bold, underlined* and *centred*, then all these changes will be made at once. Moreover, if we change our mind about what style we want our headings to be, we can redefine the style, and all the headings in our document will change instantly – we would not have to change each heading.

Conceptual understanding underpins the learning of techniques, and enables transfer of learning. As Kennewell *et al.* (2000) explain:

> The *high-road learning* of techniques is supported by the progressive understanding of key concepts . . . and general ICT principles, which enable ICT-capable learners to explore confidently

when solving problems. If we encourage pupils to reflect on the use of techniques across contexts and situations, they are more likely to generate principles, ideas and strategies that are widely applicable (Salomon and Globerson 1987: 631).

It is much easier to use a technique than it is to describe or explain it. However, making techniques explicit or stateable is likely to support concept development and the possible transfer of techniques to new situations. The techniques we selected in a particular problem situation are a function of the context, the resources available and our strategic knowledge. They are underpinned by concepts, but their application depends also on the features and the structure offered by the technology, and the knowledge the user has of these.

For example, when we first show a child how to insert an image into a publication, it is helpful to talk about *selecting* the object by *clicking*, and to refer to *handles* and *dragging* when sizing or moving the object. If we use the same words in another context – or, better still, prompt the child to use the words – the concepts should start to develop.

Processes

These are key to the ICT National Curriculum, and the attainment target level descriptions are essentially descriptions of processes, or sets of processes.

As Kennewell *et al.* (2000: 22–3) explain:

Processes are multi-stage procedures for achieving specified goals. For example, the process of developing a publication would, in the case of a desktop publishing package, involve a sequence of techniques such as:

■ select the page to work on;
■ create a number of frames;
■ enter text into frames;
■ choose text style;
■ import images into frames;
■ adjust size/position of frames.

The particular techniques and the sequence are not fully determined by the goal, and the user needs an understanding of both the goal and the tools available in order to make appropriate choices. Sometimes the choice made will not produce the desired effect, and a different technique will be tried. Reflection on this mistake will lead to learning which improves the user's ability to make an appropriate choice in the future.

Processes represent a significant part of the knowledge, understanding and skills described in the strands of the National Curriculum for ICT. It is the nature of these general processes that should be the basis for deciding which subjects might best incorporate pupils' work within the strands. They are often very complex and require a sound conceptual base in order to manage them effectively. Learning such processes requires a substantial degree of personal autonomy and active involvement on the part of the pupil. They are not associated purely with ICT, as they deal with the way in which ICT interacts with problem-solving situations in other disciplines or in the real world, rather than the technology itself. It is this aspect of ICT that distinguishes it from other subject disciplines – in its most significant aspects, it exists only in juxtaposition with other disciplines or real-world situations.

That is not to say that ICT is not a real discipline: the lines of progression described by the National Curriculum are legitimate and meaningful. Rather it is to point out that progression in knowledge and understanding in ICT takes a form very different from progression in the other subjects of the curriculum, demanding both an authentic context and a far higher level of pupil autonomy and problem-solving skills than is usually the case in school. It is difficult to discuss the learning of such processes in isolation from the other higher order skills, knowledge and understanding involved in ICT capability: metacognitive skills and metacognitive knowledge.

Producing a class magazine is not simply a question of children being able to string together a series of techniques in a predetermined manner. Rather it is a process, which *includes* being able to put together a number of techniques, but also being able to choose the appropriate techniques. Part of being ICT-capable is being able to decide which tool, and which feature of which tool, to use for oneself.

Higher-order skills

In order to execute processes the pupil has to be able to apply higher-order skills. These include (see Kennewell *et al.* 2000:23):

- recognising when the use of ICT might be appropriate or effective;
- planning how ICT resources, techniques and processes are to be used in a task;
- conjecturing, discussing and testing the strategies and data to be used;
- monitoring the progress of problem-solving activities;
- making and testing hypotheses;
- evaluating the outcomes of using ICT for a task;
- explaining and justifying the use of ICT in producing solutions to problems;
- reflecting on the learning that might have occurred during the task.

Higher-order skills, processes, concepts and techniques

The relationship between these different elements can best be explained with some examples. Let us take the example above, namely the process of producing a publication. As has been mentioned, this would involve using a sequence of techniques with a desktop publishing package such as:

- selecting the page to work on;
- creating a number of frames;
- entering text into frames;
- selecting the text style;
- importing images into frames; and
- adjusting size/position of frames.

But the process goes beyond mechanically following a predetermined sequence of techniques; it involves making decisions along the way. First of all, whether or not to choose to use a DTP package. Then, decisions such as:

- making choices as to how many frames, in what position, and what size to create;
- making choices as to which text styles to use in different places;
- making choices as to which images to import;
- making choices as to the size and position of the frames.

In order to make these choices the pupil has to use higher-order skills, such as those mentioned above, for example:

- recognising when the use of ICT might be appropriate or effective;
- planning how ICT resources, techniques and processes are to be used in a task

It is in using these *higher-order skills*, in order to make choices as to how to apply the *techniques* they have learned, that enable the pupil to execute the *process*, and in so doing the pupil demonstrates their *ICT capability*.

It is of course possible to imagine a situation where the pupil unquestioningly follows a list of instructions devised by someone else as to what to do, but in that case the pupil would not demonstrate their ICT capability and would not be executing the process in the sense that it is being used here.

To take another example, consider a child learning to cut and paste text in a word processor. The *concept* of what is happening is fairly easy for the children to understand. It is very similar to what they do on paper, although with paper they cut out the text, move the text, and then stick (paste) it. The equivalent is slightly different with a word processor, as the text actually disappears, and only the caret is moved to a new position. Children have to be reassured that the writing has not disappeared for good!

The *techniques* used can differ. With most word processors in current use, we normally teach the techniques of:

- highlighting the text;
- clicking on the scissors icon;
- moving the mouse to the desired position, and clicking on the left button;
- clicking on the clipboard icon.

There are alternatives, of course. Instead of the scissors and clipboard icons, we can:

- select **Copy** and **Paste** from the **Edit** drop down menu; or
- use the short cut keys on the keyboard, **Ctrl + X**, then **Ctrl + V**.

Or we can simply highlight the text and drag it to the new position with the mouse.

Deciding to cut and paste a section of text is a choice the child will have made, for a particular reason, perhaps because the *process* was to write a series of instructions for how to make a kite, and they had chosen to revise the order of the instructions to improve them.

In making the decision to revise these instructions, the children would have used *higher-order skills*, including evaluating their writing, and planning which techniques are to be used in the task. They would also, earlier, have recognised that ICT was appropriate and effective for this task.

ICT capability, the ICT National Curriculum and possible misconceptions

The distinction between a process and a technique is fundamental to understanding the nature of the ICT National Curriculum, and the QCA Scheme of Work.

Techniques are a means to an end, whereas processes are ends in themselves. The attainment target level descriptions describe sets of processes, not techniques.

The integrated tasks in the QCA Scheme of Work (1998) describe processes, whereas the short, focused tasks are concerned with techniques (and key ideas, or concepts).

If we examine the attainment target level descriptions of the ICT National Curriculum, nowhere is there any reference to techniques, nor to programs. What we do find are statements such as the following: *They use ICT to generate, develop, organise and present their work.*

This statement describes a class of processes. One such process, in relation to using a word processor, might be to write a set of instructions to make a kite. They write their first draft (*generate*), revise these instructions (*develop, organise*), before publishing them (*present their work*).

In order to be successful the children need to have the relevant techniques, concepts and higher-order skills, as we saw earlier.

Some of the wording in the statutory orders and the guidance provided by QCA can be misleading if the reader is not clear about the distinction between processes and techniques. We shall be discussing this further in subsequent chapters, but one such relates to what constitutes work at level 4 relating to *combining different forms of information from a variety of sources*.

The attainment target level description for level 4 includes the statement that

> [Pupils] add to, amend, and combine different forms of information from a variety of sources. They use ICT to present information in different forms and show they are aware of the intended audience and the need for quality in their presentations.

As we have seen, the attainment target level descriptions describe *processes*, not *techniques*.

Now, many pupils are able, at Year 3, to insert an image into a word processor or DTP package. Indeed, one of the techniques taught in unit 3A of the QCA Scheme of Work is precisely that. Moreover, it is now possible to insert a sound into many word processors just as easily, for example with Microsoft Word or Textease 2000. The *techniques* are almost identical. With Word:

- to insert an image, from the **Insert** drop down menu select **Picture, From File**. Then locate the desired file;

- to insert a sound, from the **Insert** drop down menu select **Object, Create from File**. Then locate the desired file.

A not uncommon misconception is that in doing the above, children would be working at level 4, because they are combining different forms of information from a variety of sources.

This is not so, however, as what we have described are the *techniques* of combining different forms of information from a variety of sources, whereas work at level 4 is about the children making choices as to which forms of information to combine in order to communicate most effectively with the chosen audience, which is a *process*.

In other words, not only do the children need to know the techniques described above, which, as we have seen, are not very difficult, but they also need to have used their higher-order skills to make decisions as to which medium will best convey the information to the audience in question.

This is very different from simply inserting an image of, say, a pyramid to improve the presentation of some work on the Egyptians.

Atherton (2002) provides an excellent account of what it really means to achieve levels 4 and 5 in this respect, and we urge the reader to read her article. In her account she explains how the children in her Year 6 class took into account the audience when making choices as to which media to select to communicate particular ideas. The children carried out two multimedia projects. The first project, on Shakespeare's Tudor London, was one which had as its audience a peer group (Years 5/6), and the second (Rainforests) had as its audience younger children (Years 2/3). We also recommend Lachs's (2000) book, *Making Multimedia in the Classroom*.

We have just emphasised the fact that ICT capability goes beyond the ability to use certain ICT techniques; it includes having conceptual understandings and making use of higher-order skills. But this is not to deny the central role of techniques, routines or basic skills.

Imagine a situation in which someone, perhaps a teacher, is familiar with a variety of multimedia CD-ROMs on various topics aimed at children of different ages and abilities. In the course of evaluating these multimedia CD-ROMs, the teacher has gained a good understanding of what can be done with multimedia, and the suitability of different media for different audiences. Suppose the teacher does not know any of the techniques involved in multimedia authoring. We would not want to say that the teacher was ICT-capable, even though he or she had all the conceptual understandings and the higher-order skills.

It is the mix of techniques, routines, concepts, processes and higher-order skills that, together, make for ICT capability. It is the ability to carry out the sets of processes defined in the attainment target level descriptions that constitute ICT capability.

An analogy with reading may help; we would not say that a child knows how to read if they 'bark at print', knowing how to decode the words but not understanding what they are reading. But neither would we say they knew how to read if they could not decode the words, no matter how good their comprehension was, were somebody to decode the words for them.

Routines

In one sense there is not much to say about routines, as they are simply techniques that have become automatic. Neither is there much to say about how to ensure that techniques become routines; it is really just down to ensuring that children get enough practice.

Because of this, routines tend to be ignored. The QCA Scheme of Work is singularly lacking in its attention to them.

Yet there is a huge difference between a child who carries out the techniques in a laborious and halting manner, perhaps needing to refer to prompt sheets, and the child who can carry out these techniques in a fluent manner, where the techniques have become routines/basic skills. It is the same sort of difference between a child who reads in a laborious and halting manner and the child who reads fluently.

Activities

1. Primary schools will organise their ICT resources in different ways. For example, some will opt for pupils having a weekly timetabled lesson in an ICT suite while others will prefer to have classroom-based PCs. What impact might these two different scenarios have on the way a teacher develops each component of Kennewell's (2000) capability? For example, is it possible for pupils to learn and use confidently an appropriate number of techniques without access to an ICT suite? Are pupils more likely to develop good conceptual understanding when the teacher explains, demonstrates and models to the whole class, without them having access to computers?

2. Select one or more units from the QCA Scheme of work for ICT and identify the techniques, concepts, processes and any higher-order skills. Are each of these components developed in particular sections of a QCA unit? For example, are processes and higher-order skills only ever related to the integrated task? Are the short, focused tasks the only opportunity to learn a new technique?

3

Progression in *Exchanging and sharing information*

Objectives

- To understand progression (in *Exchanging and sharing information*) in terms of the characteristics of the ICT National Curriculum at the different attainment target levels, as outlined in SCAA (1996) and the QCA (2003)

- To understand that for pupils to be functioning at the higher levels (4 and 5), they need to be applying higher-order skills and not just demonstrating knowledge and use of a wide range of techniques

As was explained in detail in Chapter 1, the NC ICT Programme of Study specifies, at Key Stage 1, that pupils should be taught:

3a) how to share their ideas by presenting information in a variety of forms [for example, text, images, tables, sounds]

3b) to present their completed work effectively [for example, for public display]

and Key Stage 2, that pupils should be taught:

3a) how to share and exchange information in a variety of forms, including e-mail [for example, displays, posters, animations, musical compositions]

3b) to be sensitive to the needs of the audience and think carefully about the content and quality when communicating information [for example, work for presentation to other pupils, writing for parents, publishing on the internet].

From the very beginning, *Exchanging and sharing information* includes communicating 'information' in a variety of forms, using such programs as word processors, paint programs, graphing software and music programs. The choice of the term 'information' is perhaps unfortunate in that it implies the transmission of facts, whereas music composition and paint programs are more concerned with expressing feelings and emotions, and word processors may be used to create poetry. So we need to bear in mind that 'information' is here being used in the broadest sense.

While pupils in Year 1 will begin by using programs that are only concerned with one medium, by the end of Year 6 they should be able to use a multimedia authoring program or a web authoring program to communicate more effectively to their audience by combining different forms of information.

In order to do this they will clearly be having to learn more complex programs, and the techniques associated with them, but as we saw in Chapter 2, the learning of these techniques is a means to an end, not an end in itself. Therefore, progression in the ICT National Curriculum is not about a progression in terms of ICT techniques, but in terms of progression in ICT capability.

In order to better understand progression, it is helpful to consider the characteristics of the ICT National Curriculum at the different attainment target levels (and hence the key stages), as outlined in SCAA (1996) and the QCA (2003).

Level 1	is characterised by the use of ICT to **explore options** and **make choices** to **communicate meaning**. Children develop **familiarity** with simple ICT tools.
Level 2	is characterised by **purposeful** use of ICT to achieve **specific outcomes**.
Level 3	is characterised by the use of ICT to **develop ideas**.
Level 4	is characterised by the ability to **combine and refine** information from various sources.
Level 5	is characterised by **combining the use of ICT tools** within the **overall structure** of an ICT solution. Children critically evaluate the **fitness for purpose** of work as it progresses.

Level 1: Initial exploratory use

AT level description: They use ICT to work with text, images and sound to help them share their ideas.

This is easier to explain in relation to the use of paint and music programs. For example, with a paint program it is just a question of exploring ('playing with') some of the tools. There is no requirement that the end-product be used for any particular purpose. Children use a paint program to make marks, in the same way as they would with actual paint. Their end-product may not resemble anything in particular, but they will be able to describe to the teacher what the 'painting' represents. With a music program the children would just create sounds, in the same way as they will with a glockenspiel or a drum. The end-product may not be very tuneful. This use of ICT corresponds to the scribbling stage in early literacy development; these scribbles may not reflect any of the normal outlines of the alphabet, but children will be able to read aloud to the teacher the 'story' they have written.

Strictly speaking, for children to explore a standard word-processing program with a keyboard in this way would mean that they would simply press keys at random, and they would then read their work back to the teacher. This is because in the early stages of writing development they would be unable to spell the words, or even read more than a few words.

However, it is possible to combine the use of a word processor with a word bank, either a separate word bank program (such as *Clicker*) or a word bank feature incorporated within the word processor itself (as with *Write Away*). In this manner, children can use the word processor to create texts before they are able to spell, in the same way as they could with *Breakthrough to Literacy* (1979). In fact, the use of word-bank facilities with word processors is a form of Electronic Breakthrough to Literacy. This use tends to be what characterises level 1 work with word-processing programs, although strictly speaking, this use has much in common with level 2 work (see below).

Perhaps the best way of thinking about level 1 work in Exchanging and Sharing Information is that the end-product does not matter, it does not have to have a particular purpose; whatever the child produces is OK.

Level 2: Purposeful use

AT level description: They use ICT to help them generate, amend and record their work and share their ideas in different forms, including text, tables, images and sound.

As pupils move on to level 2 they begin to use ICT for specific purposes. They will use a word processor to write stories and compose other narratives, and also write accounts of work done in class – i.e. to **generate** and **record** their work (cf. attainment target level 2 description). They will edit their work, make minor changes by using the delete key to replace one word with another, or to correct a spelling – i.e. **amend** their work (cf. attainment target level 2 description).

They will also use a graphing program to record and present the data generated in other subjects, for example in Maths, and may need to edit/amend the data if any are entered incorrectly.

They may even use both a word processor and a graphing program to record work done in, for example, science, but at this stage they will use each program separately. Later on they will insert the graph into the word processor.

They will use a computer graphics package to create a picture. Here the emphasis will be on the ways that feelings – anger, sadness, fear and joy – can be represented visually. They will examine the work of artists and see how they use line, colour, shape and texture to create effects from the examples collected. Again, they will generate and amend their work.

They will use a music program to create music to express feelings, and may use a music program in which a picture represents a musical phrase. They choose pictures (musical phrases) that sound happy/sad, fast/slow, or sound like the beginning/middle/end. They would create a musical sequence by ordering a few pictures. They might compose lyrics to fit in with the melody, and, after rehearsal, they may perform the song.

Level 3: Using ICT to develop ideas

AT level description: They use ICT to generate, develop, organise and present their work. They share and exchange their ideas with others.

What distinguishes level 3 work is that it involves pupils making significant changes to their work in order to **present** their work more effectively to an audience, rather than just making minor changes. For example, pupils will use word processors to **revise/redraft** their writing, making more substantial changes, including changes to the **organisation** and structure of their work. Successive drafts will be evaluated, allowing the user to **develop their ideas**, to **try out** different ways of communicating or presenting their ideas (including changes to the use of different fonts, section headings, and layouts of pictures and charts, where appropriate, where the word processor has simple DTP facilities).

In order to be able to revise their work they need to know how to save successive drafts, to know how to highlight and change the font style and/or size, to be able to cut out a section of the text and paste it elsewhere. They will also be able to insert images, in order to complement the text. They will be able to insert a chart they have created with a graphing program into their document, or incorporate an image into their magazine article. In other words, they will need to learn certain new **techniques**. Associated with these techniques are the relevant **concepts**.

In order to know what revisions to make, they need to be able to evaluate their work and judge whether the proposed changes will enhance their communication, and whether they will enhance the presentation. The ability to evaluate their work is a **higher-order skill**, and is associated with their literacy development.

The pupils will also be revising the work they do with sounds and images.

They will use ICT to create, organise and reorganise sounds with a music program. They will evaluate their composition, and revise it in order to present their ideas more effectively (see, for example, QCA Unit 3B: Manipulating sound).

They will use ICT to create, organise and reorganise images with a graphics program. They will evaluate their work, and revise it in order to present their ideas more effectively (see, for example, QCA Unit 4B: Developing images using repeating patterns).

In both cases what distinguishes this work is that they are evaluating their work (a higher-order skill) and applying the new techniques they have learned to revise their work, in order to communicate more effectively, in order to present their ideas more effectively.

Level 4: Combining information to take into account the audience

AT level description: They add to, amend, and combine different forms of information from a variety of sources. They use ICT to present information in different forms and show they are aware of the intended audience and the need for quality in their presentations. They exchange information and ideas with others in a variety of ways, including using e-mail.

Previously, when working at level 3, pupils reorganised their work in order to present their work more effectively. This meant that they were aware of the need to make changes because there would be an audience, whoever that audience may be.

When working at level 4 they begin to take into account the needs of a particular audience, the needs of their *intended* audience. They also combine different forms of information by using a multimedia authoring program, or a web authoring program. Using such programs enables them to select from a greater variety of media, including speech, sounds, animation, video clips, etc., as well as text and images, in order to communicate effectively. They also will record their own speech in order to communicate effectively with children who have limited reading skills.

A good way to start is by pupils authoring for their peers. Pupils can first evaluate work done by some of their peers, and develop criteria in this manner.

The children will, of course, need to learn some new ICT *techniques*, specifically those which relate to how to use the multimedia authoring program – such as inserting links etc. They will also need to learn associated *concepts*, a crucial one being a mental map of a hypertext environment. The key to children being able to work at this level is not just the techniques they are learning, but also their ability to choose the appropriate media to include in order to best communicate with their chosen audience, which is a *higher-order skill*.

For example, Atherton (2000:138) reports that, when designing multimedia for a peer group audience, her class came up with the following points to consider:

- The piece needs to look good. We want to impress other 10/11-year-olds with our artistic skills.

- Don't put them off with too much text. Use other media to explain and inform, or 'hide' the text in some way.

- Grab their attention by challenging them. Set them tasks to do but make it like a game.

- Make sure they really pay attention by forcing them to engage with the content by creating interactive elements. An example from the Globe stack illustrates such dual interactivity. The user clicks on any of five Shakespearian characters to hear them speak a line from the relevant play or see the quote appear in a pop-up text box. They then match the name of the character to the correct image by dragging and dropping name labels. A further example is the Tudor Clothes Quiz where the user reads several 'Amazing Tudor Fashion Facts' and clicks a button to say whether they believe each fact to be true or false.

As one of the girls in Lachs's class, working on a multimedia project called 'Chromosomes', explained (Lachs 2000:53):

> When I'm explaining it I have to have in mind I'm making it for younger children so I have to make . it interesting, not too much writing, a lot of pictures to show what I'm talking about and make it clearer.

E-mail

We consider the reference to e-mail as part of the level 4 attainment target description to be out of place. Technically, sending an e-mail is simple; just enter the text and click on *send*. Granted, it is conceptually slightly more complex than entering text on screen and then printing it out, as the child has to imagine where the e-mail has gone, but children are familiar with telephones, and with texting, and they can easily understand e-mails by sending them to each other in the same room.

Moreover, we, as a rule, use e-mail purposefully, rather than to develop our ideas, and certainly not to combine information from different media in order to communicate more effectively to our chosen audience. Hence it fits better in the description for level 2.

It is worth noting that the QCA (1998) place the unit relating to e-mail at Year 3, thus acknowledging that it fits more comfortably with the level 2 attainment target description.

Level 5: Increased rigour

AT level description: They use ICT to structure, refine and present information in different forms and styles for specific purposes and audiences. They exchange information and ideas with others in a variety of ways, including using e-mail.

The real defining difference between this level and the previous one is greater precision and increased rigour, both in terms of their *higher-order skills,* and in terms of *techniques* and the associated *concepts.*

In terms of new techniques they may learn how to create animations, or virtual reality resources to insert into their multimedia project.

Whereas, at level 4, pupils were able to take into consideration the needs of a peer group audience, here they are able to consider the needs of an audience of a different age, e.g. another class in the school. They may even author for a mixed audience, and offer different options to the user by making screens at different levels of complexity, or by communicating the information in different ways, for example by having the option to have the text read out aloud.

Atherton (2000:142) reports that, when designing multimedia for a younger audience, her class came up with the following points to consider:

■ Make it easy for them to understand by using clear images and easy-to-read fonts. *(It is interesting to note that the class on the whole were less concerned about impressing a younger age group with stunning artwork. Although they still wanted it to look good they presumed that your average seven-year-old would be sufficiently impressed by an average 11-year-old's artwork! However, they did acknowledge that even seven-year-olds would like a little visual variety.)*

■ Use a range of visual images to hold their attention and bring the subject to life.

■ Combine the media to reduce the amount of text used: seven-year-olds will be even less inclined to read lots of text than 11-year-olds.

■ Listen to our audience, they know what they like. Get feedback from the target audience so we can review the work as we go along.

■ Remember the purpose of the work. Make sure we teach our audience what they need to learn. But how do we know if they've learned something?

Atherton's pupils were not only careful to get feedback from their target audience; they also acted upon it in earnest. After one of the 'focus groups', a Year 3 pupil, Daniel, gave the following feedback: 'I can't be bothered to read all them words [he meant the labels] so I can't do the game bit'. She reports the action that Samuel took (Atherton 2000:143):

> Samuel took this very much to heart, and produced two cards to teach the life cycle of a caterpillar – one with an animation of the life cycle, and a voice over, and other with a drag and drop game, again using sound rather than text.
>
> Daniel approved wholeheartedly when he came to 'test' the work and he was able to describe and explain in detail what he had learned about the life cycle of a caterpillar, without having to read at all!

Techniques and higher-order skills, and ICT capability

As we have just seen, in order for a child to be judged to be functioning at levels 4/5 they need to be applying higher-order skills, and making choices as to which forms of information to combine in order to communicate most effectively with the chosen audience.

If they simply know the techniques of combining different forms of information, then no matter how good their techniques, they could not be said to be functioning at this level.

The difference between children functioning at levels 4 and 5, however, is not just a question of them being more refined in their ability to take into account different audiences; it is also a question of them being more refined in the number of techniques they use, and how skilled they are in using them.

Nowhere can one find definitive guidance on which techniques go with which level, and it is unfortunate that there is not such guidance. This is not surprising, because with the technological advances, techniques that were at one time too hard for the younger child are now within their reach. For example, products such as *Digital Blue* allow Key Stage 1 children to work with digital video simply by pressing a button to start, a button to stop, and placing the camera on a base unit to automatically download the video clip. Depending on the context this may be exploratory or purposeful use of ICT (level 1 or 2). What we present in Table 3.1 is therefore a very rough-and-ready guide to the differences between level 4 and level 5 work.

TABLE 3.1 *Exchanging and sharing information* at levels 4 and 5

	Higher-order skills	Concepts	Techniques	Routines
Level 4	Taking into account peer audience	Understanding of hyperlinks and having mental map of structure	Create and insert text, images and sound	These techniques are carried out reasonably fluently
Level 5	Taking into account an audience of younger children	Understanding of hyperlinks and having mental map of structure	The techniques used go beyond the above (e.g. they create animations, **or** video clips, **or** virtual reality clips, **or** ...)	These techniques are carried out in a fluent manner

In table 2 we summarise progression in *Exchanging and sharing information* throughout Key Stages 1 and 2.

The QCA Scheme of Work, ICT capability, and progression

If we examine the QCA units relating to *Exchanging and sharing information* we can see how they are designed to progressively prepare the children to work at level 4/5 in Year 6 (Unit 6A: Multimedia Presentation).

In order for this plan to work, it is essential that the teacher understands the main point of each unit, its rationale in the wider scheme.

TABLE 3.2 Progression *Exchanging and sharing information*

SCAA (1996)/QCA (2003)	Explication	Attainment target level description
Level 1 is characterised by initial **exploratory use** of ICT.	This is easier to explain in relation to the use of paint and music programs. For example, with a paint program it is just a question of exploring some of the tools to make marks etc. There is no requirement for the end-product to be used for a particular purpose. It corresponds to the scribbling stage in early literacy development. It is difficult to really explore a text-processing program if you are in the early stages of writing development, so the approximation to this exploratory use of ICT is the use of a word bank with a word processor.	Level 1: They use ICT to work with text, images and sound to help them share their ideas.
The characteristic which differentiates **level 2** from Level 1 is the more **purposeful** use of ICT to achieve specific outcomes.	This would include writing stories and other narratives, and also accounts of other work done in class (**generate** to **record**). Some editing of their work (using the delete key to replace one word with another) is done – **amend**. Copy typing would not go beyond this stage.	Level 2: They use ICT to help them **generate, amend** and **record** their work and share their ideas in different forms, including **text,** tables, images and sound.
The characteristic which differentiates **level 3** from level 2 is that ICT is used to **develop ideas.**	The key here is reworking a piece of writing – save and go back to later. They would use ICT not only to edit (amend) but also to **revise/redraft (develop)** their writing. For this a key technique they would have to learn is that of cut-and-paste. They also not only record their work (for their own and the teacher's benefit), but they also **present** it to share with others. So another key technique at this level is to be able to insert a **graphic** (either a picture or a chart). Also use *Save As* to save drafts.	Level 3: They use ICT to generate, **develop, organise** and **present** their work. They share and exchange their ideas with others.
The characteristic which differentiates **level 4** from level 3 is the ability take into account the **audience.**	The key here is not that they have learned the technique of combining different forms of information they have already learned how to combine text and graphics to present their work (see above) and the technique for combining sound etc. is no more difficult). Here they need to demonstrate that they can choose which forms to combine to take into consideration the audience. N.B. The reference to e-mail seems out of place in this level description, as discussed earlier in this chapter.	Level 4: They add to, amend and combine different forms of information from a variety of sources. They use ICT to present information in different forms and show they are aware of **the intended audience** and the need for quality in their presentations. They exchange information and ideas with others in a variety of ways, including using e-mail.
The characteristic which differentiates **level 5** from level 4 is its **increased rigour,** and by **combining the use of ICT tools** within the overall structure of an ICT solution.	The difference here is that they are now able to go beyond a familiar audience (such as their peers) to take into account audiences such as children younger than themselves.	Level 5: They use ICT to structure, refine and present information in **different forms and styles** for **specific purposes** and **audiences.**

TABLE 3.3 The QCA units and progression in *Exchanging and sharing information* relating to text

QCA unit	Comments – what is important in these units is to ensure that the **key processes are learned**, rather than simply the key techniques.	Attainment target level description
Using a word bank (1B)	This is an approximation to an exploratory use of a word processor.	level 1
Writing stories: communicating information using text (2A)	This is purposeful use of a word processor, where ICT is used to **record** – to write a story, or an account of some work done in class, where there is no suggestion of an audience (it would actually be the teacher or the child themselves). The **key techniques** relate to selecting a word or phrase and correcting, changing or deleting it. The **key process** relates to **editing/amending** the text, and using ICT to **record purposefully**.	level 2
Combining text and graphics (3A) *A better title would be* ***Using ICT to present work, including inserting graphics to improve their presentation (3A)***	Again this is purposeful use of a word processor, but here ICT is used to **present** information to others. The children understand that there is an audience. Hence the **key technique** is of **inserting graphics**, such as including pictures in a magazine to add interest, to grab the reader's attention, or a chart in the report of a science experiment, to communicate the results of the experiment more clearly. A better title would be inserting graphics to improve the presentation, rather than combining text and graphics, as the latter suggests level 4/5 work, which it is not. Otherwise it is still only amending text – selecting a word or phrase to correct or change (editing the text). The **key process** relates to **presentation** (in addition to editing/amending).	level 2, working towards level 3
e-mail (3E)	Again this is purposeful use of an e-mail word processor. In this unit the children are also introduced to evaluating the first drafts of someone else's writing (sent by e-mail), as a way of working towards the process of developing their ideas in the unit 4A. The fact that this unit includes both evaluating drafts and the use of e-mails is simply a pragmatic decision by the QCA – there is no necessary connection between the two (children could be introduced to evaluating drafts in another way). While the **key technique** here is **learning to use e-mail** (including attachments), the **key process** is learning **to evaluate drafts**, as a prerequisite to developing their ideas.	level 2, working towards level 3
Writing for different audiences (4A) *A better title would be* ***Using ICT to develop written language (4A)***	The **key technique** here is learning to cut and paste. The **key process** is learning **to develop their ideas, to revise/redraft** their work. Here again the title is very misleading, giving the impression that this is concerned with different audiences, whereas it is **not** concerned with writing for **different** audiences, it is simply that they are **presenting** their work more effectively **to** an audience. They are working towards level 4, in that they show they are aware of the intended audience and the need for quality in their presentations	level 3
Multimedia presentation (6A) *A better title would be* ***Using Multimedia to Communicate with different audiences (6A)***	The **key techniques** here are combining text/graphics/sound/animation/videoclips, and creating hyperlinks in a multimedia authoring program – i.e. learning to work with hypermedia. The **key process** is learning which forms to combine to **take into consideration the needs of the audience**. Level 4 work would typically be authoring for their peers, level 5 for other audiences (e.g. younger children).	level 4 or 5 – see Table 3.1

Table 3.3 summarises the progression in the QCA scheme relating to *Exchanging and sharing information* with text.

Other units prepare the children in relation to *Exchanging and sharing information* with media other than text, in particular those outlined in Table 3.4:

TABLE 3.4 QCA and *Exchanging and sharing information* other than text

Creating pictures (2B)	This is concerned with purposeful use of a paint package, making amendments. The integrated task is *to select and use different techniques to communicate ideas through pictures.*
Manipulating sound (3B)	This is concerned with using a music program to develop their ideas, to create, amend and revise, or 'redraft', their work. The integrated task is *to use ICT to create, organise and reorganise sounds.*
Developing images using repeating patterns (4B) *The title is misleading, it is about digital art. A better title would be:* **Developing images and digital art (4B)**	This is concerned with using a paint program to develop their ideas, and to create, amend and revise, or 'redraft', their work. The integrated task is *to use the skills and techniques learnt to organise, reorganise and communicate ideas, and to select suitable information and media and prepare it for processing using ICT.* The main focus here is to explore the use of a paint program as an artistic tool in its own right – creating digital art, if you like. The suggested teaching activity in the integrated task communicates the rationale and purpose of this unit more effectively than the title: *Show the class a mixed-media collage, such as 'Guitar' by Pablo Picasso, and discuss some of the techniques used. Encourage children to find material that can be scanned, e.g. from newspapers or magazines.* *Ask children to use the various techniques learnt to incorporate the scanned images in order to create composite images, based on direct observation of musical instruments. Encourage them to focus on particular details, such as tuning pegs or keys. Each child could be given a different viewpoint. Remind them of the importance of saving drafts.* The subject matter does not, of course, have to be musical instruments. The title for this unit is misleading, as it is about *developing images*, not really about repeating patterns at all. The focus on repeating patterns is to ensure that the children know how to copy and paste, and hence can build up a *mixed-media collage*, building up their digital art work by using images from various sources, including scanned images, images taken with digital cameras, etc.

Unit 4B, Developing images using repeating patterns, is all about developing images, digital art, rather than repeating patterns. What matters is that children use a paint package to develop their ideas. The integrated task is described as follows:

Show the class a mixed-media collage, such as 'Guitar' by Pablo Picasso, and discuss some of the techniques used. Encourage children to find material that can be scanned, e.g. from newspapers or magazines. Ask children to use the various techniques learnt to incorporate the scanned images in order to create composite images, based on direct observation of musical instruments. Encourage them to focus on particular details, such as tuning pegs or keys. Each child could be given a different viewpoint. Remind them of the importance of saving drafts.

Ask children to print out multiple copies of their work and use the printouts, together with other collected images, to make a mixed-media collage.

The reader is referred to Loveless (1997) and Wood (2003) for a fuller discussion of digital art, and of how ICT can help develop their artistic ideas, but essentially it is all about *trying things out* with graphics programs, scanners and digital cameras, of *developing their artistic ideas*. It is *not* about using the copy-and-paste tool to create patterns on wrapping paper.

As Wood (2003:11) observes, one great advantage of computers is that it frees them from the fear of making mistakes:

> Computers don't just offer new tools and the ability to test ideas quickly. They also make spontaneity safer than it used to be. Mistakes no longer matter. A keystroke erases them, restoring the previous version. The 'undo' button may be technology's greatest gift to art students. Jan McGranaghan explains: 'Kids are frightened to death of making marks that might be wrong. They're afraid to make the first stroke on a blank canvas or the first cut in a large piece of paper. The undo button takes away that terror.' . . . Experimentation is at the heart of any creative endeavour. Computers make it easier – both psychologically and technically – to try things out. They let art students work noncommittally – hence, fearlessly and with greater excitement.

This is true for digital collage. As Wood reports (2003:10):

> Jan McGranaghan and Sue Crudgington share an enthusiasm for digital collage. Sue writes: 'This is a totally new language and the possibilities are vast. New techniques are now possible that were unavailable with traditional media.' In particular, students can 'layer' images, readily 'cutting and pasting, moving bits, putting in, taking out'. The speed and ease with which this can be done 'gives a totally different dimension', according to Sue. Significantly, she adds: 'Now parts can be removed without losing everything. You can rub out what you've done without affecting the layer underneath.'

This ability to experiment with changing images unleashes the creative potential of young artists, by manipulating an existing image to create original works, (*ibid.*: 6):

> Human contact and collaboration are at the heart of Phil Callow's approach, both as Head of Art and Design at Christ the King Catholic High School, Merseyside, and as an artist in his own right. Dozens of students of all ages – and their teachers – enter an annual digital art competition run by Phil from his website [www.treacletart.net]. He provides a 'starter' image which young entrants can manipulate to create original works. The website doubles as an online gallery for displaying students' entries. Site visitors vote to select the winning work. One starter image, for example, was a digital photograph of a tiger's head. The winning entrant – a 17-year-old girl from the Outer Hebrides – used software to strip away the background of the photograph and substitute an urban night scene. She added a neon glow to the tiger's stripes.

Phil Callow's website is well worth a visit.

The scanner has been used in a way that was never intended (*ibid.*: 8):

> Jan McGranaghan began by scanning images onto her school's intranet for students to use as starting points. Then students scanned in their finished work, which in turn became starting points for other students. 'Next we moved from images to objects. We put fruit onto the scanner, with clingfilm underneath to protect the scanning mechanism. We rapidly discovered that accidental wrinkles in the clingfilm gave the scanned image a more interesting quality, with wonderful textures and creases. So,

having first tried to smooth the cling film, we now began crinkling it deliberately to see what we would get. We then extended this to other materials – scrunching up acetates and bits of foil. A lot of this came from the students saying, "What if?" They sparked off each others' ideas.' ... Having first used the scanner simply as a recording device, Sue discovered it could be 'a great tool for inspiring creativity'. Her students use scanned images in collages and other mixed media work. She enjoys merging novel processes with more familiar ones.

Other characteristics of *Exchanging and sharing information*

Techniques learned in other units are also important, for example being able to create graphs and charts with databases and spreadsheets, and in particular using an object-based drawing program as in Unit 5A: Graphical modelling. The main aim of this unit is that children learn the value of using a drawing program to solve a problem, such as deciding on the best layout of a classroom. But drawing programs can, of course, also be used to exchange and share information.

We consider that there is a lack of balance in the units. A lot of emphasis is given to exchanging and sharing information with programs relating to text, as opposed to images, tables, sounds, charts/graphs etc. In Chapter 8 we discuss how a better balance can be restored, and how this would better prepare children for Unit 6A: Multimedia Presentation. For example, there is no reason why a sound recorder program cannot be used from the start, as it is no more difficult to use than a tape recorder. It even has the same kind of icons for Play, Record, Fast Forward etc. In Year 1 the teacher would have to set the program up for the children, but there is no reason why, working in pairs, they could explore this resource, and record and play back their own voices.

Progression and techniques

Given that we have been careful to emphasise the point that the ICT National Curriculum is not just about techniques, it may come as a surprise to the reader to learn that we consider that not enough attention is paid to techniques in the QCA Scheme of Work.

For example, it can be quite appropriate for children to learn about bulleted lists at the time that they are introduced to unit 4A. Having entered their text and evaluated their first draft they may consider that their points would be expressed more clearly as a bulleted list.

Given that many programs now used for word processing are, to all intents and purposes, simple DTP packages, children need also to be introduced to creating frames, and how to lay these out.

Some teachers will, in fact, teach these sorts of techniques, but it is still important to note that the QCA Scheme of Work provides guidance to teaching ICT, and does not provide an ICT curriculum.

Activities

1. Examine the content of QCA unit 4B – Developing images using repeating patterns. The outcome of the integrated task is for pupils to create a mixed-media collage. The resources listed on the front of the unit include a scanner, a digital camera or clip art. How might the short, focused tasks be adapted or extended to reflect the use of the suggested resources, and to better prepare pupils for the integrated task?

2. Can you think of a different focus for the integrated task? For example, what images could be used as a stimulus instead of Picasso's 'Guitar'? What theme could the composite images be based on instead of musical instruments? You might find it helpful to look through the Art QCA units of work, and to search the internet for visual stimuli.

Progression in *Finding things out*

Objectives

- To understand progression (in *Finding things out*) in relation to the characteristics of the ICT National Curriculum as outlined by SCAA (1996) and the QCA (2003)

- To understand that the reason why databases are difficult is because of the conceptual understandings and the higher-order skills that are necessary in order to create and use them effectively, whereas the techniques involved are relatively simple

- To understand the difficulties that pupils might have in using Boolean searches, creating databases and interpreting and using graphs

- To understand what constitutes following a line of enquiry, and differentiate between conducting, or following, a straightforward line of enquiry, which is a process, and carrying out a simple search, which is a technique

As was explained in detail in Chapter 1, the National Curriculum ICT Programme of Study specifies, at Key Stage 1, that pupils should be taught to:

1a) gather information from a variety of sources [for example, people, books, databases, CD-ROMs, videos and TV]

1b) enter and store information in a variety of forms [for example, storing information in a prepared database, saving work]

1c) retrieve information that has been stored [for example, using a CD-ROM, loading saved work]

and at Key Stage 2, that pupils should be taught:

1a) to talk about what information they need and how they can find and use it [for example, searching the internet or a CD-ROM, using printed material, asking people]

1b) how to prepare information for development using ICT, including selecting suitable sources, finding information, classifying it and checking it for accuracy [for example, finding information from books or newspapers, creating a class database, classifying by characteristics and purposes, checking the spelling of names is consistent]

1c) to interpret information, to check it is relevant and reasonable and to think about what might happen if there were any errors or omissions.

We will, again, consider progression in relation to the characteristics of the ICT National Curriculum, as outlined by SCAA (1996) and the QCA (2003), after an overview of the kinds of activities that are expected of pupils at Key Stage 2.

Finding things out is concerned with locating and handling data held in electronic databases, be they flatfile databases, branching databases, a CD-ROM, the Web, etc. We shall begin by considering the use of flatfile databases in detail, and then consider the use of other tools for *Finding things out*, such as graphing programs, spreadsheets, branching databases, and CD-ROM and web-based search engines.

Strictly speaking, a database is a collection of information organised in such a way that it can be easily accessed by a computer program, and this program is called a *database management system*. In general usage, however, the program is usually now referred to as a database (although, strictly speaking, it should be referred to as a database program).

There are different kinds of databases, including relational databases, flatfile databases, branching databases, and Hypertext databases. Relational databases, one example of which is Access, are not appropriate for use in primary schools, and, consequently, are not considered here. Branching and Hypertext databases, and graphing programs and spreadsheets, will be considered later in this chapter.

Flatfile databases

A flatfile database stores data in a structured manner. These raw data can be represented as a list, as in a telephone directory, or as a set of records, as in a library card index. Flatfile databases are organised by *fields*, *records* and *files*. A field contains a single item of data, a record is a set of fields, and a file is a collection of records.

One example of a flatfile database in printed form is a telephone book, which in its electronic form would be a file. This file is made up of a list of records, each of which is made up of three *fields*: *name*, *address*, and *telephone number*.

Another example of a flatfile database in printed form is a library card index, where each record contains such information (in 'fields') as *title*, *author* and *classification*.

The fact that library card indexes are virtually obsolete testifies to the power of electronic databases – how soon before the personal address book joins it (it has for those with electronic personal organisers)? From here on, a flatfile database and the program for accessing the data will be referred to simply as a database, to reflect common language use.

Let us consider a very simple, even trivial, database of information about four children. When represented as a list it looks like Figure 4.1.

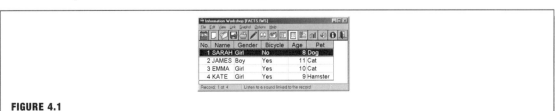

FIGURE 4.1

It can also be represented as a set of four records, one of which would look like Figure 4.2.

FIGURE 4.2

The data can be stored in three basic formats

- as text (e.g. letters/words, or a combination of letters and numbers);
- as a number; and
- as a multiple choice entry (e.g. Yes/No, Girl/Boy).

The data can be accessed and processed quickly and easily. Basic functions in databases in current use in primary schools include the ability to:

- sort
- search
- display data in graph/chart form.

The techniques involved here are relatively simple, as we shall demonstrate in the next few pages. The reason why we are taking the trouble to spell out the techniques concerned will become clear in due course. The reader familiar with using databases designed for use in primary schools can skim read the next few pages.

Sorting

For example, with the database program Information Workshop, the data can be sorted by age as in Figure 4.3.

Five clicks are all it takes. The techniques are simple, and it does not take much practice to turn these techniques into routines.

Simple searches

The techniques involved in searching the database are just as simple. Let us say we wanted to search for all the girls. Of course, with such a simple database it is far simpler just to look at the list, but we have chosen this simple database precisely to make it easier to explain, and discuss, the sorting and searching techniques. The procedure would be as in Figure 4.4.

Just seven clicks in all, or six clicks and typing in one word (see stage 4).

N.B. When searching it is sometimes necessary to enter a search term, and sometimes the user only has to make a choice between alternatives (e.g. Boy/Girl, Yes/No), depending upon how the database has been set up.

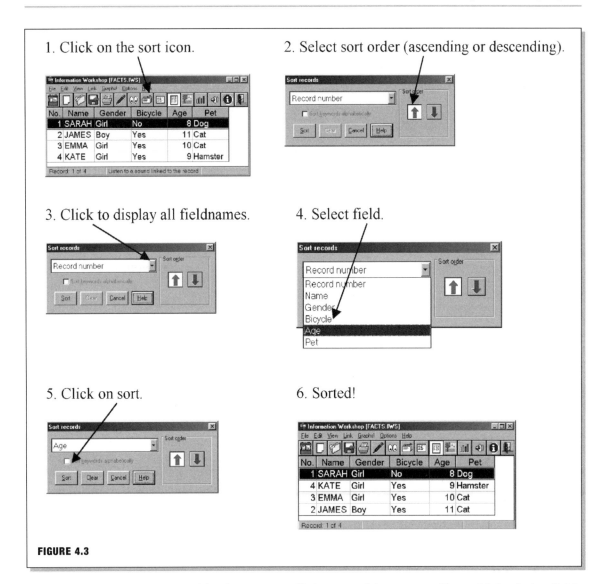

1. Click on the sort icon.

2. Select sort order (ascending or descending).

3. Click to display all fieldnames.

4. Select field.

5. Click on sort.

6. Sorted!

FIGURE 4.3

It is good practice, and leads to more efficient searching, to specify multiple choice fields (e.g. Boy/Girl, Yes/No) when the entries are restricted to a finite limited set of alternatives. Otherwise 'text' fields would be used; fields where the entries can be composed of letters or letters and numbers. In the example above, it would be appropriate to specify *Gender* and *Bicycle* as multiple choice fields, whereas *Pet* would be a text field.

Complex (Boolean) searches

An example of a complex search with this database would be to search for all the girls who had bicycles. To do this we would have to search under both the Gender and the Bicycle fields, to find all records in which **Gender = 'Girl' AND Bicycle = 'Yes'**. Again, the techniques involved are very simple. The first four stages, and the last three, are the same as the simple search. There are just five extra clicks (stages 5a–5e), as shown in Figure 4.5.

1. Click on the search icon.

2. Click to display all fieldnames.

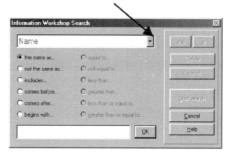

3. Select field.

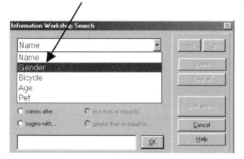

4. Enter/select* search term.

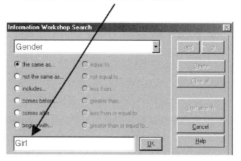

5. Click OK.

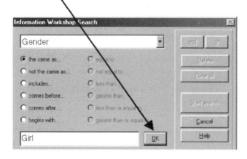

6. Click 'Start search'.

7. Click OK.

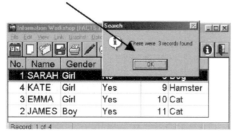

8. Done!

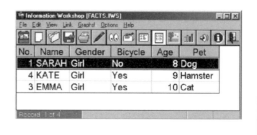

FIGURE 4.4

5a. Click 'and'.

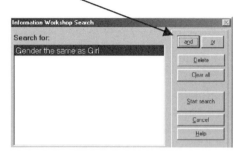

5b. Click to display all fieldnames.

5c. Select field.

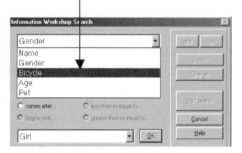

5d. Enter/select* search term.

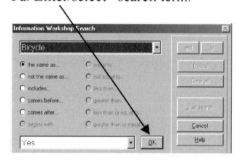

5e. Click OK.

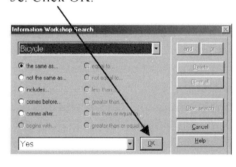

6. Click 'Start search'.

7. Click OK.

8. Done!

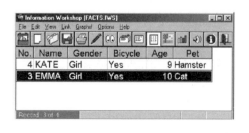

FIGURE 4.5

A complex search using the Boolean operator **OR** is technically just as simple.

Suppose we wanted to select all children who had a cat or a dog as a pet. There would be exactly the equal number of stages to go through as when using the Boolean operator AND. The differences would be as follows:

At stage 3 we would select the field *Pet* (instead of *Gender*).

At stage 4 we would enter *Cat* (instead of *Girl*).

At stage 5a above we would click on *OR* (instead of *AND*).

At stage 5c we would select the field *Pet* (instead of *Bicycle*).

At stage 5e we would enter *Dog* (instead of *Yes*).

Displaying the data

Displaying the data in the form of a graph or chart is just as simple. For example, to create a pie-chart of *Pets* we simply follow the steps outlined in Figure 4.6.

Creating a database

The techniques involved in creating a database are just as simple, as can be seen in Figure 4.7. After a few clicks and typing in a few words the structure of the database is defined. Adding information about each entry is even easier.

Searching databases

We have taken the trouble to spell out the techniques involved in accessing information in a database, and creating such a database, in order to emphasise the point that the techniques are relatively simple.

This is not to say that learning to access information from a database, and creating useful databases, is simple. Far from it. The difficulties they pose are recognised by the fact that the ICT National Curriculum identifies different stages of its use in the primary and secondary years of schooling and the fact that there are four medium-term plans devoted to them in Key Stage 2 alone by the QCA Scheme of Work.

The reason why databases are difficult is because of the conceptual understandings, and the higher-order skills, that are necessary in order to create and use them effectively.

Perhaps the easiest way to demonstrate this is to consider the difference in difficulty children have with **AND** and **OR** complex searches. Whereas even fairly young children can conduct a complex search using AND (perhaps even as young as seven, though one would not expect that until Year 4), a complex search using **OR** poses difficulties for children even at Year 6. It is not really until they are of secondary school age that they are at ease with such searches. Yet, as we saw earlier, the techniques involved are not only exactly similar but are, to all intents and purposes, **identical** – the only difference being whether at step 5a the user clicks the **AND** button or clicks the **OR** button.

Among others, Smith (1997; 1999) and Underwood and Underwood (1990) have reported the difficulties children have with complex searches involving the operator **OR**. As they point out, queries such as 'How many children go swimming **and** play football?' do not cause any difficulty, as the wording of the question matches the correct operator.

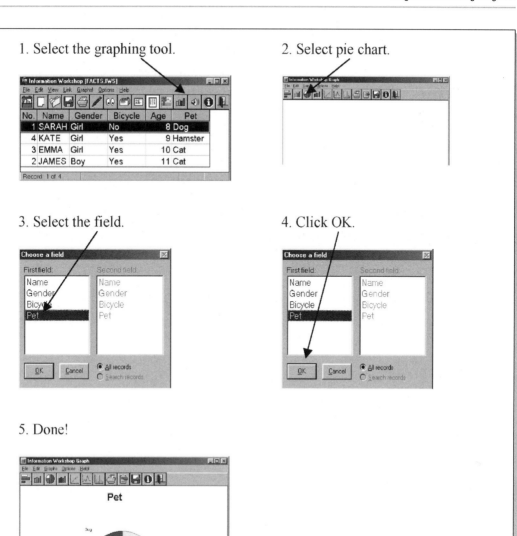

FIGURE 4.6

There are two reasons why **OR** causes difficulty:

1. Sometimes in natural language we use **'and'** where the operator needs to be **OR**. If we wish to search a database of paintings to find paintings by Rembrandt **and** paintings by Monet, the operator needs to be **OR**, namely *'Select all records where the entry is Rembrandt OR Monet'* (a painting by Rembrandt cannot also be a painting by Monet!).

2. In ordinary language we often use **'or'** exclusively, for example in the sentence *'Is Hilary a boy or a girl?'* There is no suggestion s/he could be both! Hilary is either a boy or a girl. The operator **OR**, however, is inclusive. If we conduct the following search in a database *'Select all records where the entry is football OR swimming'* the results will contain all children who play football, all children who swim, and all children who do both.

---

1. Select **New** from the **File** drop down menu.

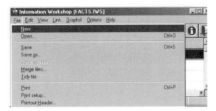

2. Choose to use the advanced file and click on Next.

3. Enter information about the file and click OK.

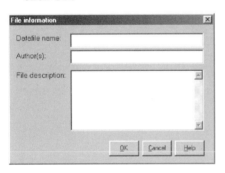

4. Enter the fieldnames, state type and size of fields etc, then click on exit.

5. Type in, or select (if multiple choice) the information about each entry.

FIGURE 4.7

When children are asked which of the two searches (**AND** or **OR**) would yield the larger number of records, they usually say **AND**. This reflects what they have learned from their work in maths and their general use of English.

'What is 6 and 5' yields a larger answer. *'Do you want an apple or a banana'* usually means you can choose one or the other.

One helpful strategy is to ask children to stand up if certain statements apply to them and compare the results between, say, 'Who has a dog OR a cat?' with 'Who has both a dog AND a cat?'

We have been describing a difficulty that children have which is related to their developing conceptual knowledge about Boolean operators – what a Boolean operator actually does.

A lack of conceptual understanding, a lack of a clear model of the database structure, is probably also the cause of the following confusion between the fieldname and the entry (Smith 1997:54):

> Where details of each country's cheapest fruit needed to be added to the 'Shopping' file, one child suggested 'pears' as the heading (field), since her letter gave pears as the cheapest fruit. Others disagreed:
>
> Josephine: When we do the other ones, it might not be pears, say in Spain or somewhere […]
> Nicola: 'Cos that's what we want to try and compare […] We want to keep the pears there [as the data entry; cheapest fruit] can be the heading for the next one.

Smith (1999:179) reports other difficulties children have with searches, which are not so much conceptual difficulties as to do with their need to learn appropriate strategies.

Sometimes the difficulties children have relate more to whether they are using the most appropriate strategy, rather than to a conceptual misunderstanding. The query *'Which is the largest/smallest'* is best answered by sorting the data, but the way the question is worded suggests a search, especially if it is phrased as *'**Find** the largest/smallest'*. Smith (1999) reports that on many occasions pupils attempted to estimate the highest (or lowest) value, then search the file. This is usually a much less efficient strategy.

Another example concerns a child who wanted to find out *'Which children have dogs as pets'*. He realised that he would have to enter the search term *'dog'* rather than *'dogs'*, although it is not uncommon for less-experienced users to enter *'dogs'*, as this matches the wording of the question they want to answer, whereas if the question were to be formulated as *'Which children have a dog as a pet?'* it would be easier to answer. This is one example of the need for children to *understand the need for care in framing questions when … interrogating information* (level 4 attainment target). One useful strategy is to select 'includes' rather than 'exact matches'.

Smith (1999) gives another example that illustrates the difficulty children sometimes have with converting the question into the appropriate search. The children had constructed a database in which they could enter more than one pet for each record. Thus one entry might be: *Pets: cat, fish, dog* (meaning the child in question had three pets – a cat, a dog and a fish). Smith (*ibid.*:179) made the following observations, in relation to asking the question *'Who has a cat and a dog?'*:

Here, narrowing-down is implied. Fewer people are likely to have both animals, than dogs or cats alone. In this case, a special difficulty arises because the field must be searched twice. To find who has a dog and a cat, (ii) below is correct. Placing 'and' in the text to be matched, as in (i), is a common error. Read aloud, (i) and (ii) seem to mean more or less the same. The outcomes of the searches may be quite different:

(i) Pets / includes / dog and cat
(ii) Pets / includes / dog **AND** Pets / includes / cat

Laura emphatically urged others in her group not to enter (i). She did not explain, but supported another child's suggestion to use (ii). This incident reveals the emerging formal thinking ability of a capable 11 year old, aided by the scaffolding of group interaction. From her experience of searching the file, Laura had been able to make the distinction between the functional parts of the search query.

Children have little difficulty with mathematical relations in numeric searches. However, the retrieval of a range of values using *less than* or *greater than* is not so straightforward. For example, one pupil wanted to find adults in the age group 35–39, and was able to narrow down the same by carrying out the following search:

Age is less than 40 AND Age is greater than 34.

Smith (1999:177–8) reports, however, that not all pupils grasped this strategy:

A Year 6 class compiled a database of performance times. They had devised a stiff endurance test which involved hanging from wall bars! A histogram showed two records in the highest range, 200 to 219 seconds. To identify the two children, one group entered the search:

Arm hang / greater than / 200

To the pupils' surprise, only one record was matched. Going back to the source data, they found the lower of the two times was exactly 200 seconds. However, they could still not correct the search.

It is not clear from Smith's report whether the reason for this failure was a lack of conceptual understanding (about the distinction between *greater than* and *greater than or equal to*) or a failure to apply the correct strategy (a higher-order skill).

From the description we gave earlier of the techniques, and the problems children actually have with databases, it is clear that the difficulties arise through a lack of conceptual understanding and a lack of knowing and applying appropriate search strategies, which involve the use of higher-order skills, rather than any difficulty with the techniques.

This is also true for children attempting to interpret their graphs and charts, and knowing which graphs and charts are appropriate to test their hypotheses etc.

Interpreting graphs

As we have already seen, it is easy to produce graphs and charts with the databases used in primary schools. However, we have to be careful that this ease of production does not lead us to overlook difficulties in interpretation.

Column charts are familiar enough at Key Stage 1. Children find these easy to interpret when each column represents a category, for example a mode of transport (like 'car'), when they are doing a survey on how the class travels to school. They are used to categories being represented by (e.g.) rows of cubes – the more cubes, the greater the number of children who travel to school that way.

When the category is a number, however, this can cause difficulties in interpretation. It is the fact that there are two numbers together that causes the problem.

Smith (1999) reports that a Year 6 class had, over a period, gathered some weather data, and created a file which included the midday temperature for each day, and displayed this as a chart. Each column therefore represented the number of days on which this temperature was recorded. The tallest column represented the most frequently recorded temperature, yet they were convinced that it represented *'the hottest day'*.

Histograms present the same problem (each column in a histogram represents a range of values, rather than one value). The computer automatically constructs these for numeric fields. Smith (1997) reports that, for the data in Figure 4.8, one child thought that someone took 32 minutes to travel to school.

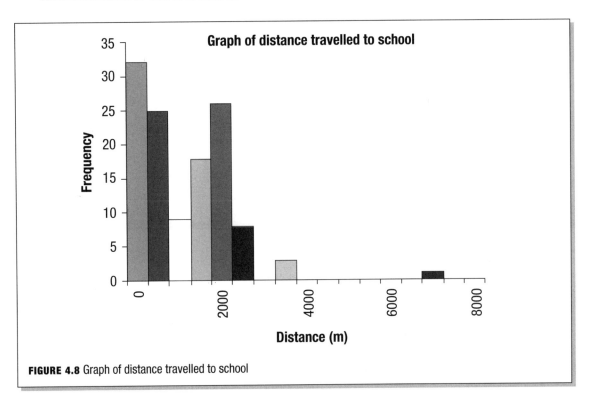

FIGURE 4.8 Graph of distance travelled to school

However, even young children can be helped to interpret such charts, for example the one in Figure 4.9. Smith (1997) reports that Ryan, a seven-year-old in a low-ability group, thought that the chart showed that one person had lost three teeth (more than anyone else). When the structure of the graph was pointed out, the pupils adjusted their view. Even as the teacher began to explain, Ryan pointed to the third bar and said *'Oh, that's me then, I've lost three teeth'*. This is the advantage of using such personal data. It is more concrete, and children find it easier to process, easier to think about.

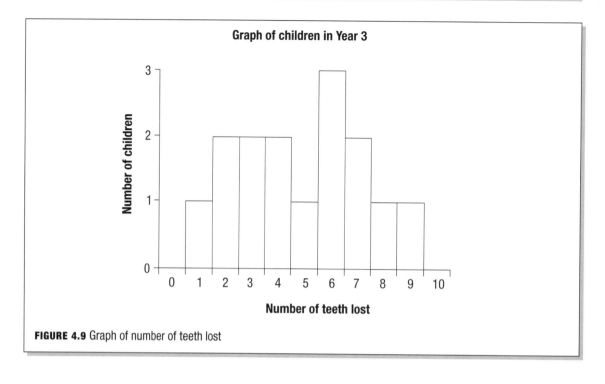

FIGURE 4.9 Graph of number of teeth lost

As Smith points out, the difficulty in interpretation is related to the difficulty in describing the chart: *'the hottest day'* is easier to grasp than *'the most frequently recorded temperature'*, and describing what the mode in Figure 4.9 represents is even more difficult. It does not show that most children have lost six teeth!, and we cannot use the words 'favourite' or 'commonest' in these sorts of situations, which is what children are used to. The best way to explain it may be to say *'The largest set is the set of children who have lost six teeth'*.

One great advantage of computers is that graphs can be drawn quickly and easily, allowing the emphasis to be placed on interpretation. However, if we are not careful, this very ease can hide difficulties of interpretation.

As was the case with searching, the techniques for creating graphs and charts are relatively easy, it is the conceptual understandings that pose the difficulties. As we have seen, numeric fields present special difficulties. It is easier for children if teachers use personal, concrete data (at least to begin with), and to articulate clearly what the graph shows.

Fair comparisons

To make sense of the data children also need the appropriate higher-order skills, which include making a fair comparison, and understanding whether one is making valid assumptions about the data.

Consider a database of census information about families living in Bourneville 100 years ago (this database can be downloaded from the **Cadbury Learning Zone** website). The database includes the following fields:

Name	
Surname	
Gender	Male/Female
Cadbury's worker	Yes/No

Let us suppose the children wanted to question the data to find out whether men living in Bourneville were equally likely to have worked for Cadbury's as women. Even adults may not always test this hypothesis correctly – the hypothesis, that is, that *Men at Bourneville were equally likely to have worked for Cadbury's as women.*

Some initial training students made the incorrect assumption that, as the file was about families living in Bourneville, all of them must have worked at Cadbury's. They therefore simply displayed a pie-chart for the field *'Gender'*. The graph displayed approximately the same number of men and women, and so they concluded, incorrectly, that the hypothesis was true.

Other students, by conducting a simple search, selected all the Cadbury's workers, and then displayed a pie-chart for the field *'Gender'*. This showed that about three-quarters of the Cadbury's workers were men, and so they concluded that the hypothesis was false, that men in Bourneville were more likely to work at Cadbury's. In fact what they had shown was that Cadbury workers in Bourneville were more likely to be men, which is not the same thing. Perhaps they had made the implicit assumption that there were an equal number of men and women in the database, which is, in fact, approximately true, so their conclusion was correct, even thought the reasoning was incorrect.

This was the actual data:

	Cadbury's worker	Not a Cadbury's worker
Men	27	36
Women	9	45

Suppose, on the other hand, that this had been the data:

	Cadbury's worker	Not a Cadbury's worker
Men	9	12
Women	9	45

Here the implicit assumption is now false, even though the proportion of men working at Cadbury's is still the same. Now the pie-chart would have shown an equal number of men and women working at Cadbury's, and they would have concluded that the hypothesis was true, whereas, in fact, the hypothesis is false (as 43% of men work at Cadbury's, whereas only 17% of women do so).

The correct way to test the hypothesis is to compare two graphs, one showing the proportion of women who are Cadbury's workers, the other showing the proportion of men who are Cadbury's workers. To do this, we first have to filter out all the women, by conducting a simple search, and create a pie-chart for the field *'Cadbury's worker'*. We then repeat that process for men. The result is as in Figure 4.10:

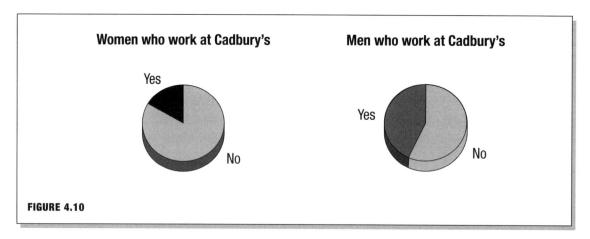

FIGURE 4.10

Creating databases

As we saw earlier, the techniques involved in creating a database are simple. It will come as no surprise to the reader to learn that, just as was the case with searching and interpreting graphs, the difficulties in creating a database are more in terms of the conceptual understandings and the higher-order skills involved.

As Smith (1999) has pointed out, much of the work in creating a new database takes place away from the computer:

- pupils identify and articulate a problem;
- brainstorm, prioritise, articulate a problem;
- collect the information, organised into categories, deciding which attributes are relevant to the enquiry.

When all this difficult work has been done, requiring conceptual understanding and higher-order skills, the actual entering of the data into the computer is an almost trivial task, albeit sometimes quite time-consuming, given the limited keyboard skills of some children.

In fact, if the thinking and planning is not done carefully enough, the whole enterprise can become a sterile, trivial, 'box-filling' exercise. As Underwood and Underwood (1990:77) point out, children need a purpose for classifying, and the act of creating a datafile should require children to set goals or pose a problem, collect and select data, and organise those data in such a way that the initial question can be resolved. They give examples of more and less successful attempts of children creating databases.

One successful experience involved children investigating pedestrian safety around their village school. They attribute the success to the nature of the problem. Crossing the road had meaning for these children – they knew what the goal was – and it was within their power to manipulate the material into an appropriate form.

The unsuccessful experience involved similar children, of the same age, creating a datafile relating to their topic on transport which included such fields as speed, cost and number of passengers. On a technical level the file was highly successful, but it had little real-world meaning, as they did not operate a consistent criterion for their choice of exemplar vehicles, choosing to compare Concorde with 'an average family car' (where the choice of a Ferrari or a Rolls-Royce would have been more consistent and appropriate). Underwood and Underwood (1990) concluded that the lack of clear, articulated goals for collecting the data on transport must have had some bearing on the matter, as well as the fact that the teacher seemed to be defining the goals in terms of ICT skills/techniques rather than ICT capability.

Sometimes, in order to ensure a successful outcome, the data need to be revisited and (re)coded. In the successful road safety investigation referred to above, the children had a clear research goal – to identify accident black spots and safe places to cross the road. At first they were not successful at retrieving this information because the nature of the data format inhibited access to the information the children knew was in the file. They had entered the data in lengthy text fields rather than using numeric variables. The children therefore coded the data relating to how heavily used a road junction was. They employed a five-point scale, where 1 represented a junction with low flow and no commercial traffic, and 5 a junction with plenty of heavy commercial vehicles.

Smith (1999) gives other examples of the difficulties children face when creating databases, none of which relate to techniques, but rather to conceptual understanding and higher-order skills:

- When pupils gathered data on hair colour they used a variety of descriptors, such that practically every entry was unique ... Pupils realised the need to group people with *similar* hair colour into a single category in order to ask questions such as 'Are there more children with fair hair than brown hair?' In the process they learned how information is lost when categorising it to ensure effective searching.

- Children have to recognise that for a good choice of fields for a datafile on mammals it is *habitat* not *tropical forest* or *desert* that constitutes the field. Children have difficulties in making the necessary abstractions.

- A Year 7 class constructed a questionnaire to find out what facilities younger children wanted in the new playground. The question they asked was 'What playground markings would you like?' The responses were too varied and so the questionnaire was redesigned to include one Yes/No question for each playground marking.

- Questions were suggested by different children in a Year 4 class that was carrying out a survey of children's journeys to school. Children agreed that the second of the two questions would yield more information:

Do your friends take you to school?

Who takes you to school?

Eventually, with guidance from the teacher, the children selected a question with a multiple choice field:

How do you travel to school? car / bus / bike / walk.

Understanding the structure of a database – having a mental map of its structure – is necessary not only for interrogating it successfully but also for constructing one (Smith 1999; Spavold 1989; Underwood and Underwood 1990:99). Yet one of the best ways of achieving this understanding is actually to construct a database. This paradox is resolved by starting with very familiar concrete data, which is why 'Ourselves' is such a popular initial topic for database work. It is also important for children to be actively involved 'in discussing what questions to pursue, and in exploring possible models for the file' (Smith 1999:171).

In terms of ICT capability, *Finding things out* makes few demands in terms of ICT techniques, but many in terms of conceptual understanding and higher-order skills. Table 4.3 summarises the techniques, concepts, processes and higher-order skills necessary for interrogating and constructing databases.

Following lines of enquiry

Before we continue we need to explain what is meant by the **processes** of *organising* and *classifying* information, and *following straightforward lines of enquiry* (see Table 4.1), as this is the key to understanding progression in *Finding things out*. In so doing, we shall explain how these processes relate to the **techniques** of sorting and searching.

TABLE 4.1 The characteristics of levels 2 and 3 and *Finding things out*

Level	Attainment target level description	Characteristic (QCA 2003)
2	**Pupils use ICT to organise** and **classify information** and to present their findings. They enter, save and retrieve work.	Level 2 is characterised by **purposeful** use of ICT to achieve **specific outcomes**.
3	**Pupils use ICT** to save information and **to find and use appropriate stored information, following straightforward lines of enquiry.**	Level 3 is characterised by the use of ICT to **develop ideas** and **solve problems. Lines of enquiry** are followed and the results taken into account in **successive steps**.

Organising and classifying information

Suppose pupils want to find out how many children in their class have blue eyes. There are three ways they can do this:

1. They conduct a simple search. They use the technique of a simple search to pick out all those children with blue eyes, to filter them out from the rest of the records of the other children in the class. They organise and classify the children in the database into those with blue eyes (those that are picked out by the search), and those with eyes of other colours (those that are not picked out by the search).

2. They can sort the data. They sort the children by eye colour. The pupils organise and classify the records of the database, and they then count the number of children with blue eyes without having to look through the whole database.

3. They create a column chart of eye colour. The information about eye colour is organised and classified, and this is displayed in graphical form.

The first and third techniques are more efficient that the second to answer this question.

Had they wanted to know *which* children had blue eyes, only the first and second techniques would be appropriate. Had they wanted to know which was the tallest child, sorting the data would be the most appropriate technique to use. Again, the process would be to organise and classify the data.

Similarly, when children are locating information in a CD-ROM encyclopaedia, they may conduct a simple search for 'whales'. Again, what they are doing is picking out, or filtering out, the sections of the encyclopaedia with information about whales from the rest of the information on the CD-ROM. Again, the *process* is organising and classifying information, and the *technique* used is a simple search.

We can think of the process of organising and classifying information as locating information; when we look for information on a CD-ROM we are clearly locating information; when we look for all the children with blue eyes we are also locating information; when we look for the tallest child we are locating information.

In each case the information we seek is in the CD-Rom or database, it is just a question of using the appropriate technique to locate it, by organising and classifying the information.

A straightforward line of enquiry

Earlier in this chapter we described how the Bourneville database was used to find out whether men living in Bourneville were equally likely to have worked for Cadbury's as women, to test the hypothesis that *Men at Bourneville were equally likely to have worked for Cadbury's as women*. This is an example of the process of following a line of enquiry. With a line of enquiry a hypothesis is formulated and the data needs to be handled, or manipulated, in order to test the hypothesis. The answer to the question posed is not actually in the database. In our example, nowhere in the database is it stated whether or not *Men at Bourneville are equally likely to have worked for Cadbury's as women*. The information cannot simply be located by organising and classifying the records. Instead, there are a series of steps that need to be followed, a line of enquiry:

1. First we classified the information to filter out all the women, by using the **technique** of *conducting a simple search*.

2. We then used the **technique** of *creating a pie-chart* to show the proportion of women who did and did not work at Cadbury's.

3. Next, we repeated that process for men.

4. Finally, we compared the two pie-charts, and concluded that the hypothesis was false.
   The next step for the children would be to ask 'Why?' *– to interpret the results – which may involve going back and following another line of enquiry.*

This explains what is meant by *following a line of enquiry*, which involved a series of steps, including two simple searches, and drawing two graphs.

It is not, however, a very straightforward line of enquiry. This is partly because it is not easy to decide which are the appropriate searches to test the hypothesis in question. It requires higher-order skills of reasoning that one would not expect of Year 4 children.

An example of a more straightforward line of enquiry is to determine whether the balance between boys and girls in their class is the same as for the school as a whole, by creating pie-charts, one for the class and one for the school (this example is taken from *Unit 4D, Collecting and presenting information: questionnaires and pie charts*).

An even more straightforward line of enquiry would be to answer the question 'Do children with brown eyes have brown hair?' This can be approached by searching for all children with brown eyes and seeing whether they have brown hair, or by sorting by eye colour and looking through the bunch of children with brown hair.

If we refer back to Table 4.1 we can see that the level 3 attainment target refers to *following straightforward lines of enquiry*, and is characterised by *the use of ICT to develop ideas and solve problems. Lines of enquiry are followed and the results taken into account in successive steps.*

It is not simply a question of using the *technique* of a simple search. The *technique* of a simple search was used to organise and classify the information (e.g. filtering out all the children with brown eyes in the first step of the latter line of enquiry).

As we discussed earlier, higher-order skills are necessary in order to select the most appropriate line of enquiry, including being able to reason what would constitute a fair test of the hypothesis.

Lines of enquiry involve testing hypotheses, and one would expect lines of enquiry to be embedded in a *Process Loop* (Gifford 1995). Indeed when ICT is embedded in such a process loop it almost automatically ensures that a line of enquiry is followed. The stages in the Process Loop are (*ibid.*:2):

A: Starting Point
What are the prerequisite skills/knowledge/experience that pupils need?
Finding starting points – a context for study; looking for readiness to proceed.

B: Engagement
Establishing children's interest and involvement in the task.
Defining a purpose (in general terms) and deciding what data to look at.
Gathering data and freely exploring it.

C: Looking for connections

Sorting/classifying/browsing through data.

Asking purposeful questions and asking about relationships.

D: Asking questions

Taking an inquisitive look at the organised data.

Asking purposeful questions and asking about relationships.

E: Looking for Answers

Interrogating the data in various ways.

Looking for relationships/correlations and counter-examples.

Discussing whether the answer is *yes, no* or *unproven.*

F: Interpretation

Adopting a sceptical view and questioning the validity of the finding.

Interpretation and explanation – from *what* to *why.*

G: Product

New knowledge and a deeper engagement leading to further enquiry.

IT capability.

Steps A to G form a progressive sequence. However, in some investigations it may be necessary to take a step backwards or to re-run the centre of the loop (steps C to E).

The higher-order information-handling skills involved are (*ibid.*:18):

- **Decision-making skills** – the ability to decide what data will serve the purpose of the enquiry and what sources are appropriate.
- **Classifying skills** – the ability to adopt a variety of approaches to the sorting, searching, organisation and presentation of data, to understand a range of classification systems and to seek out connections.
- **Questioning skills** – the ability to ask pertinent questions that will probe the data and lead to meaningful answers.
- **Analytical skills** – the ability to make inferences from information in a reasoned and logical manner.
- **Explanatory skills** – the ability to apply existing knowledge to draw conclusions about the nature and significance of what has been observed and to put forward a reasoned case to help explain new findings.

In this chapter we have repeatedly argued that the difficulties and challenges that relate to the use of databases concern the conceptual understandings and higher-order skills that are needed, rather than the techniques.

The implication for teaching is that any work with databases needs to be embedded in realistic, purposeful activities. In other words, what is sometimes called the *contextual* or *integrationist* method of teaching (Lodge 1992), rather than the *didactic* or *separatist* method of teaching information skills. The didactic style uses specific lessons for the purpose of imparting *information skills* to the pupils; the contextual style teaches *skills* in any lesson where a need to handle information arises (where the term skills refers to higher order information skills, not basic ICT skills).

A straightforward line of enquiry with no searching

A straightforward line of enquiry need not involve searching at all. For example, suppose the children wanted to know, from their 'Ourselves' database, whether taller children weighed more. One way is to plot a scattergram, but the interpretation of scattergrams is not something that one can expect from Year 4 children. An alternative is to sort the data by height, and then look at the top and bottom ten records. This might yield the information presented in Table 4.2.

TABLE 4.2 A line of enquiry using the technique of sorting the data

	cm	kg
Julia	115	26
Sam	117	21
Shanna	118	24
James	118	23
Thomas	119	23
Peter	121	21
Dani	123	29
Terry	124	26
Matthew	124	15
Jenny	125	25
Joe	152	45
Greg	153	32
Kate B	154	36
Simon	154	35
Joe	154	36
Sophie	154	39
Ruth	154	32
Kate	156	38
Nathan	159	28
Simon	160	29
Julia	162	41

By inspecting the weights of the top and bottom ten children it can be seen that, on the whole, it is true that taller children weigh more.

Complex searches and complex lines of enquiry

A complex, or Boolean, search is a technique that includes an operator, such as **AND**, **OR**, or **NOT**.

Complex search techniques using **AND** are not beyond the ability of Key Stage 2 children, as evidenced by the fact that the QCA Scheme of Work introduces them in Year 5 (Analysing data and asking questions: using complex searches, 5B).

Following a complex line of enquiry, however, is not expected until Key Stage 3 (level 5 attainment target description: *Pupils develop and refine their work to enhance its quality, using information from a range of sources. Where necessary,* **they use complex lines of enquiry** *to test hypotheses*).

Just because children can carry out a complex search does not mean that they can undertake a complex line of enquiry.

If we are clear about the distinction between a *search* (a technique) and a *line of enquiry* (a process) then we can avoid such misconceptions.

Conversely, a complex search (a technique) does not necessarily mean that there is a straightforward line of enquiry (a process), let alone a complex line of enquiry. Searching a database to see if there are any children with blue eyes and black hair is a complex search, but, in itself, is not a line of enquiry at all. The process is organising and classifying information (level 2) – picking out, filtering out, all children with blue eyes and black hair.

It would be a somewhat arbitrary decision where to draw the line between a simple line of enquiry and a complex line of enquiry. The number of steps involved is one factor, the logical reasoning involved is another (including being able to reason with **OR** and **NOT** Boolean operators). Greater understanding of the subject matter is another factor. The section above on searching databases will give the reader an idea of the kinds of lines of enquiry that can be expected in the primary school, and the difficulties that children have.

The reader is referred to Chapter 5, 'Questioning the File', of Underwood and Underwood (1990) for further discussion of the processes involved in interrogating databases.

Table 4.3 summarises the distinctions made between the techniques, concepts, processes and higher-order skills relating to interrogating and constructing databases.

Attainment target levels and progression in *Finding things out*

As we did in relation to *Exchanging and sharing information*, so again we shall consider progression in relation to the characteristics of the ICT National Curriculum, as outlined by SCAA (1996) and the QCA (2003).

Level 1: Initial exploratory use

AT level description: Pupils explore information from various sources, showing they know that information exists in different forms.

At this exploratory stage the pupils are simply learning that information exists in a variety of forms, including text, images, sounds (including speech and music), and icons.

TABLE 4.3 ICT capability and databases

	Routines / basic skills	Techniques Knowing how to …	Concepts Understanding …	Processes Being able to …	Higher-order skills Knowing what/that …; deciding that …

Interrogating a database	*As per techniques*	sort data
		search data (simple keyword search)
		search using AND, OR, NOT
		create graphs/charts
			record
			list
			field
			entry
			Boolean logic
			  AND, OR, NOT
			bar chart
			histogram
				organise information
				classify information
				locate information
				conduct a straightforward
				  line of enquiry
				display information
				interpret information
				checking the accuracy of the
				  data
					making and testing hypotheses
					knowing when it is appropriate to organise, classify,
					  conduct line of enquiry to test hypothesis
					knowing what technique(s) to use to test hypothesis
					knowing what data to display to test hypothesis
					knowing what a fair comparison is
					interpreting the result of the line of enquiry
					knowing that one needs to check the plausibility /
					  accuracy of the data
					see also (2) – (5) below

Constructing a database	*As per techniques*	specify field size and type (text, number, and multiple-choice fields)
		enter data
			text field
			numeric field
			multiple-choice field
			field length and units
				creating a database structure
				constructing questionnaires
				entering data in a database
				checking the accuracy of the
				  data
					deciding which fields are necessary, and whether they
					  should be text, number, or multiple-choice fields
					knowing that one needs to check the accuracy of the
					  data
					see also (2) – (3) below

Higher-order skills

1. recognising when the use of ICT might be appropriate or effective;
2. planning how ICT resources, techniques and processes are to be used in a task;
3. conjecturing, discussing and testing the strategies and data to be used;
4. monitoring the progress of problem-solving activities;
5. making and testing hypotheses;
6. evaluating the outcomes of using ICT for a task;
7. explaining and justifying the use of ICT in producing solutions to problems;
8. reflecting on the learning that might have occurred during the task.

It is not so much the children using the computer at this stage, as the teacher drawing attention to the fact that information exists in a variety of forms, whether it be the teacher or the children using the computer. Attention will also be drawn to forms of information off computer.

A talking book is an example of an ICT resource with text, images, spoken language, icons and animations. The teacher might draw their attention to the different forms when the pupils are using this resource, and/or when the teacher is using the talking book as a 'Big Book'.

Other examples might include:

- The teacher using a CD-ROM encyclopaedia to locate information. Using a computer connected to a data projector the teacher could show the pupils information about an animal, reading the text out to them, and letting them see and hear any video or audio clips (e.g. of a lion).

- The teacher taking digital photos on a school outing, and the pupils viewing them on their return to the classroom.

- The teacher recording sounds in the classroom at different times of the day. The children work out when the sound may have been recorded, what information/clues the sound gives us. This can be useful for getting across the idea that the absence of sound can provide information as well!

- The teacher and children using a pictogram graphing program to display results of a simple survey, for example of the children's favourite food.

Level 2: Purposeful use

AT level description: Pupils use ICT to organise and classify information and to present their findings. They enter, save and retrieve work.

As pupils move on to level 2 they begin to use ICT for specific purposes.

They use a graphing program to find out answers to questions, such as 'How do most children travel to school?' By examining the graph they are able to find out the answer to their question – and also, of course, subsequently *exchange and share this information* with other children.

They will also use a simple database to sort and search, in order to find out answers to questions. For example, using a database with information about themselves, they might:

- sort the data to find out who is the tallest in the class (the *process* is using ICT to organise information, and to do this they use the *technique* of sorting the data);

- search the data to locate all children with blue eyes (the *process* is using ICT to classify children by eye colour, and to do this they use the *technique* of a simple search to filter out children with blue eyes – it is also possible to use the *technique* of sorting the data, as all the children with blue eyes will then be bunched together).

They also learn to use menus, indexes, hyperlinks and key words to search for pictures and gather information held on a CD-ROM. For example, they may search for information about an animal, where the *process* is to *locate information* (technically, this is the same as *classifying* information – the keyword will *filter out* all the pages with references to the keyword in question), either:

- by using the *technique* of clicking on links (e.g. from a menu); or
- by using the *technique* of entering a keyword to carry out a search.

They also use branching database programs to identify (classify) objects, by answering yes/no questions. The process is to *classify* the object, and with most branching programs the technique needed is simply to click on an icon or link.

Level 3: Using ICT to develop ideas, following lines of enquiry

AT level description: Pupils use ICT to save information and to find and use appropriate stored information, following straightforward lines of enquiry.

The characteristic which differentiates level 3 from level 2 is that IT is used to develop ideas. Lines of enquiry are followed, and the results are taken into account in successive steps.

Up to now, information has been located in a single step, be it by entering a key word in a search, or by sorting the data, or by drawing a graph. What characterises children at level 3 is that they are able to find things out in a series of steps – namely by *following a line of enquiry*. We explained what constitutes a straightforward line of enquiry earlier in this chapter.

One example we gave concerned finding out whether the balance between boys and girls in their class was the same as for the school as a whole, by comparing two pie-charts. This would require a series of steps:

1. drawing a pie-chart for the field 'Gender' for all the children in the school;
2. conducting a simple search for the children in their class;
3. drawing a pie-chart for the field 'Gender';
4. comparing the two pie-charts.

Other examples of straightforward lines of enquiry include testing the following hypotheses:

- Do taller people weigh more? At this stage children would not be able to interpret scattergraphs, but could proceed to answer the question by comparing the weights of the ten tallest and ten shortest children (as was explained earlier in this chapter).
- Do children with brown eyes have brown hair? This can be approached by searching for all children with brown eyes and seeing whether they have brown hair (or, again, by sorting by eye colour and looking through the bunch of children with brown hair).

It is helpful at this stage to consider the research and analysis undertaken by Underwood and Underwood (1990), who produced a classification of the complexity of the strategies used by children to question databases (see Table 4.4), and who make a distinction between *fact seeking retrieval* and *relational retrieval*.

One way of thinking about the difference between finding things out at levels 2 and 3 is that at level 2 information is merely located, but at level 3 information has to be processed or handled in order to find the answer to the question.

At level 2 a database might be searched in order to find which *animals are marsupials* – this information is there and can be located. When the record for a particular animal has been located, the information as to whether or not it is a marsupial is there. This is what Underwood and Underwood call *fact seeking retrieval*.

At level 3 nowhere in the database can the fact that *large dinosaurs are (or are not) meat eaters* be located. Instead the information has to be processed, a line of enquiry has to be followed.

TABLE 4.4 Fact-seeking retrieval, relational retrieval and the attainment target level descriptors

Underwood and Underwood (1990:94–95)	Comments
1. *Page the data retrieval* – moving from one record to another. This is analogous to looking for information in a dictionary or telephone directory by turning the pages one by one.	**Level 1** This is **exploring** the data, which is level 1 NC AT.
2. *Fact-seeking retrieval.* This was done either: **Fact1** by sorting the data by the field 'type of animal', which enabled all the instances of (e.g.) marsupials to be grouped together in the list; or **Fact2** by a simple search for (e.g.) animals which are marsupials (i.e. by identification questions to find the animals which posses the property of being marsupials).	**Level 2** These are both **purposeful.** Fact1 is using ICT to **organise** and classify information, by using the *technique* of sorting the data; and Fact2 is using ICT to organise and **classify** information (filtering out those animals which are marsupials), by using the *technique* of a **simple search** (this is not the same as the *process* of following a straightforward line of enquiry). One way of thinking about this is that information is *located*.
3. *Relational retrieval.* In these questions children looked for relationships and patterns within the data through the testing of hypotheses, which might be fallacious but legitimate – for example, that large dinosaurs are meat-eaters. Sometimes the testing of the hypothesis might be implicit (implied by the question asked), and sometimes explicit (clearly articulated). Sometimes children might ask questions with two variables (e.g. of size and eating habits) but with no specific question in mind other than a feeling that this could be interesting, implicitly indicating a belief in a relationship.	**Level 3** This is **developing** ideas, lines of enquiry are followed, decisions are made, the results are taken into account In successive steps, and the use of IT is described (SCAA 1996; QCA 2003). This is the *process* of following a straightforward line of enquiry. One way of thinking about the difference between this and fact-seeking retrieval is that this goes beyond merely locating information. Nowhere in the database can the fact that large dinosaurs are (or are not) meat-eaters be located.

Level 4: Interpreting and questioning the plausibility of information

The characteristic which differentiates **level 4** from level 3 is the ability to *interpret* the information obtained by using IT tools, and *question the plausibility* of information.

AT level description: Pupils understand the need for care in framing questions when collecting, finding and interrogating information. They interpret their findings, question plausibility and recognise that poor-quality information leads to unreliable results.

Up to now the teacher will either have set up the structure of the database (i.e. selected of fields etc.), or have guided the pupils in how to set it up themselves. When they are able to do this for themselves they will be working at level 5 (see below), and so one feature of working at level 4 is pupils becoming progressively more independent in this respect (*Pupils understand the need for care in framing questions when collecting, finding . . . information*).

Another feature of children working at this level is that they become more efficient at following lines of enquiry, and are more able to work out how to work out the appropriate search to answer a specific question, even when the wording of the question may not be helpful, for example knowing the query *Which is the largest / smallest* is best answered by sorting the data, as was discussed earlier (see the section on searching databases in this chapter). (*Pupils understand the need for care in framing questions when . . . interrogating information*).

Up to now the pupils have been using existing databases, or creating simple databases of information relating to the particular topic being studied, and then, after the event, formulating and testing hypotheses. Now they collect the data they need in order to test a hypothesis.

The reader is referred to two activities described by Ross (1989) which exemplify this distinction. He worked with three classes of children, one Year 4 class (demonstrating evidence of working at level 3), and two Year 5 classes (working at demonstrating evidence of working at level 4).

The Year 4 class collected fossils under his guidance, and the individual pupils entered information on about six fossils each. When the information had been collected and entered into the database, the children browsed through the data looking for connections and formulating hypotheses (*Ibid.* 1988:111):

> Groups of children came up with different ideas of what to look for. Some searched for the distribution of dimensions and averages of each particular species, discovering the typical size of each. Others searched for the different kinds found, showing them as histograms or pie charts. And others looked at the distributions on the sketch of the quarry, seeing if there was any pattern in where species were found. They found that most of the Inoceramus were in the lower of the two strata, and that the Entolium and Rhynchonella were found in both layers. Bellemites were only in the lower level. As each discovery was made, the children came up with new ideas to try out. Their hypothesising was firmly rooted in the data, with which they were quite familiar, but they nevertheless were encouraged to speculate freely because there was very little penalty in testing a 'wrong' hypothesis – the computer did the boring searches, and did it accurately and without wasting time.

In contrast, the two Year 5 classes started out by collecting the data necessary in order to answer specific questions, one of which was *What are the characteristics of a strong conker?* and the other, *What makes a good parachute?*

These children had to decide what data to collect, to collect it, and then decide how to interrogate it (level 4: *Pupils understand the need for care in framing questions when collecting, finding and interrogating information*).

At level 4 they also question the accuracy and plausibility of data, whether this information is in a database, on a CD-ROM, or on the Web. For example they would become aware that, when using an American CD-ROM encyclopaedia, or an internet search engine, that some of the information about Birmingham would be about Birmingham in Alabama, and that if they wanted to search for information about football they would need to enter the search term 'soccer', otherwise some of the information they locate would be about American football. They learn to work around this problem in various ways, including the use of complex searches, for example using the Boolean search 'Birmingham AND England' (see QCA unit 5B) (*Pupils understand the need for care in framing questions when collecting, finding and interrogating information*).

They also check for incorrectly entered and implausible data, and recognise that such poor-quality information leads to unreliable results. For example, they check for incorrect spellings, implausible data (for example, 1 metre for the length of a river), and incorrect field types (for example 'ten' in a number field or 'girl' in a field where 'f' for female is required) (see QCA unit 5B). (*They interpret their findings, question plausibility and recognise that poor-quality information leads to unreliable results*).

They will also be evaluating the information they find on the Web for bias. For example, part of the suggested integrated task in *Unit 6D, Using the internet to search large databases and to interpret information*, is the following:

> As part of a literacy topic on developing journalistic style, use the internet to research events of public interest. Discuss how the children can refine the search to get suitable information and which sites may be appropriate. Ask the children to work in groups to interpret the information, checking for balance and ethical reporting. Discuss the impact on individuals of inaccurate reporting.

In this connection the reader is referred to the framework developed by the BFI (Bazalgette 1989, 1990) for critically evaluating media texts (whether this is books, newspapers, television, film or electronic texts). This framework takes the form of a set of signpost questions which should be asked of any text, whatever the medium, in order to be able to evaluate it, see Table 4.5.

TABLE 4.5 The BFI's 'Signpost' questions

WHO is communicating, and why?	Media agencies
WHAT TYPE of text is it?	Media categories
HOW has it been produced?	Media technologies
HOW do we know what it means?	Media languages
WHO receives it, and what sense do they make of it?	Media audiences
How does it PRESENT its subject to us?	Media representations

Level 5: Increased rigour, combining the use of ICT tools

AT level description: Pupils select the information they need for different purposes, check its accuracy and organise it in a form suitable for processing.

The characteristic which differentiates **level 5** from level 4 is its **increased rigour**, and by **combining the use of ICT tools** within the overall structure of an ICT solution.

The defining difference between this level and the previous one, apart from greater precision and increased rigour, is that children are able to create their database independently. They are also able to deal with less-straightforward lines of enquiry. In addition, they combine the use of ICT tools.

The latter can be exemplified by the following scenario (from the National Curriculum in Action *Football Investigation* scenario – see *http://www.ncaction.org.uk/*):

Football investigation

Pupils were shown how to use a spreadsheet as part of a mathematical investigation into probability.

Using a prepared spreadsheet, the teacher threw a die 30 times and demonstrated to the class how to transfer information from a tally into a spreadsheet. Pupils were asked to repeat the activity. They were asked to predict the average frequency for each number. In groups, pupils threw dice and recorded their results. This information was entered into the prepared spreadsheet. The teacher pointed out the actual results ranged from 2 to 10. The teacher then taught the class to use the AVERAGE function within the spreadsheet. As a class they discussed results and created a chart showing the frequency of each number.

Later, the pupils were given a number of scenarios to investigate using a spreadsheet. Pupils were encouraged to collect their own data and design their own spreadsheets. They created charts, using them to identify patterns in the data. The pupil, in this example, chose to investigate the frequency and timing of goals in the Football Premiership.

Commentary

In this example, the pupil has created and entered data into a spreadsheet. He has collected information from newspapers and designed his own spreadsheet, choosing to enter data about the frequency of goals at five-minute intervals. He has used the charting facilities of the software to look for patterns in the data. He has used the chart to hypothesise that 'most goals are scored just before half-time and in the last ten minutes of a match'.

The teacher encouraged him to question the plausibility of the hypothesis by searching for more statistical data using the internet. With some support, he has used the internet to find an additional source of football statistics. He printed out a graph titled 'When the goals go in'. He compared this new information with his own to question the plausibility of his hypothesis. He noted that the pattern found in his data was reflected by the more extensive data set on the website.

This actually exemplifies work at level 4, as the pupil was not working independently, and had to be guided by the teacher. The teacher was scaffolding the learning. Had the pupil been working independently, this would have demonstrated work at level 5.

Activities

1. In this chapter we have said that the techniques in creating a database are simple and that the difficulty is in terms of the conceptual understanding and higher-order skills involved. We also made the point that if the thinking and planning associated with creating a database is not done carefully enough the whole enterprise can become a sterile, trivial, 'box-filling' exercise. Children first need a purpose for classifying, and the act of creating a datafile should require children to set goals or pose a problem – they collect the data needed to test an hypothesis. (Underwood and Underwood 1990).

   Think of a purposeful reason for the creation of a database, and explain how it links to another area of the primary curriculum. You could make reference to a particular Programme of Study from the National Curriculum – such as geography or science, or to a QCA scheme of work from a foundation subject within the curriculum.

2. Analyse the content of one or more of the following QCA units: 2C, 3C, 5B or 6D to decide what National Curriculum level pupils could attain if they completed the unit of work. Ensure that you include a justification for the level that you assign. How might the work within a particular unit be adapted or supplemented to facilitate higher levels of attainment?

5

Progression in *Making things happen*

Objectives

- To understand progression (in *Making things happen*) in relation to the characteristics of the ICT National Curriculum as outlined by SCAA (1996) and the QCA (2003)

- To understand that, as was true with *Exchanging and sharing information* and *Finding things out*, it is also the case that much of the difficulties concerning *Making things happen* relates to the higher-order skills that are needed rather than the ICT techniques involved

- To understand the importance of pupils using control boxes to give instruction to models (such as model traffic lights) that are external to the computer, in order for them to understand at a concrete level how computers control devices and respond to inputs (sensors)

As was explained in detail in Chapter 1, the National Curriculum ICT Programme of Study specifies, at Key Stage 1, that pupils should be taught:

> 2c) how to plan and give instructions to make things happen [for example, programming a floor turtle, placing instructions in the right order];

and at Key Stage 2, that pupils should be taught:

> 2b) how to create, test, improve and refine sequences of instructions to make things happen and to monitor events and respond to them [for example, monitoring changes in temperature, detecting light levels and turning on a light].

As with the other aspects, as children progress through Key Stage 1 and Key Stage 2, so they learn more complex programs, and the techniques associated with them. But as we saw in Chapter 2, the learning of these techniques is a means to an end, not an end in itself. Therefore, progression in ICT is not about a progression in terms of ICT techniques, but in terms of progression in ICT capability.

As we shall see, progression in relation to *Making things happen* is relatively straightforward, but there are questions concerning whether the level descriptions realistically map onto what one should expect at particular ages.

We shall first explain what is expected of children at the end of Key Stage 2. It will then be easier to see the rationale for the activities in the previous years.

As we saw in Chapter 1, part of *Making things happen* is concerned with children understanding that computers can be programmed to sense physical data (e.g. changes in light, movement etc.) and to automatically respond to this by controlling devices. Examples include alarms responding to intruders, the street lights turning on and off in response to changes in the amount of light, supermarket doors opening automatically when customers approach, etc.

In Years 5 and 6 children have hands-on experience by creating models or simulations of such systems. A simple system would be a model lighthouse, with the main light being activated by lack of sunlight, i.e. when it gets dark, the light flashes. The equipment needed for this includes:

- a control box;
- a model lighthouse (*ideally this will be constructed by the children themselves with corriflute, but it is possible to buy a ready made model*);
- a bulb;
- a light sensor (an LDR, or light-dependent resistor);
- a program to control the lighthouse, and a computer.

The program for controlling the lighthouse is shown in Figure 5.1.

The main program is shown on the left, and the subroutine (or procedure) is shown on the right. The rhombus is a decision symbol. At this point in the program a test is made to see if input 1 is on (i.e. is the sun out?). If it is, then it returns to the start and makes the test again. This loop will continue until input 1 is turned off (i.e. the sun goes down), at which point the subroutine 'Flash' will run. This turns the main light on, waits one second, turns it off, waits another second, then stops and returns to the main program, where the test 'Is input 1 on?' is again made. This loop will continue until input 1 is turned on (i.e. when the sun rises).

With such a simple series of instructions, this could be written as one single program, without needing to call a subroutine, but it is good practice to break down programs into procedures/subroutines as they are then much easier to write, to follow and to debug.

At Year 6 the expectation is that most children would be able to write a more complex program than this (with inputs and outputs). The QCA (1998) guidance states that most children should be able to *produce simple procedures to turn on lights and sound alarms; need help with their program and will need to make amendments* (Unit 6C: Control and monitoring – What happens when . . . ?). The description of the integrated task for this unit is as follows:

- Explain to the class that they are going to make a house security system with a floodlight and house lights that come on after dark and go off in the morning, a window alarm based on a magnetic switch, a door alarm based on a pressure pad and a burglar alarm with a loud buzzer and flashing lights.

- Ask the children to work in groups to build a model of a house with a variety of input and output devices attached. This could just be the front façade, built out of cardboard or other material. The house will need a floodlight and light sensor outside and lights at one or more windows inside. The front door will need a pressure pad under the door mat and the window will need a magnetic switch. Both door and window will need to open. There should be a coloured light and buzzer on the front of the house marked 'alarm'.

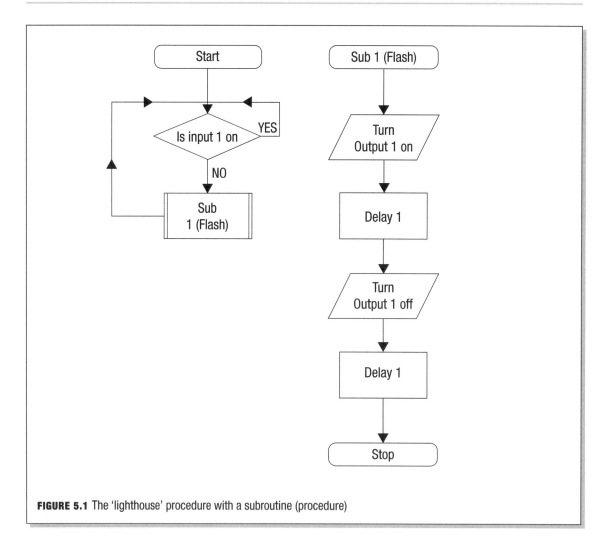

FIGURE 5.1 The 'lighthouse' procedure with a subroutine (procedure)

- Ask each group to write a sequence of instructions to switch lights on at night and off in the morning, and for the alarms to sound if the door or window is opened. They should write separate sequences for each event, not try to combine them all. Ask them to record their programs, draw and annotate a diagram, and describe the results.

However, it should be noted that the QCA does not expect all children to be able to do this independently at this age – in the QCA unit it does say that most children will *need help with their program.*

It can readily be seen that writing a program for the house security system is more complex and more difficult than writing the program to control the lighthouse. Yet the basic building blocks are identical, and hence the techniques the children need to know are exactly the same. What creates the difficulty is the complexity of the system, not the techniques. The difficulty is one of procedural thinking; it relates to the higher-order skills needed, in particular to (cf. Kennewell *et al.* 2000:23):

- planning how ICT resources, techniques and processes are to be used in a task;
- conjecturing, discussing and testing the strategies and data to be used;
- monitoring the progress of problem-solving activities;
- making and testing hypotheses;
- evaluating the outcomes of using ICT for a task.

As was true with Finding Things Out, so here it is also the case that much of the difficulty concerns the higher-order skills that are needed, rather than the ICT techniques involved. Anyone who has used LOGO or Flowol will attest to this. The number of commands that need to be learned are relatively few, and are not difficult. But putting them together in a sequence that works is more problematic, and the difficulty increases with the complexity of the problem, not the techniques involved.

Let us consider how competent Year 6 children would tackle the problem of writing a program to make the house security system mentioned in Unit 6C. We would expect them to plan it on pencil and paper, and use procedures/subroutines where appropriate (the QCA states that the children *should write separate sequences for each event, not try to combine them all*). They might write the instructions on paper first, some of which might look like this:

1. Is it dark?
2. If 'Yes' turn the lights on.
3. If 'No' go back to 1.
4. Is it light?
5. If 'Yes' turn the lights off.
6. If 'No' go back to 4.

or they might plan it on paper as a flow chart, as in Figure 5.2.

Either way, they will plan it in advance, before going to the computer.

A program that responds to inputs (such as changes in light intensity) as well as controlling outputs (such as turning a light off) is more complex conceptually than a program with only outputs.

A program with procedures is more complex conceptually than one without procedures. This is because the procedures have to be thought of independently of the main program, although once children are comfortable with the concept of a procedure, then it becomes easier to write them, follow them and debug them.

This might not, at first, appear to be true, as the 'lighthouse' program written without any subroutines/procedures seems to be simpler to follow (as in Figure 5.3) than the same program written with a subroutine (as in Figure 5.1).

However, this is only because the program is so simple that we can keep all the individual steps in mind at once. Once there are more than seven or so steps to the program it is difficult to keep them all in mind, and so it then becomes easier to think in terms of the main program and subroutines/procedures separately. This is because of a limitation of our working memory, and is a feature of the way we cope with many different tasks – as was originally

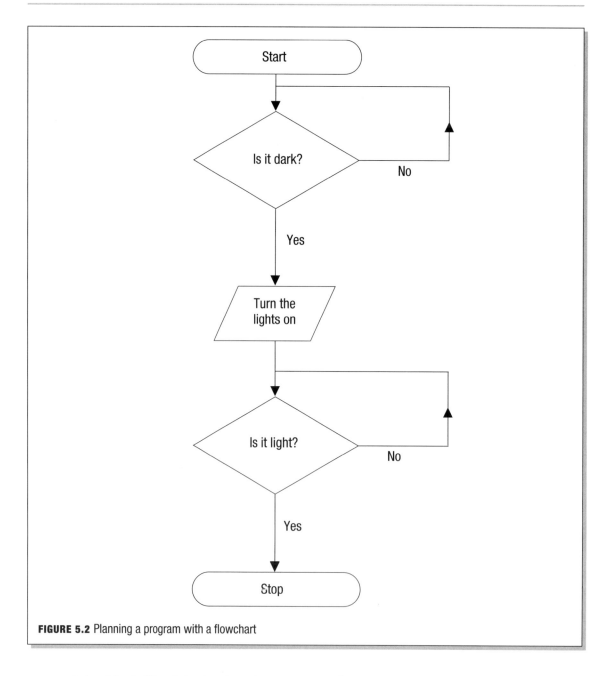

FIGURE 5.2 Planning a program with a flowchart

explained by Miller (1956) in his classic article 'The magical number seven, plus or minus two'.

Consider how to program a computer to play backgammon. It is simple, really. Here is the program:

1. Display the backgammon board on the screen.
2. Place the pieces in their starting positions.

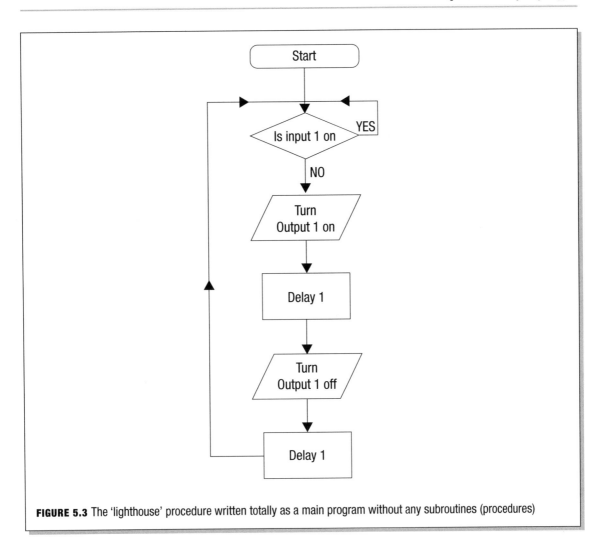

FIGURE 5.3 The 'lighthouse' procedure written totally as a main program without any subroutines (procedures)

3. Shake the dice to see whose turn it is to go first.

4. Display the dice.

5. If it is the computer's turn, then go to subroutine/procedure 'My turn', ELSE go to subroutine/procedure 'Your turn'.

6. If no-one has won, then go to subroutine/procedure 'Change turns' and go to step 5, ELSE go to subroutine/procedure 'Game over' and STOP.

This can be represented by the flow diagram in Figure 5.4.

All that remains is the minor matter of writing all the subroutines/procedures!

This illustrates the way it is possible to plan how to write a program by breaking down the problem into a number of manageable steps. We can envisage how the program will work, as there are only a limited number of steps to consider. This also illustrates what is meant by the attainment target *They use ICT systems to control events in a predetermined manner...* **(level 4).**

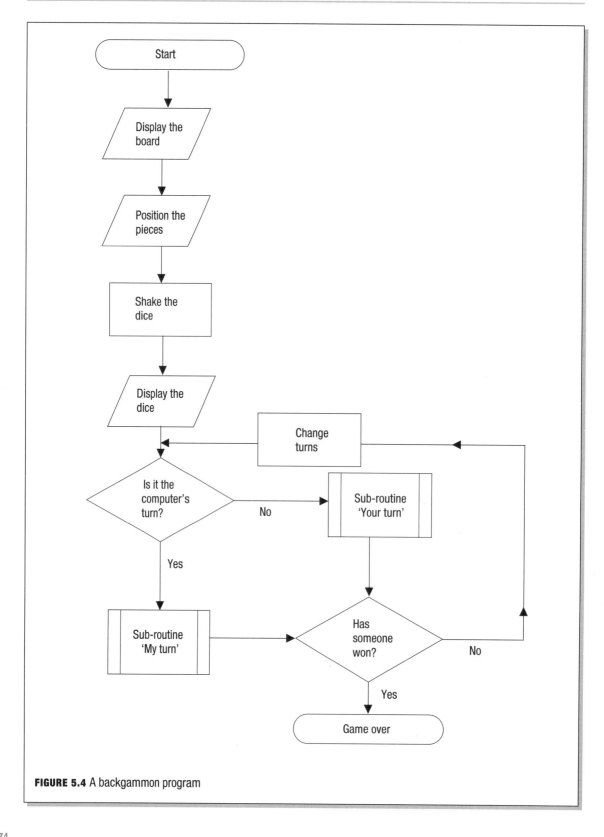

FIGURE 5.4 A backgammon program

Let us now consider two different ways (as in scenarios 1 and 2, below) of using a floor turtle, such as a Roamer, with a course such as the one in Figure 5.5:

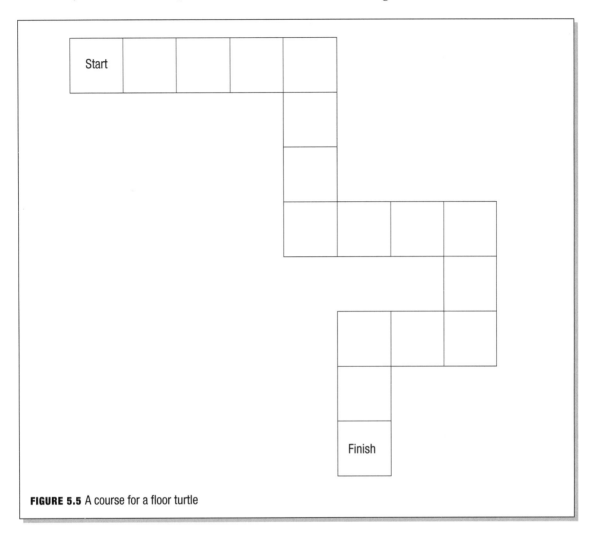

FIGURE 5.5 A course for a floor turtle

Scenario 1

One child might create a sequence of instructions, without procedures, to program the floor turtle to follow a track from the starting grid to the finish line, by counting the squares, and arrive at the following sequence:

Forward 5
Right 1
Forward 4
Left 1
Forward 4

Right 1
Forward 3
Right 1
Forward 3
Left 1
Forward 3

Having planned the sequence on paper, the child then enters the instructions into the Roamer. When she has entered all the instructions, she tests them by pressing 'GO'.

She finds the sequence does not work. She has failed to take into account that, as the Roamer starts on the first square, it only needs to go forward four steps, not five.

So she changes the first instruction accordingly. She tests it again, and finds that it still does not work. Now the problem comes at the second stage. She now realises that it is the same basic error and that this is going to be a problem all the way through the sequence. She improves and refines the whole sequence, and tests the following revised set of commands:

Forward 4
Right 1
Forward 3
Left 1
Forward 3
Right 1
Forward 2
Right 1
Forward 2
Left 1
Forward 2

The child is able to *create, test, improve and refine sequences of instructions to make things happen*, which is what is expected in the Programme of Study at Key Stage 2. She is working at level 3 of the National Curriculum: *[Pupils] use sequences of instructions to control devices and achieve specific outcomes.*

Scenario 2

Consider another child, working on the same problem. This child counts the number of squares, writes down the instruction *Forward 5*, enters the command into the Roamer, and observes the effect. He sees that it has gone too far, so he amends the command to *Forward 4*. He tests this and observes that it now works. He then decides that the Roamer needs to turn Right once. He records this on paper, enters the command into the Roamer and presses 'GO'. He sees that it works. He continues entering and testing each command, one at a time, testing each one in turn after he has entered it. He records the effect, amending and re-entering it where necessary.

This is a more time-consuming and cumbersome procedure, but is conceptually easier to manage.

This child is able to *plan and give instructions to make things happen*, which is what is expected in the Programme of Study at Key Stage 1, and he is working at level 2 of the National Curriculum: *[Pupils] plan and give instructions to make things happen and describe the effects.*

Note that the difference between the child working at level 2 and the child working at level 3 has nothing to do with their learning new techniques; it is a matter of what higher-order skills are used, the way the child is *conjecturing, discussing and testing the strategies and data to be used.*

We have now illustrated what constitutes progression, apart from at the very first stages. In terms of actually making something happen, not much is expected at level 1; it is more a matter of the children realising that devices can be controlled. All that is required is that children should be able to enter single commands – for example the children might move the Roamer forward and back along a number line. Attainment target description for level 1 states that: *[Pupils] recognise that many everyday devices respond to signals and instructions. They make choices when using such devices to produce different outcomes.*

Before we summarise the progression in *Making things happen* and relate it to the guidance in the QCA, we should like to discuss the importance of using control boxes and external devices, the use of LOGO, and the use of data-logging equipment.

Control boxes and external devices

First, it is very important that children use control boxes to give instructions to models (such as model traffic lights) that are external to the computer, in order for them to understand at a concrete level how computers control devices, and respond to inputs (with sensors).

We consider it necessary to emphasise this point as it is possible to have on-screen mimics of traffic lights for children to control (see Figure 5.6). If these are used, however, children do not actually experience, at first hand, that computers control *external* devices, and therefore are not having the full hands-on experience, and consequently are not so able to *investigate and compare the uses of ICT inside and outside school* (*Breadth of study*, Key Stage 2).

Another reason for not using the on-screen mimics is that there is a limited choice of such mimics, but most important of all is the fact that if they use the ready-made mimics they will not actually be designing their own external device, and hence this would be limiting the Design and Technology opportunities.

This is not to say that mimics should never be used in a primary classroom, as it is one way that children can test, improve and refine a sequence of instructions quickly and easily, without having to connect up the control box and the external devices (e.g. bulbs, motors). As a learning experience for a short, focused task, it may be acceptable, but as an integrated task it surely is not.

LOGO and *Making things happen*

We consider that the point we have made above, concerning the importance of external devices, also has implications for the use of LOGO in relation to *Making things happen*.

Even though the difference between working at level 2 and level 3 can be demonstrated by the ways in children approach a Roamer task (see scenarios 1 and 2 above), children are

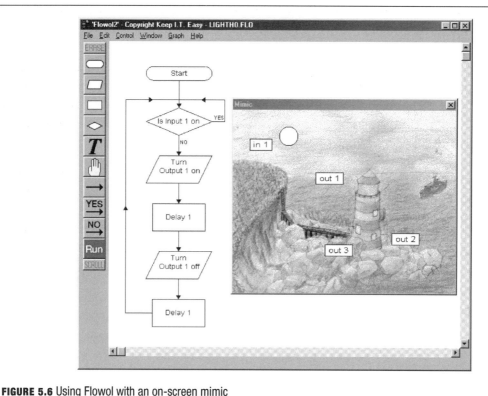

FIGURE 5.6 Using Flowol with an on-screen mimic

normally introduced to LOGO and screen turtles at Key Stage 2, rather than continuing work with floor turtles. This is partly because it is unrealistic to manage work with more than one or two floor turtles in a classroom, and much easier to manage half a class (say) in a computer suite using LOGO. But it is also because children get feedback much more easily, quickly and accurately with a screen turtle, as there are no inaccuracies introduced by the floor surface being a bit slippery etc.

LOGO, however, suffers from the same disadvantage as the mimics. It is not, in a concrete sense that is easily understandable for children, controlling an external device. Of course, in a very literal sense, the computer is controlling an external device – the computer monitor. But if one is going to allow that, then whatever use one puts the computer to would count as *Making things happen* – clicking the print icon in a word processor, playing sound through a speaker, pressing a key on the keyboard etc.

If LOGO were to be used to control a floor turtle, or a control box, then the situation would be different, as it would be clear to the children that the computer was controlling an external device. In the early days, this was possible, and, indeed, it actually took place. The BBC micro-computer would be connected with leads, or by infrared signals, to a floor turtle, and would control it. The BBC micro was also used to control external devices such as bulbs and motors via a control box. But not all implementations of LOGO are programmed in such a way that this is possible; they tend only to be able to program a screen turtle. Even were it possible, many would consider a program such a Flowol a better program for children to use to control external devices.

We therefore recommend that a program such as Flowol, connected to a control box and external devices, should be used as the follow-up work in *Making things happen* after Roamer work at the end of Key Stage 1. This is certainly within the ability of Year 3 and Year 4 children, and fits into the work they can do in Design and Technology in those years. For example:

- At Year 3 they will be able not only to programme a simple output such as turning the lights on and off at a zebra crossing, but also to enter commands to turn the lights on and off on a model traffic light, using trial and error to determine the correct sequence.

- At Year 4 they would be able to enter commands to turn the lights on and off on a model traffic light, having planned the sequence of commands in advance.

A note concerning SCAA (1996) and QCA (1998)

SCAA and the QCA are, for our current purposes, effectively the same organisation, SCAA having been merged with the National Council for Vocational Qualifications (NCVQ) to form the QCA in 1997. It is interesting to note the change in guidance between SCAA (1996) and QCA (1998), which we have summarised in Table 5.1.

It can be seen that QCA (1998) have higher expectations of children than do SCAA (1996), and we have followed the guidance of the former, given that it is more recent. It is likely that, if anything, we can have even higher expectations now, in 2004, given the substantially greater investment in ICT resources over the last five years, and the improved ICT capability of both pupils and their teachers.

Developing ideas and *Making things happen*

Making things happen is not separated from *Developing ideas* in the National Curriculum. One of the reasons for this is that the children will be programming models/simulations of traffic lights (for example). Another reason is that when the children engage in the process of creating, testing, improving and refining instructions (at level 3) this is referred to as the characteristic of *Developing ideas* by the QCA, as we have already seen in relation to *Exchanging and sharing information*.

The reason why we find it helpful to separate *Developing ideas* and *Making things happen* into 'sub aspects' will become clearer in the next chapter, where we discuss *Progression in developing ideas*.

Table 5.2 outlines the progression in relation to the guidance provided by the units in the QCA scheme of work.

TABLE 5.1 A comparison of the guidance provided by SCAA (1996) and QCA (1998)

SCAA (1996)	QCA (1998) and our comments
Level 1 *They recognise that many everyday devices* (such as a remote control toy car) *respond to signals and commands, and that they can select options when using such devices to produce different outcomes,* for example changing channel or altering the volume or brightness on a television.	**Implicit level 1 for QCA** (at year 1 the expectation is level 1) Unit 1F: Understanding instructions and making things happen Use a tape recorder with the children to record sounds. Show the children how the tape recorder buttons are used in the correct sequence to record and play back sound. Divide the class into small groups, give them a simple diagram of a tape recorder and ask them to record some sounds. Ask them to label the buttons on the diagram and write down the order in which they are pressed. Recognise that some machines and devices work by using a sequence of physical actions. **Comment:** The expectations of SCAA and QCA do correspond at this level.
Level 2 *Pupils control devices* (which may be real or simulated) *purposefully,* typically entering single instructions and then describing what happens.	**Implicit level 2 for QCA** (at year 2 the expectation is level 2) Unit 2D: Routes: controlling a floor turtle In this unit children learn how to create, test, modify and store instructions to control the movements of a floor turtle. They learn to programme the floor turtle to move around an area by using single instructions, a sequence of instructions and repeated sequences. To develop and record sequences of instructions to control the floor turtle, and predict and test results. **Comment:** The expectation described by QCA does not match the expectation described by SCAA. Create, test and modify a sequence of instructions is definitely more than a single instruction, and corresponds to the level 3 expectation of SCAA (see below left).
Level 3 *They understand how to control equipment to achieve specific outcomes by giving a series of instructions,* typically entering instructions in sequence one at a time, correcting any mistakes and recording them on paper.	**Implicit level 3 for QCA** (at year 4 the expectation is level 3) Unit 4E: Modelling effects on screen [Using a screen turtle pupils] learn how to write a procedure that 'teaches' the computer a new word and will be asked to write short sequences to produce particular shapes on screen. **Comment:** The expectation described by QCA does not match the expectation described by SCAA. A procedure is definitely a set of instructions that are predetermined, and corresponds to the level 4 expectation of SCAA (see below left).
Level 4 *Pupils use IT systems to control events in a predetermined manner,* typically creating a set of instructions which can be followed at a later time.	

TABLE 5.2 Comments concerning the units relating to *Making things happen* (QCA; 1998)

	QCA units	Comments
Year 1	Understanding instructions and making things happen (1F)	In the first exploratory phase children learn that devices respond to signals and instructions. At this stage the distinction is not made between ICT devices and other devices (such as a light switch). The teacher will discuss with the children: ■ what technology that they see or use, e.g. televisions, video recorders, microwaves, washing-machines, toys, traffic lights, supermarket checkouts. The teacher will explain how this equipment is operated, e.g. by pressing on/off buttons, turning dials, remote control; ■ the importance of putting a sequence of instructions in the correct order, for example by giving the children a set of cards showing pictures of the stages in a recipe to make sweets, and asking the children to identify the correct sequence by putting the cards in order. The teacher will also play People LOGO with the children, perhaps in a PE lesson, where they give each other instructions to go forward a certain number of paces, to go backward (paying due regard to Health and Safety), and to turn left and to turn right. The children will write down a set of instructions to move someone from one place to another, and discuss ways of standardising the instructions. The children may also control some devices in a simple manner, for example by programming a 'floor turtle' to move forward or back.
Year 2	Routes: controlling a floor turtle (2D)	Here they will not simply be moving a floor turtle forward or back – not simply exploring the controls on a floor turtle – but will be putting together a simple sequence of instructions (including using the repeat command). For example, they might programme a floor turtle to move round the room but avoiding obstacles such as tables and chairs – or to purposely hit obstacles such as skittles. Here they will be working as the child in scenario 1 above.
Year 3		**As explained in the text we would favour simple work with control boxes and external devices.**
Year 4	Modelling effects on screen (4E)	The children are here introduced to the screen turtle, and in addition to the repeat command, are also introduced to procedures. Here they should be working as the child in scenario 2 above. **As explained in the text we would favour simple work with control boxes and external devices.**
Year 5	Controlling devices (5E) Monitoring environmental conditions and changes (5F)	The children are introduced to a control box and some output devices, such as lights, buzzers and motors. They programme the computer to operate some of these devices, for example by creating a sequence of instructions to control an advertising display with lights, motors and buzzers to draw attention to the product being sold. They are also, on another occasion, introduced to a data-logging device, which is able to monitor light and temperature levels. They use this to help carry out some science experiments.
Year 6	Control and monitoring – What happens when …? (6C)	In Year 6 they combine sense and control. The key element in the progression is the addition of inputs as well as outputs to the program. Not only do the children programme the computer to control the device(s), they also programme it to respond to inputs – for example changes in the intensity of light. For example, they might make a model house security system with a floodlight and house lights that come on after dark and go off in the morning, a window alarm based on a magnetic switch, a door alarm based on a pressure pad and a burglar alarm with a loud buzzer and flashing lights.

TABLE 5.3 Comments concerning progression in *Making things happen*

SCAA (1996)/QCA (2003)	Explication	Attainment Target level description
Level 1 is characterised by initial **exploratory use** of ICT.	In the first exploratory phase, children learn that devices respond to signals and instructions, and the teacher will discuss with the children technology that they see or use, e.g. televisions, video recorders, microwaves, washing-machines, toys, traffic lights, supermarket checkouts. The teacher will explain how this equipment is operated, e.g. by pressing on/off buttons, turning dials, remote control. At this stage the distinction is not made between ICT devices and other devices (such as a light switch). The children may also control some devices in a simple manner, for example by programming a 'floor turtle' to move forward or back.	**Level 1:** They recognise that many everyday devices respond to signals and instructions. They make choices when using such devices to produce different outcomes.
The characteristic which differentiates **level 2** from level 1 is the more **purposeful** use of ICT to achieve specific outcomes.	Here the children will be entering instructions one at a time, observing and recording the effects (i.e. **describing** them – see Attainment Target level description), and building up a sequence as in scenario 1 above (see p. 75), by making amendments to their sequence. The key words here are **record** and **amend** (as they were also in *Exchanging and Sharing Information*).	**Level 2:** They plan and give instructions to make things happen and describe the effects.
The characteristic which differentiates **level 3** from level 2 is that IT is used to **develop ideas**.	The key words here are creating, testing, improving and refining their instructions, as in scenario 2 above (see p. 76). This is equivalent to reworking a piece of writing, as we saw characterised level 3 of *Exchanging and Sharing Information*), where children use ICT not only to edit (amend) but also to **revise/redraft (develop)** their writing.	**Level 3:** They use sequences of instructions to control devices and achieve specific outcomes.
We do not consider the way this is phrased by the QCA is helpful in relation to Making Things Happen.	At this level children are not only able to use ICT to control devices, but they also on other occasions use data-loggers to sense physical data. They are also able to programme using procedures/subroutines, and hence to plan a sequence of instructions in a predetermined manner (see pp.71–5).	**Level 4:** They use ICT systems to control events in a predetermined manner and to sense physical data.
The characteristic which differentiates **level 5** from level 4 is its **increased rigour**, and by **combining the use of ICT tools** *(here sense and control)*.	At this level they are able to combine sense and control, and can programme a computer to respond to an input and control a device, within the same program (as with a decision box in a flow diagram, or an *If...then...else* statement with a program code (e.g. LOGO). They also are able to produce more complex programs (e.g. the house security system mentioned on p. 69), including using variables in procedures (SCAA 1996:7).	**Level 5:** They create sequences of instructions to control events, and understand the need to be precise when framing and sequencing instructions. They understand how ICT devices with sensors can be used to monitor and measure external events.

The characteristics of the ICT National Curriculum

We will again consider progression in relation to the characteristics of the ICT National Curriculum, as outlined by SCAA (1996) and the QCA (2003). Whilst SCAA (1996) and QCA (2003) state that the characteristic which differentiates level 4 from level 3 is the ability to combine and refine information from various sources, this does not really seem to apply for the aspect of *Making things happen*. Otherwise, the characteristics do help in gaining an understanding of the features of the levels in relation to this aspect. Table 5.3 outlines progression in *Making things happen* in relation to the SCAA (1996)/QCA (2003) characteristics.

Activities

1. Imagine that, for a half-term, you are going to have the theme of 'pirates' in your Year 2 class. Outline the learning objectives and possible activities that could take place for the numeracy, literacy and ICT (including using a floor turtle) work in your classroom that would relate to the topic. Can you extend your range of activities to cover any of the foundation subjects within the primary curriculum? What displays might you and the children produce?

2. Review the content of QCA ICT Units 5E and 6C. Can you find a suitable Design and Technology context for each ICT unit? The contexts might come from specific D&T QCA units or be your own ideas. The relevant contexts may not necessarily be found in the Year 5 and 6 D&T QCA units, so do not limit your search to work in those particular year groups. In light of your chosen contexts, how will you adapt the QCA ICT integrated tasks?

6

Progression in *Developing ideas*

Objectives:

- To understand the ways in which pupils develop their ideas using ICT, and how this all relates to progression in the other aspects in the Programme of Study for ICT

- To understand that for this aspect of the ICT curriculum, ICT is helping pupils to solve a problem and that unless this is a realistic activity it can become a trivial task – there needs to be an actual problem to solve

- To understand the role of spreadsheets, object-based drawing programs, LOGO, and simulations and models in developing ideas

- To understand the original concept underlying using LOGO to develop mathematical thinking; how this differs from the approach to LOGO outlined in the QCA Scheme of Work, and the implications for the role of LOGO in the ICT National Curriculum

As was explained in detail in Chapter 1, the ICT Programme of Study specifies, in relation to *Developing ideas* and *Making things happen*, at Key Stage 1, that pupils should be taught:

2a) to use text, tables, images and sound to develop their ideas

2b) how to select from and add to information they have retrieved for particular purposes

2c) how to plan and give instructions to make things happen [for example, programming a floor turtle, placing instructions in the right order]

2d) to try things out and explore what happens in real and imaginary situations [for example, trying out different colours on an image, using an adventure game or simulation];

and at Key Stage 2, that pupils should be taught:

2a) how to develop and refine ideas by bringing together, organising and reorganising text, tables, images and sound as appropriate [for example, desktop publishing, multimedia presentations]

2b) how to create, test, improve and refine sequences of instructions to make things happen and to monitor events and respond to them [for example, monitoring changes in temperature, detecting light levels and turning on a light]

2c) to use simulations and explore models in order to answer 'What if...?' questions, to investigate and evaluate the effect of changing values and to identify patterns and relationships [for example, simulation software, spreadsheet models].

In Chapter 1 we discussed the nature of the developing ideas, with particular reference to models and simulations – including the use of models in weather forecasting – and in kitchen layout simulations; here we shall begin by considering simulations and models at Key Stage 2 (see Programme of Study 2c above). We shall then consider other ways in which children develop their ideas using ICT, how this all relates to progression in the other aspects we have so far considered, and to the aspect of *Reviewing, modifying and evaluating work as it progresses*. We shall then relate this to ICT capability, and suggest a different way of conceptualising the aspects to help get a better understanding of the ICT National Curriculum.

The key characteristics of ICT that make computer models and simulations so helpful are:

- **provisionality** – the function of ICT which allows changes to be made easily and enables alternatives to be explored readily;

- **speed and automatic functions** – the function of ICT which enables routine tasks to be completed and repeated quickly, allowing the user to concentrate on thinking, and on tasks such as analysing and looking for patterns within data, asking questions and looking for answers, and explaining and presenting results; and

- **interactivity** – the function of ICT that enables rapid and dynamic feedback.

These characteristics allow us to *try things out* easily and quickly, and to get feedback.

Models and simulations enable us to solve problems, and to explore patterns and relationships. We shall illustrate this by reference to spreadsheet activities that children typically undertake in primary schools.

Models and simulations at Key Stage 2

Using spreadsheets to solve problems

This example is taken from *Approaches to IT Capability* (SCAA 1996) and is similar to the integrated task in *Unit 5D, Introduction to spreadsheets* (QCA 1998). It concerns the children planning a Christmas party (SCAA 1996:27):

> The children were shown how to enter data into a spreadsheet and how to use the formula function to carry out simple calculations. They were asked to work in pairs to decide what should be bought for a school Christmas party. They were told the price of individual items and given a budget of £33.
>
> Mark and Amy wanted to include chicken drumsticks, but predicted that this would use more than one third of the budget. They made some initial estimates and created the spreadsheet. As a result of a class vote they found that the most expensive drink was the least popular, and decided not to include it. This gave them more money for the more popular items. They adjusted quantities, predicting the changes that would result, and used the spreadsheet to check that they did not exceed the budget.

The spreadsheet helps because the children can make changes easily, and they are given immediate feedback as to the effect this will have on the total cost of the party. They can change the number of mince pies they buy and the computer automatically calculates the total. In this example, they still have £3 to spend, and they can try out different alternatives easily and quickly before finally deciding what more to buy.

The spreadsheet is a computer model. The children are not actually going to the shop, buying the items and seeing what they all cost. Instead, they are simulating what would happen should they make these purchases.

ICT is helping them to solve a problem, the problem being how to buy the food that would be the most popular with the class, and still keep within their budget.

At this point it should be emphasised that unless this is a realistic activity it can become a trivial activity. Note that the children conducted a survey to determine the class's food preferences. This constrained the choices they could make.

Had this activity not been constrained in this way it could easily have become a trivial activity, in which any choice would do, and the children might just have made choices at random until the total came close to £33. In that case, it would not have been a valuable ICT experience, as it would not have demonstrated the value of ICT in helping them to solve a problem.

In other words, activities such as this rely on there being realistic activities and on there being actual problems to solve.

In the example above, the children were functioning at level 3: *They make appropriate choices when using ICT-based models or simulations to help them find things out and solve problems.*

Using spreadsheets to explore patterns and relationships

We shall illustrate this with the ubiquitous problem of the farmer and his sheep pen. The farmer has a fixed amount of fencing and wants to use it efficiently to build a sheep pen with the largest possible area. In addition to the fencing, he can make use of a stone wall which runs all the way along one side of the field, and he can use this as part of the enclosure. This is similar to the integrated task in *Unit 6B, Spreadsheet modelling* (QCA 1998).

A spreadsheet model can be set up to solve this problem. Often the initial hypothesis is that the most efficient shape will be a square, one side of which would be formed by the stone wall. Suppose the farmer has 120 metres of fencing available. To form a square, 40 metres of fencing would be needed for each of the three sides of the square enclosure, in addition to using 40 metres of the stone wall. The area of this sheep pen would then be 1600 m² (40 x 40).

If a square is the most efficient shape, then any rectangle with a side longer or shorter than this should result in a sheep pen with a smaller area. (The children could use a spreadsheet to check this by entering sides of length 37, 38, 39, 41, 42 and 43.) However, by examining the spreadsheet it can be seen that this is not the case. The children will notice that the area is greatest for width 37. They might then enter values from 28 to 37 for the width, to check which value results in the greatest area. The spreadsheet would then be as in Table 6.1.

They would notice that the greatest area is achieved when the width of the fence is 30 metres. When the values are displayed as a line graph this can be seen very clearly.

So far the children have made good use of a spreadsheet model to solve the problem of how to find the maximum area that can be enclosed with 120 metres of fencing. They have found out the most efficient shape is not a square, as they had originally thought.

TABLE 6.1 Sheep pen problem

	A	B	C	D	E	F
1	**Total amount of fencing Available**	**Width of pen**	**Length of pen**	**Width of pen**	**Length of pen (walled side)**	**Area of pen in m²**
2	120	28	64	28	64	1792
3		29	62	29	62	1798
4		30	60	30	60	1800
5		31	58	31	58	1798
6		32	56	32	56	1792
7		33	54	33	54	1782
8		34	52	34	52	1768
9		35	50	35	50	1750
10		36	48	36	48	1728
11		37	46	37	46	1702

They might then go on to attempt to discover a general rule as to the most efficient shape. To do this they could take different lengths of fencing and determine the maximum areas that could be enclosed by these different lengths. Let us suppose they have done this for 100 metres of fencing and found the maximum area to be 1250 for width 25. They then do the same for 140 metres of fencing.

They begin to see a pattern emerging – the most efficient width of fencing seems to be a quarter of the amount of fencing available. They go on to test this for 200 metres of fencing, and predict that the most efficient width would be 50 metres. This is confirmed, and they therefore conclude that their hypothesis was correct.

This illustrates the use of an ICT model to explore patterns and relationships, and in this example the children were therefore functioning at level 4: *They use ICT-based models and simulations to explore patterns and relationships, and make predictions about the consequences of their decisions.*

Modelling with an object-based drawing program

Unit 5A, Graphical modelling, in the QCA scheme is concerned with using *an object-based graphics package to produce and explore a graphical model.*

Object-based graphics programs, or *drawing* programs, differ from *paint* programs.

In a paint program the image is defined as a series of dots, known as pixels, much as a picture in a newspaper. The picture is called a bitmap image, and the computer stores the colour of each pixel. A computer screen is typically composed of 480,000 pixels (a resolution of 800 x 600) or more often now of 786,432 pixels (a resolution of 1024 x 768). When the image is enlarged the quality is lost.

An example of a paint program is *Paint*, which comes as one of the accessories in Windows (known as Paintbrush in early versions of Windows).

In an object-based drawing program the objects are defined mathematically, for example by the start and end points of straight lines, by the way a line curves, and by the colour of the shape in question. These are known as vector-based formats. A picture is built up of many such defined objects, and the computer stores the formulae for creating the objects, and recreates the image from a series of instructions each time it is displayed. This is a very efficient way of storing the information, and one consequence is that the file size is typically much smaller. Another consequence is that an image can be enlarged with no loss of quality – as the instructions are almost identical, the only difference being the factor of size (e.g. make it twice as big). Much clip art is vector based.

An example of an object-based graphics program is the drawing tools in *Word*.

Another advantage of an object-based program is that each object can be manipulated independently of the other elements. Objects can be moved without affecting the other objects. This makes *drawing* programs ideal for trying things out, for trying out different layouts. Changes are made very easily.

In *Unit 5A, Graphical modelling*, the suggested integrated task is the following: *Ask the class to think of ways to improve the school site. Ask them to produce maps showing the site as it is, and their proposals. Tell them that they need to show that their proposals will not disrupt requirements, e.g. access and parking.*

The maps are produced with an object-based drawing program, and the children are required to solve a problem, in this case to improve the school site by moving objects around (such as the playground equipment).

Another suggested activity is how to lay out the classroom most efficiently: *Ask the children to find out how many tables would fit in the classroom using different layouts and different-sized chairs and tables.*

In both these cases the children will create a plan view of the school site or the classroom, with shapes (such as rectangles) to represent the various objects (such as chairs and tables). They can then move the chairs and tables around in their drawing program, trying out different arrangements, printing these out and comparing them, before making a decision as to which is the best arrangement, without having to actually move any of the furniture in reality.

The children in these scenarios would be functioning at level 3: *They make appropriate choices when using ICT-based models or simulations to help them find things out and solve problems.*

Breadth of study and *Reviewing, modifying and evaluating work as it progresses*

In addition to using ICT-based models and simulations to solve problems, or to explore patterns and relationships, children should be learning about how models and simulations are used in the wider world outside school; they should be *investigating and comparing the uses of ICT inside and outside school* (*Breadth of study*, Key Stage 2, 5c).

When the children are using a drawing program to try out different layouts of a classroom (or a school playground etc.) their attention can be drawn to the use of similar kinds of programs in the wider world. A business specialising in selling and fitting kitchen units will use a kitchen design program, producing a number of different kitchen layouts for their customers.

Programs such as *Spex+* and *The Model Shop* are available, which can help children understand how these more professional programs work. *Spex+* and *The Model Shop* both have simulations of a classroom layout program (for *Spex+* this is an additional 'environment' that is purchased separately). Both are valuable in that they are less abstract than using a drawing program, in that the children can see the actual objects, and *Spex+* has the added virtue of showing both the plan view and the 3D view of the objects – and a spreadsheet facility so that children can see what the cost is, and if they are within budget. However, neither have the flexibility of a drawing program: the classroom is a fixed shape, the furniture is predetermined and of a fixed size. So neither would enable the children to solve a realistic problem for their classroom, unless by some remote chance their classroom was the exact shape and size as the one in the program, and the objects were also the exact same shape and size.

So *Spex+* and *The Model Shop* are not substitutes for using a drawing program, but they are helpful in two ways. Not only do they provide a better idea of what these kinds of programs are like in the wider world, they also provide opportunities for children to *describe and talk about the effectiveness of their work with ICT, comparing it with other methods* (*Reviewing, modifying and evaluating work as it progresses*, Key Stage 2, 4b). By comparing these programs with a drawing program, they are able to gain a better idea of the advantages and disadvantages of a drawing program, the latter having more flexibility. If the class can visit a kitchen design shop and see what a professional program of this sort can do, that is, of course, ideal. They will then be able to compare the strengths and limitations of the various programs and also have firsthand experience of the use of ICT in the wider world outside school.

At this point it is worth mentioning the drawing program *Black Cat Designer*. This object-based program includes pictures of the furniture in a classroom, which are objects that can be re-sized, as in Figure 6.1.

We have discussed the role of spreadsheets and object-based drawing programs, as well as some simulation programs (*Spex+* and *The Model Shop*), in delivering the element of Programme of Study 2c (*Developing ideas*) at Key Stage 2, and have linked this to Programmes of Study 4b (*Reviewing, modifying and evaluating work as it progresses*) and 5c (*Breadth of Study*). In so doing, we have illustrated progression in relation to the attainment targets, namely *using models and simulations to solve problems* (level 3), and *using models and simulations to explore patterns and relationships* (level 4).

We shall discuss and evaluate this in more detail later in this chapter, and also discuss at length the role of LOGO in relation to developing ideas with simulations and models. For the moment, suffice it to say that LOGO is centrally concerned with exploring patterns and relationships.

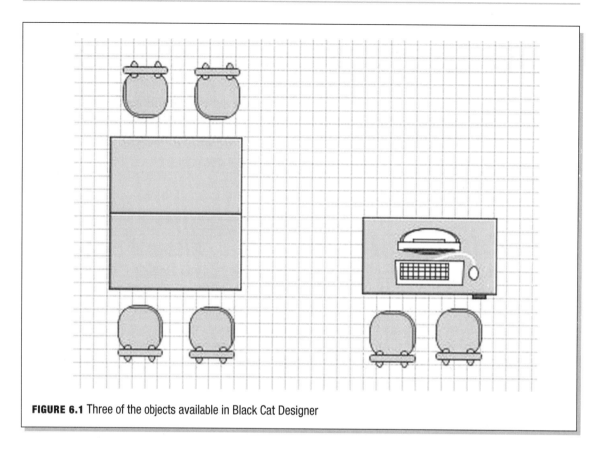

FIGURE 6.1 Three of the objects available in Black Cat Designer

We would also like to reassure the reader that we will also be discussing, later in this chapter, the elements 2a (*how to develop and refine ideas by bringing together, organising and reorganising text, tables, images and sound . . .*) and 2b (*how to create, test, improve and refine sequences of instructions . . .*).

We consider it more helpful to examine first what children are expected to do at Key Stage 1 in relation to simulations and models, and to illustrate the progression throughout the primary phase of this element of this aspect.

Models and simulations at Key Stage 1

We have seen that children at Key Stage 2 are expected to use models and simulations to solve problems and explore patterns and relationships, and to learn about how simulations and models are used in the wider world outside school.

At Key Stage 1 they are only expected to explore models and simulations, *to try things out and explore what happens in real and imaginary situations* (Programme of Study for Key Stage 1, 2d). As we shall see, the teacher will also discuss with the children how such models and simulations differ from reality, as any computer model or simulation is only an approximation of reality (as we have seen in relation to *Spex+* and *The Model Shop*).

First, though, we need to explain why the SCAA (1996) and QCA (2003) characteristics of the level descriptions, which we have found so helpful in relation to other aspects, do not match the attainment target level descriptions for *Developing ideas*.

TABLE 6.2 Attainment target level descriptors and SCAA/QCA characteristics

	Attainment target level description	**SCAA (1996) and QCA (2003) characteristics**
Level 1		Initial exploratory use
Level 2	They use ICT to explore what happens in real and imaginary situations.	Purposeful use
Level 3	They make appropriate choices when using ICT-based models or simulations to help them find things out and solve problems.	Using ICT to develop ideas

For the other aspects, and for the SCAA (1996) and QCA (2003) characteristics, level 1 corresponds to the initial exploratory stage, and level 2 to purposeful use. In relation to the use of models and simulations, however, level 2 corresponds to the initial exploratory stage. The reason for this is that any purposeful use of a model or simulation is, by definition, 'developing ideas'. This means that the level descriptions and the SCAA/QCA characteristics have, of necessity, to be 'out of sync'. This need not trouble us, and it does explain why at Key Stage 1 children will tend to be only exploring models and simulations.

Typical exploratory activities include using exploring *My World* screens, and exploring adventure programs.

A particularly good *My World* screen for models and simulations is *Find Ted*. The children have to find where Teddy is hidden. One reason that this is a good screen is that Teddy can be hidden behind the picture, under the rug or in the wardrobe. This provides an ideal opportunity to discuss the difference between this particular two-dimensional model and three-dimensional reality. In reality, a 3D Teddy could not be hidden behind a picture, and if placed under a rug there would be a bump. This particular activity is suitable for Year 1 children.

Another suitable activity for Key Stage 1 children is exploring an adventure program. One such is *Freddy Teddy's Adventure*. In this program, the bears have lost their honey, and anyone who finds it is invited to their special picnic tea. There are eight different places children can choose to go to, one of which is a tree trunk. If they choose to go there, they can hear a loud buzzing sound, which could mean that there are bees there, and bees mean honey. But until the children have solved some puzzles the honey will not be visible.

Just as with the *My World* screen, the teacher can discuss with the children the difference between this computer simulation and reality. For example, it is not possible, in reality, to be transported at the click of a mouse from one location to another.

At this point it is appropriate to alert the reader to a possible misconception concerning the use of adventure programs and the attainment target level descriptions: the fact that children, when exploring adventure games, are solving problems, sometimes leads to a misconception that the children are functioning at level 3, the description of which states that pupils *make appropriate choices when using ICT-based models or simulations to help them find things out and solve problems*. When exploring an adventure game, however, the computer program is *posing the problem*. The children are not using the adventure program to help them solve a problem in the real world, which is what would need to be happening were they to be functioning at level 3.

We are now in a position to summarise progression in the elements of Developing Ideas relating to models and simulations, the Programme of Study 2d, at Key Stage 1, and 2c, at Key Stage 2, and relate that to all the relevant units in the QCA scheme of work (see Table 6.3).

The role of feedback in simulations and models

One of the advantages of using a spreadsheet model is that any changes are made easily, and the spreadsheet automatically recalculates the contents of the cells, for example recalculating the total cost of the food for the party speedily and automatically. This gives rapid and dynamic feedback to the user.

One of the advantages of using an object-based drawing program to design the layout of the classroom is that it allows changes to be made easily, and for the different layouts to be printed out. Note that this program does not do anything automatically. The user moves the objects around, and the program is completely passive, but the user still obtains some feedback. We like to think of this as passive feedback, to contrast it with the *rapid and dynamic feedback* mentioned in the previous paragraph.

Most computer simulations provide dynamic feedback, but the value of *passive* programs should not be underestimated. The reader is referred to the article by Finlayson and Cook (1998) for an experimental report and an interesting discussion of the value of such passive software.

How do the level descriptions relate to competence in the use of ICT techniques?

Earlier, we described spreadsheet scenarios illustrating children functioning at level 3 and level 4, and it is clear that using spreadsheets and drawing programs is fairly demanding in terms of the ICT techniques that are required. Consider, however, the following scenarios:

Spreadsheet modelling

A spreadsheet is set up by the teacher, and children are encouraged to enter different numbers in the cells indicated, and to observe the result of multiplying by ten, seeing if they can discover a pattern, and then make a prediction for what would be the result if they (say) entered the number 14.

TABLE 6.3 QCA Units Relating to *Developing ideas*

QCA unit	Attainment target level description and comments
An introduction to modelling (1A)	**AT level 2:** They use ICT to explore what happens in real and imaginary situations. **Comment:** One of the examples in this unit is the *My World* screen *Find Ted*, described above. Another example is an adventure program, such as *Freddy Teddy's Adventure*.
—	N/A
Exploring simulations (3D)	**AT level 2:** They use ICT to explore what happens in real and imaginary situations. **Comment:** The kind of simulation is not specified, and it is implied that it would be helpful if simulations of real situations could be used. *The Model Shop* is one possibility, which has a number of such simulations, including *Paint mixing, Ball throwing, Plant growing* and *Traffic lights*. These simulations are appropriate for work at, but not beyond, this level. The advice given is that children should be encouraged to recognise patterns within simulations and make and test predictions — this is preparation for subsequent units.
Modelling effects on screen (4E)	**AT level 2:** They use ICT to explore what happens in real and imaginary situations. **Comment:** Even though we stated earlier that LOGO is centrally concerned with exploring patterns and relationships, we will argue later in this chapter that this unit is mainly concerned with teaching the techniques of LOGO, and exploring what can be done with it.
Graphical modelling (5A)	**AT level 3:** They make appropriate choices when using ICT-based models or simulations to help them find things out and solve problems. **Comment:** As discussed earlier, this unit is concerned with using an object-based drawing program to solve problems (e.g. finding out the best layout for the furniture in the classroom).
Introduction to spreadsheets (5D)	**AT level 3:** They make appropriate choices when using ICT-based models or simulations to help them find things out and solve problems. **Comment:** As discussed earlier, this unit is concerned with using a spreadsheet to solve a problem (e.g. getting the best value for money for the Christmas party with a limited budget).
Spreadsheet modelling (6B)	**AT level 3:** They make appropriate choices when using ICT-based models or simulations to help them find things out and solve problems. **Comment:** This unit is concerned with using a spreadsheet to solve a problem (e.g. finding the maximum area that can be included in a rectangular field of fixed perimeter). This is the first part of the 'Sheep Pen' example discussed earlier. If the unit of work had gone on to explore patterns and relationships, as discussed earlier, it would have exemplified work at level 4.

	A	B	C
1	**Enter your numbers in the cells below**		**Can you discover a pattern?**
2	5	× 10 =	50
3	5	× 10 =	60
4	5	× 10 =	30
5	5	× 10 =	80
6	5	× 10 =	90
7	5	× 10 =	20
8	5	× 10 =	60
9	5	× 10 =	120
10	5	× 10 =	70
11	5	× 10 =	150

FIGURE 6.2 A simple spreadsheet model

All the children do is enter whatever numbers they like in column A (they might have found it is easier to discern a pattern had they entered the numbers 1 to 10 in sequence). In terms of 'trying things out', are they not using an *ICT-based model to explore patterns and relationships, and make predictions about the consequences of their decisions (level 4)*?

Similarly, consider a classroom design program which has been programmed in such a way that it makes virtually no demands in terms of the ICT techniques needed. Would using such a program to choose the layout of the classroom be equivalent in terms of the level description as using an object-based drawing program?

Consider also the difference between using a spreadsheet to solve a problem (as in the Christmas party example) with using a spreadsheet to explore patterns and relationships. The same ICT techniques are needed, the only difference being the higher-order skills that are needed.

Yet again, consider a simulation of a nuclear power station. If its use required an understanding of nuclear physics, it would be well beyond the average Year 6 child even if the ICT techniques were simple enough.

The point we are making here is that there is something complex about defining progression in the use of models and simulations, in that the conceptual understanding of the subject matter is a crucial factor.

Rather than attempting to discover a conceptually coherent account of progression in relation to models and simulations, we have concluded that it is best to take a pragmatic view. This pragmatic view is that we aim to provide the sort of experiences outlined by the QCA in Years 5 and 6:

■ using a drawing program to solve a realistic problem, such as design a classroom layout that will actually be enacted;

- using a spreadsheet to solve a realistic problem, such as planning the food to be bought with a limited budget – which includes conducting a survey of food preferences, and if necessary going back to the class to take a vote on different alternatives;

- using a spreadsheet to explore patterns and relationships, going beyond the integrated task in the unit *Spreadsheet modelling*, 6B, to include what we described earlier (to find out the general rule concerning the relationship between the width and length of fencing).

We consider this pragmatic view important, as it safeguards the use of a drawing program and a spreadsheet, and we consider that it is important for children to be competent in using such programs, as they are central to ICT as a subject.

But if we take this pragmatic view, why are the introduction of drawing programs and spreadsheets left until Year 5? Surely children's ICT capability would be better served if they knew how to use these programs before they were introduced for the integrated tasks in the Year 5 units; the children could then focus on the content of the integrated tasks, rather than struggling with the techniques and being in danger of succumbing to the *ICT interference factor* (cf. Kennewell *et al.* 2000). In addition, as the children would already be familiar with the programs, the teacher could get the children to think about which program would be appropriate for the tasks in question, rather than telling them which program to use. Making choices as to which ICT application to use is an essential element of ICT capability.

It is realistic to introduce such programs before Year 5, as long as appropriate contexts can be found for them, and these can be provided in the Maths and DT curriculum. Indeed, it is advantageous for children to know how to use spreadsheets earlier on in Key Stage 2. One context is for creating graphs, instead of using a simple graphing program. Drawing programs can be used for creating *developments* in DT, and for creating diagrams in a variety of subjects.

Modelling with LOGO

In the previous chapter we concluded that LOGO was not best suited to exemplifying *Making things happen* in the primary school, unless it could be used to control external devices. This is probably one reason why the QCA unit concerned with LOGO has the title *Modelling effects on screen* (Unit 4E), rather than a title which relates to *Making things happen*. Certainly, LOGO's origins are all about *Developing ideas* rather than control; trying things out rather than *Making things happen*.

Papert (1980) designed LOGO for children to *explore patterns and relationships*. For him, LOGO was a tool to help children develop their ideas. LOGO was, for him, essentially *a tool for thinking*, in the same way that other more concrete models are tools for thinking. He reports that when he was a young child he was fascinated by cars and that he found particular pleasure in such systems as the differential gear, and that this helped him to think about maths and made maths more concrete. He wrote (*ibid.*:vi–vii):

> I believe that working with differentials did more for my mathematical development than anything I was taught in elementary school. Gears, serving as models, carried many otherwise abstract ideas

into my head. I clearly remember two examples from school math. I saw multiplication tables as gears, and my first brush with equations in two variables (e.g. $3x + 4y = 10$) immediately evoked the differential. By the time I had made a mental gear model of the relation between x and y, figuring how many teeth each gear needed, the equation had become a comfortable friend.

In the same way that the differential became 'an-object-to-think-with', so Papert considered that the screen turtle in LOGO could be such 'an-object-to-think-with', and that LOGO could be a tool for thinking. One of the reasons Papert gives for why the gears served as 'an-object-to-think-with' is (*ibid.*:11):

> I could use my body to think about the gears. I could feel how gears turn by imagining my body turning. This made it possible for me to draw on my 'body knowledge' to think about gear systems.

Children can, in the same way, imagine how a turtle turns by imagining their body turning. In the same manner, LOGO can be 'an object to think with', and can serve as a model for abstract mathematical ideas. In this way LOGO can help children concretise and personalise the formal. In so doing, children are able to deal with abstract mathematical ideas earlier than they otherwise would.

When LOGO is used as a tool to think with it is not being used as a tool to create, for example, triangles, squares, heptagons etc., which would be drawn far more quickly and easily using a graphics program. Rather, it is being used as a tool to explore and further the mathematical understanding of the user (e.g. of angles).

Papert did not think that LOGO was only of use to help children understand mathematical ideas. He also gives examples of how some LOGO implementations can help children learn about physics and about language.

In Chapter 5 of his book he discusses how LOGO can help children think about Newton's laws of motion. The new turtle that is needed for this is the Dynaturtle, a turtle that not only has a *position* and a *heading* but also *mass* and *velocity*. These Dynaturtles can help children explore and discover Newton's laws of motion.

In Chapter 2 of his book, he also discusses how exploring the list-processing features of LOGO can help children explore language and thereby gain a better understanding of grammatical categories, of parts of speech. Some 12-year-old students had been working on what they called 'computer poetry', using computer programs to generate sentences. They programmed the computer with some simple grammatical rules, and the computer then chose words at random from the given lists of words. Papert reports (*ibid.*:48):

> One day Jenny came in very excited. She had made a discovery. 'Now I know why we have nouns and verbs,' she said. For many years in school Jenny had been drilled in grammatical categories. She had never understood the differences between nouns and verbs and adverbs. But now it was apparent that her difficulty with grammar was not due to an inability to work with logical categories. It was something else. She had simply seen no purpose in the enterprise. She had not been able to make any sense of what grammar was about in the sense of what it might be *for*.

In the process of having to program the computer, she had learned the importance of these categories, she had learned what these categories were for. The program would not work if she placed the words in the wrong categories. This enabled her to learn the difference between them, between the different parts of speech.

The key to LOGO being 'a tool for thinking' is that the child programmes the computer, as opposed to the computer programming the child, as is the case with drill and practice programs. Papert argues that this can also help children learn how to learn (*ibid.*:23):

> I began to see how children who had learned to program computers could use very concrete computer models to think about thinking and to learn about learning and in doing so enhance their powers as psychologists and as epistemologists. For example, many children are held back in their learning because they have a model of learning in which you have either 'got it' or 'got it wrong'. But when you learn to program a computer you almost never get it right the first time. Learning to be a master programmer is learning to become highly skilled at isolating and correcting 'bugs', the parts that keep the program from working. The question to ask about the program is not whether it is right or wrong, but if it is fixable. If this way of looking at intellectual products were generalised to how the larger culture thinks about knowledge and its acquisition, we all might be less intimidated by our fears of 'being wrong'. This potential influence of the computer on changing our notion of a black and white version of our successes and failures is an example of using the computer as 'an-object-to-think-with'.

LOGO was very much designed with a constructivist approach to learning in mind. Children were meant to use LOGO as a tool to think with, constructing hypotheses and then testing them by programming the computer. If their program did not do what they thought it would, it was either because of an error in their program or because their construct of the microworld needed refining or restructuring.

So, for example, suppose children have successfully drawn a square by entering the instructions:

forward 100
right 90
forward 100
right 90
forward 100
right 90
forward 100
right 90

They then attempt to draw a triangle and enter the instructions:

forward 100
right 60
forward 100
right 60
forward 100
right 60

What they see appear on screen is shown in Figure 6.3.

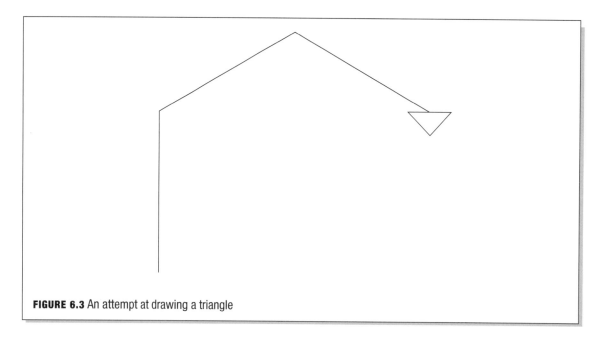

FIGURE 6.3 An attempt at drawing a triangle

After some trial and error, they fix their sequence of instructions, and in so doing learn something about internal and external angles.

This is a different way of using LOGO than what we find in the guidance produced by the QCA (1998 and 2003).

In Unit 4E, Modelling effects on screen (QCA 1998), the integrated task is described as follows:

- Explain to the class that they will create a number of 'crystal flowers' on screen. Tell them that they will need to write a number of procedures, such as square, rectangle, triangle, pentagon, and that they will combine the shapes into a larger procedure; the larger procedure will allow them to rotate the shapes 360 degrees and produce a flower. An example procedure might be: repeat 36 [square, right 10] which would produce 36 squares with a rotation of 10 degrees in between, producing a flower effect.

- Ask children to work in pairs to create their own flowers and get them to print out their work. They could colour in their flowers and produce a garden display for the classroom.

The children have previously been taught the instructions for creating the procedures. One of the short, focused tasks is:

- Prepare a worksheet with a few simple repeat sequences on it. These could include:
  repeat 4 [forward 100, left 90];
  repeat 3 [forward 150, right 120];
  repeat 6 [forward 100, right 60];
  repeat 360 [forward 1 right 1];
  repeat 10 [forward 50, right 36].

Discuss with the children their previous experiences with a repeated sequence and demonstrate the instruction: repeat 5 [forward 80, right 108]. Ask the children how many sides they think the shape will have. Type the instruction into the computer and show the children what happens.

- Using the prepared worksheet when the instructions are entered, ask the children to predict what will appear on screen and give them a chance to work in pairs at the computer to test their hypotheses.

This kind of activity is too directed, and not in tune with the constructivist approach of Papert. Neither are the children really using a computer model to solve problems or explore patterns and relationships. The children are being told what instructions to enter into the computer, and then to see if they can see a pattern; the whole activity is back to front. What they are doing is applying their knowledge of what they have learned in maths, rather than learning maths through LOGO.

The update of the teacher's guide to the QCA Scheme of Work (QCA 2003:36) is similar. The guidance to the teacher is to:

- Explain that there are 360 degrees or four right angles in a whole turn or circle . . .
- Ask the children to try out the following sequence: repeat 4 [forward 100 right 360/4]
- Ask the children to predict what will happen if they enter the following sequence: repeat 5 [forward 100 right 360/5]. Ask them to test their hypotheses.

This is very directed, not what Papert intended. The QCA (2003:36) goes on to comment (bear in mind this is a Year 4 unit):

> Children may be confused when they consider what has happened, given the work they have carried out on measuring the angles of a triangle. Internal and external angles are not covered until year 6, but you may wish to point out that the turtle is turning around the outside of the angles of the triangle.

But, as we have commented above, the whole point of LOGO is that it can help children concretise and personalise the formal and, in so doing, children will be able to deal with abstract mathematical ideas earlier than otherwise. The point is that, if LOGO were used as Papert intended, rather than as the QCA recommend, the children would learn about internal and external angles through using LOGO, rather than being confused.

The QCA is recommending that LOGO is used to apply what is learnt in the maths curriculum, rather than using LOGO as a tool for thinking.

The integrated task in unit 4E (Modelling effects on screen) relates to the Year 5 outcome in the National Numeracy Strategy (DfEE 1999:111): 'As outcomes, Year 5 pupils should, for example Make patterns by rotating shapes (e.g. rotations of 90°, rotations of 45°)'.

Why then does the QCA recommend this way of using LOGO, and why is there only one suggestion for an additional integrated task for LOGO in the supplementary guidance (QCA 2003)?

The reason is probably that LOGO work is time-consuming, and does not fit into the very directed approach of the National Numeracy Strategy. If we are to develop ICT capability we need to have realistic contexts in which to use the ICT tools, including LOGO. If this is not possible, does LOGO really belong in the ICT National Curriculum?

Our answer to this question is a resounding 'Yes', because programming is central to ICT as a subject, and LOGO is the sensible language with which to introduce programming in the primary school, perhaps in conjunction with a program such as Flowol. Commands are entered as words in LOGO, and as objects in a flow diagram in Flowol. It is helpful to the children to encounter both ways of representing instructions.

This, however, changes the objective of using LOGO. It is no longer primarily using LOGO as a tool for thinking, which relates to ICT capability. Rather, it is primarily about using LOGO as an introduction to programming, which relates to ICT as a subject. In which case using LOGO is an end in itself. If that is the case, however, might not LOGO encompass list processing as well as turtle graphics? A simple introduction to list processing should not be beyond the capabilities of Year 5 and Year 6 children.

For example, this DAY procedure, below, prints out the day of the week:

MAKE "WEEK [MONDAY TUESDAY WEDNESDAY THURSDAY FRIDAY SATURDAY SUNDAY]

TO DAY :n

SHOW ITEM :n :WEEK

END

When the procedures and lists have been defined,

- entering DAY 1 prints *Monday* on the screen
- entering DAY 3 prints *Wednesday* on the screen
- etc.

The syntax here is the one that Superlogo and MSWLogo use. Other implementations of LOGO may differ slightly in the syntax used.

The procedure below allows the user to 'personalise' a message:

TO PERSONALISE :friend

(PRINT SENTENCE "Dear :friend ":)

PRINT [Wishing you a Happy Birthday.]

PRINT [Best wishes]

END

Entering PERSONALISE, John prints the following on screen:

Dear John:

Wishing you a Happy Birthday.

Best wishes

In this chapter we have argued that LOGO does not fit well into the 'sub aspect' of *Developing ideas* as there is not enough time, and hence not enough opportunities, to use LOGO as a tool for learning mathematics in any significant manner, although it can be used to apply what is learned in the daily mathematics lessons.

In the last chapter we argued that the use of screen turtles is not an effective way of illustrating that ICT can be used to control *external devices*, and hence that this does not provide a rationale for placing LOGO in the 'sub aspect' of *Making things happen*.

However, we have argued that LOGO still has a place in the ICT National Curriculum, but as a programming language, as this is central to learning about ICT as a subject. This, we consider, is the reason for placing it in both the 'sub aspects' of both *Developing ideas* and of *Making things happen*. When programming it is, of course, essential to *Review, modify and evaluate work as it progresses*. In terms of *Breadth of study*, when *investigating and comparing the uses of ICT inside and outside school* they can make connections with how computers work – the value of list processing is particularly helpful in this respect.

How *Developing ideas* relates to the other aspects

Developing the product

As we have seen, *Developing ideas* with ICT is about using ICT to *try things out*. It is the characteristic of *provisionality* that makes ICT so useful in this respect – the ability to make changes easily (the technical term *provisionality* is used because this emphasises that what we have produced is not set in stone – whereas text written with a word processor can be easily changed, text written with a pen cannot so easily be changed, and text carved onto a headstone is very difficult, if not impossible, to change).

When discussing progression in *Making things happen*, we saw that what distinguished level 3 from level 2 is that pupils not only use ICT to plan and give instructions, but also to create, test, **improve** and **refine** sequences of instructions. The children *create* their sequence of instructions, try them out (*test* them) and then see what happens. On the basis of the test, they make changes in order to produce a better set of instructions to control a device, to *improve* and *refine* the instructions. This process develops their sequence of instructions, which is one reason why SCAA (1996) and the QCA (2003) refer to this process as *Developing ideas*.

The product is a sequence of instructions that is clearer than it would otherwise be, and hence more likely to make the desired things happen. This is partly what is meant by the Programme of Study 2b for *Developing ideas and Making things happen* (Key Stage 2):

> Pupils at Key Stage 2, should be taught:
>
> 2b) how to create, test, improve and refine sequences of instructions to make things happen and to monitor events and respond to them [for example, monitoring changes in temperature, detecting light levels and turning on a light].

What we have described above also holds good for *Exchanging and sharing information*. For example, ICT enables us to try out, quickly and easily, many different layouts of the front page of a newspaper, before deciding on our preferred layout. Children not only use ICT to generate their work but also to *develop* and *organise* it before printing it out and publishing it (cf. ICT

NC level 3 attainment target: *They use ICT to generate, develop, organise and present their work*). The similarity between trying out different layouts of a newspaper front page and different layouts of a classroom will not have escaped the reader.

Any ICT tool that can be used to *exchange and share information* allows us to try things out in this respect:

- With a word processor we can easily change the structure of our writing, in order to communicate our ideas more clearly.

- With a graphing program we can easily change the type of graph, in order to choose the one which best communicates our idea – for example, a pie-chart may be the best for comparing proportions.

- With a music program we can easily change the tempo, pitch, type of instrument etc.

- With a paint program we can also make changes easily, in particular undo an effect easily – unlike with the medium of charcoal or watercolours or other physical paint.

- With a sound recording program, like *Audacity*, we can make changes easily.

As we saw when discussing progression in *Exchanging and sharing information*, the characteristic of children at level 3 is precisely that they use ICT to revise their work, to draft and redraft their writing, etc. – in other words to try things out, to develop their ideas. So developing ideas can also be thought of as one element of the aspect of *Exchanging and sharing information*, in the sense that children use ICT to try things out in order to communicate their ideas more effectively – for example, to produce some persuasive writing that is more persuasive than it would otherwise be to the reader (e.g. a more effective advertisement), or some instructions that are clearer than they would otherwise be to the reader (e.g. an easier-to-follow recipe). This is partly what is meant by the Programme of Study 2a for *Developing ideas and Making things happen* (Key Stage 2):

> Pupils at Key Stage 2, should be taught:
>
> 2a) how to develop and refine ideas by bringing together, organising and reorganising text, tables, images and sound as appropriate [for example, desktop publishing, multimedia presentations].

In the examples above, ICT is being used to improve the *product* (a sequence of instructions, or the layout of a newspaper page etc.); ICT is being used to *develop* the product. This relates to the Programme of Study *Reviewing and modifying work as it progresses*:

> 4. Pupils should be taught to:
>
> a) review what they and others have done to help them **develop** their ideas
>
> b) describe and talk about the effectiveness of their work with ICT, comparing it with other methods and considering the effect it has on others [for example, the impact made by a desktop-published newsletter or poster]
>
> c) talk about how they could improve future work.

Developing ideas as a process

In addition to developing the product, the tools that are used for *Exchanging and sharing information* and for *Making things happen* can also be used as **tools for thinking**. We have already seen this in relation to LOGO. The same is true for a tool such as a word processor.

In addition to communicating our ideas, writing things down can also help us clarify our thinking. In so doing writing is not just a medium for communication, it is also a tool for thinking. We have all experienced the process of writing clarifying our thinking (e.g. when writing an essay), or *developing our ideas*. This is sometimes known as the 'heuristic' function of writing, and has been encapsulated by the saying 'How can I know what I think until I see what I write?' (attributed to a number of different authors, amongst them W.H. Auden and E.M. Forster).

There are two different processes here, albeit sometimes hard to separate in practice:

- When we know exactly what we want to say, then any changes we make will be solely for the purpose of communicating more effectively to our audience. Here we are using ICT as a tool to help us communicate more effectively.

- Sometimes, however, we may simply be writing something down to clarify our thinking, with no intention of ever showing the writing to anyone else. Here we are using ICT as a tool to help us clarify our thinking; we are using ICT as a tool for thinking.

Often we make changes to our writing to both clarify our thinking and to communicate more clearly.

When using ICT to make changes easily, to try things out, the focus can be on the process or on the product. When the focus is on the product, ICT is being used as a tool for *Exchanging and sharing information* or as a tool for *Making things happen*. When the focus is on the process, ICT is being used as *a tool for thinking*, or developing ideas. This distinction is presented in Table 6.4.

TABLE 6.4 The different elements of *Developing ideas*

The Programme of Study for *Developing Ideas and Making things happen* at Key Stage 2 states that pupils should be taught:	If the focus is on the **product**:	If the focus is on the **process**:
2a) how to develop and refine ideas by bringing together, organising and reorganising text, tables, images and sound as appropriate [for example, desktop publishing, multimedia presentations]	*ICT is being used as a* **tool for Exchanging and sharing information**	*ICT is being used as a* **tool for thinking**
2b) how to create, test, improve and refine sequences of instructions to make things happen and to monitor events and respond to them [for example, monitoring changes in temperature, detecting light levels and turning on a light]	*ICT is being used as a* **tool for Making things happen**	*ICT is being used as a* **tool for thinking**
2c) to use simulations and explore models in order to answer 'What if ... ?' questions, to investigate and evaluate the effect of changing values and to identify patterns and relationships [for example, simulation software, spreadsheet models]	*ICT is being used as a* **tool for solving problems, for finding things out**	*ICT is being used as a* **tool for thinking, for exploring patterns and relationships**

For pupils to engage in the process of developing ideas, whether the focus be on the process or on the product, they need to *review, modify and evaluate their work as it progresses*. This is the fourth aspect of the National Curriculum. It is no accident that this aspect of the ICT National Curriculum includes the following phrase: 'Pupils should be taught to (a) review what they and others have done to help them **develop their ideas**.'

We have already seen that the SCAA (1996) and the QCA (2003) characteristics state that work at level 3 is characterised by the use of ICT to **develop ideas**.

We summarise the results of our analysis in Figure 6.4.

Developing ideas is central to the ICT National Curriculum, all-pervasive, and cuts across all the aspects. Similarly, *Reviewing and modifying work as it progresses* and *Breadth of study* also cut across the other aspects. We therefore offer a way of conceptualising the aspects which takes this into account (see Table 6.5).

TABLE 6.5 Developing ideas, threads and aspects

'Threads'	Aspects			
	Finding things out	Models and simulations	Making things happen	Exchanging and sharing information
Reviewing and Modifying Work as it Progresses	✓	✓	✓	✓
Breadth of Study	✓	✓	✓	✓
Trying Things Out: Developing the Product			✓	✓
Developing Ideas (Trying Things Out)	Pursuing a line of enquiry	✓	✓	✓

Activity

In this chapter we have suggested that there is no need to wait until Year 5 to introduce pupils to spreadsheets and drawing programs (QCA Units 5A and 5D), and that pupils' capability would be better served if they knew how to use these programs before they were introduced for the integrated tasks in the Year 5 units.

If it is realistic to introduce such programs before Year 5, we need to identify appropriate contexts for them, and these could be provided in the Mathematics and the Design & Technology curricula.

Outline some learning objectives and possible activities for the introduction of spreadsheets and drawing programs in Years 3 or 4. What would be the context for your tasks? What simple problems might the pupils solve using these programs, which would help to prepare them for the existing work in Year 5? (QCA Units 5A and 5D). Which curriculum subjects would provide an appropriate context for this work and what are the learning objectives for those subjects?

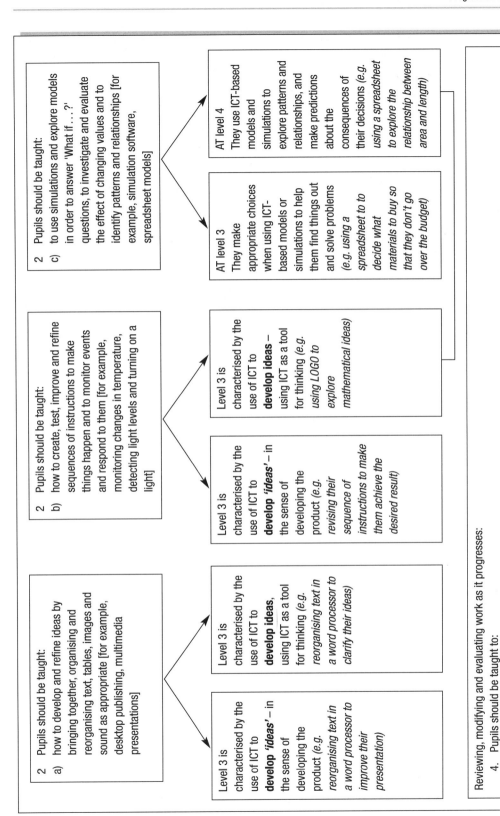

2 Pupils should be taught:
a) how to develop and refine ideas by bringing together, organising and reorganising text, tables, images and sound as appropriate [for example, desktop publishing, multimedia presentations]

2 Pupils should be taught:
b) how to create, test, improve and refine sequences of instructions to make things happen and to monitor events and respond to them [for example, monitoring changes in temperature, detecting light levels and turning on a light]

2 Pupils should be taught:
c) to use simulations and explore models in order to answer 'What if . . . ?' questions, to investigate and evaluate the effect of changing values and to identify patterns and relationships [for example, simulation software, spreadsheet models]

Level 3 is characterised by the use of ICT to **develop 'ideas'** – in the sense of developing the product *(e.g. reorganising text in a word processor to improve their presentation)*

Level 3 is characterised by the use of ICT to **develop ideas**, using ICT as a tool for thinking *(e.g. reorganising text in a word processor to clarify their ideas)*

Level 3 is characterised by the use of ICT to **develop 'ideas'** – in the sense of developing the product *(e.g. revising their sequence of instructions to make them achieve the desired result)*

Level 3 is characterised by the use of ICT to **develop ideas** – using ICT as a tool for thinking *(e.g. using LOGO to explore mathematical ideas)*

AT level 3
They make appropriate choices when using ICT-based models or simulations to help them find things out and solve problems *(e.g. using a spreadsheet to to decide what materials to buy so that they don't go over the budget)*

AT level 4
They use ICT-based models and simulations to explore patterns and relationships, and make predictions about the consequences of their decisions *(e.g. using a spreadsheet to explore the relationship between area and length)*

Reviewing, modifying and evaluating work as it progresses:
4. Pupils should be taught to:
a) review what they and others have done to help them **develop their ideas**
c) talk about how they could improve future work.

FIGURE 6.4 *Developing ideas and Making things happen*

7

Medium-term planning and the QCA Scheme of Work

Objectives

- To understand the structure of a QCA unit of work for ICT

- To understand that the integrated task is a purposeful activity, in which pupils apply their ICT knowledge, skills and understanding, i.e. in which they demonstrate their ICT capability. It should be an activity where there is an advantage in using ICT over more traditional methods

- To understand that even though the QCA scheme is a well-thought-out scheme, it should not stop us from thinking about alternative ways of delivering the ICT National Curriculum. For example, is the same way appropriate for all aspects? Is the same way appropriate for both Key Stages? We should not assume that 'one size fits all'

- To understand the pedagogical underpinning of the QCA Scheme of Work

Each unit in the QCA Scheme of Work for ICT is, in effect, a medium-term plan for teaching one aspect of the ICT National Curriculum.

The structure of each unit emphasises that the ICT National Curriculum is about teaching ICT capability, rather than skills. There are three parts to each unit:

- Setting the scene

- A series of short, focused tasks

- An integrated task.

The integrated task is a purposeful activity in which the children *apply* their ICT knowledge, skills and understanding, in which they *demonstrate their ICT capability*. It should be an activity where there is an advantage in using ICT over more traditional methods. An example of an integrated task might be to create a class magazine. Here ICT can clearly help, not only in terms of presentation but also in terms of being able to make changes more easily.

In order to create a class magazine the children need to be able to use a simple DTP application, or at least a word processor with which it is possible to insert images.

A breakdown of the techniques they need to know, i.e. a task analysis, will include such things as being able to:

1. enter text, including using the space bar;

2. use the Enter and Delete keys;

3. insert capital letters;

4. print out their work (perhaps by clicking on the print icon on the toolbar);

5. change the style and size of the font (and perhaps the colour);

6. make changes to the wording of the text;

7. insert punctuation, including exclamation marks and question marks (which involve using the shift key); and

8. insert, reposition, and re-size images.

If, for example, the children already know techniques 1–4, then they will need to learn techniques 5–8 in order to be successful at the integrated task.

In a QCA unit, these techniques would be taught in a series of short, focused tasks – short lessons where the focus is on just learning that technique. In these short, focused tasks, the emphasis would be on learning these techniques and any associated concepts (key ideas). Unit 3A, Combining text and images, does just this (see Table 7.1).

For children to be ICT-capable it is necessary, amongst other things, for them to:

1. be able to apply their techniques to a realistic, purposeful activity;

2. understand how ICT helps (part of *Reviewing and modifying work as it progresses*); and

3. make connections between what they are doing and the uses of ICT in the wider world (part of *Breadth of study*).

The *Integrated task*, which is different in content and focus to any of the short, focused tasks, is designed to ensure that the new techniques are applied to a realistic, purposeful activity. To the extent that the teaching and learning is successful, the children should be able to undertake the integrated task without any help (see point 1 above).

Both *setting the scene* and the *integrated task* provide opportunities for the teacher to discuss with the children how ICT helps (see point 2 above). In unit 3A, it is suggested that as part of the integrated task the teacher should *discuss with the class the advantages of using ICT*, and this can also be done in the section on setting the scene.

Both *setting the scene* and the *integrated task* also provide opportunities for the teacher to make the connection between what they are doing and the uses of ICT in the wider world (see point 3 above). This is not explicitly mentioned in unit 3A, but it is implicit. One of the best ways of doing this is, of course, to visit a publisher, for example the local newspaper.

There is a common misconception about the short, focused tasks; it is important to note that the short, focused tasks should *not* be treated as parts of the integrated task. It can be seen quite clearly in the above example that the short, focused tasks are quite different tasks from the integrated task. This is to avoid what Kennewell *et al.* (2000) call the *ICT interference factor* – the learning of new techniques interfering with carrying out the integrated task.

TABLE 7.1 The objectives of Unit 3A, Combining text and images

Setting the scene
Key idea: that text and graphics can be combined to communicate information ■ Show the class a range of greeting cards. Discuss the designs and point out elements, such as pictures, fonts, captions and messages. Divide the class into groups and ask each group to examine one card. Ask them to produce an annotated poster identifying the card's key features. ■ Look at messages and how they are written. Ask children to think about cards that they could design and produce.
Short, focused tasks
Technique: to alter font type, size and colour for emphasis and effect ■ Type in a number of words, *e.g. 'rainbow', 'grow', 'lean', 'high', 'low', 'stairs' and 'ghost'.* ■ Show the class font-editing features, such as how to change font type, size and colour. Ask the children to change the look of each word so that it reflects its meaning, *e.g. placing each letter of 'rainbow' in a different colour, increasing the font size of each letter in 'grow'.*
Key idea: that ICT can be used to improve text **Technique:** to amend text and save changes ■ Type in a piece of text using 'nice' as the only adjective. ■ Remind the class how to edit text by highlighting words and over-typing them. Demonstrate how to save work and give it a sensible name. Ask the children to edit the text using more varied adjectives and to save their work.
Technique: to combine graphics and text ■ Prepare examples of text which would benefit from illustrations *e.g. a description of a pyramid.* Demonstrate to the class how to locate, retrieve, insert and add a graphic into a piece of text. Show the class how to re-size a graphic so that it fits on the page. Ask the children to search a clip art file or a CD-ROM to locate graphics and copy them into a piece of text.
Technique: to use the shift key to type characters, such as question marks ■ Enter a piece of text and replace all the punctuation marks with 'x'. ■ Discuss how authors use punctuation marks for effect and remind the class how to use the shift key to type upper-case letters. Show them how the key can be used to type other characters. ■ Ask the children to replace each 'x' with the correct punctuation. Ask them to print out their work.
Integrated task
Technique: to combine graphics and text to communicate information ■ Tell the class that they are going to produce a class magazine, which will include pictures and captions, and explain that they will use punctuation and font effects. ■ Divide the children into pairs and ask them to choose a theme for a page in the magazine. Get them to create, or capture, a picture for their page and ask them to caption the picture. Tell the children to print their work and bring the work together to form the magazine. Finally, discuss with the class the advantages of using ICT.

Keeping the activities in the short, focused tasks and the integrated task separate also enables the children to demonstrate their ICT capability. Part of being ICT-capable is being able to decide for oneself which tool to use, and which feature(s) of each tool to use. So the idea is that children in the integrated task will be making choices and decisions for themselves. Producing a class magazine is not simply a question of children being able to string together a series of techniques in a predetermined manner. Rather it is a process, which *includes* being able to put together a number of techniques, but also being able to choose the appropriate techniques, as we saw in Chapter 2.

So the structure of the QCA units is designed to provide a framework for ensuring that children become ICT-capable. It was also designed to help with classroom organisation and management when only one or two computers are available in the classroom and there is no access to a computer suite (the QCA scheme dates back to 1998, when computer suites in primary schools were a rarity). The short, focused tasks are just that – short and focused, allowing all the children in the class to go to the classroom computer(s) in turn (perhaps in pairs or threes) and for all to learn a technique at various times during one week, perhaps each spending only ten minutes or so at the computer. So thirty or more children could all learn that technique within the week, even with limited ICT resources. If there were four techniques to learn in the unit, then the unit of work could be completed in about half a term. This also had the advantage that the children were not overfaced with learning too many techniques at once.

The scheme has been designed to ensure that all the ICT National Curriculum aspects are covered, and to attempt to ensure that children are able to achieve level 4 (and beyond).

So the QCA scheme of work is a well-thought-out scheme of work, and has been very well received, especially since the ICT National Curriculum was difficult to understand and still more difficult to know how to translate into practice.

This, however, should not stop us from asking the question: could there be a different and better scheme of work for delivering the ICT National Curriculum at Key Stage 1 and Key Stage 2, especially since the resources and skill levels of both pupils and teachers are so much better in 2004 than in 1998?

We should not assume that the structure and teaching methodology of the QCA Scheme of Work is necessarily the most appropriate way to deliver the content of all the elements in those units. For example:

- Is the same way appropriate for all aspects?
- Is the same way appropriate for both key stages?

We should not assume that 'one size fits all'. These are the issues we are going to discuss in the remainder of this chapter.

The difference between the aspects

We shall begin by discussing two examples, for which we argue that the QCA approach is more appropriate, namely *Unit 3C, Introduction to databases,* and *Unit 4E, Modelling effects on screen.*

In both these units there is a carefully sequenced series of short, focused tasks to introduce the children to the key ideas (concepts) and key techniques, in order to undertake the integrated task.

Unit 3C, Introduction to databases

The expectation at the end of Unit 3C (Introduction to databases) is that children should be able *to use a database to sort and classify information and to present their findings*.

In order to be able to carry out the integrated task the children have to understand:

- the structure of a database (this is addressed in the first short, focused task, in setting the scene, and in the third task);

- that information in a database can be held as numbers, choices (such as yes/no), or words (this is addressed in the second short, focused task);

- how to add a record to a file in a computer database (this is addressed in the third short, focused task);

- how to sort the records in a database, and how to carry out a simple search (these are addressed in the fourth short, focused task); and

- how to use a database to produce bar charts (this is addressed in the fifth short, focused task).

Perhaps the key element here is for the learner to create a mental model of the structure of a database, the format in which information is stored, and to understand what is happening when information in that database is being sorted and searched. This is not something trivial, and it is new to the children (despite a very short experience with a database the year before). Added to that, the children have to learn how to add a record and also to produce bar charts. These latter elements are not challenging in themselves, but all add to the complexity of the task. Introducing all these elements in a carefully structured, sequential manner is more likely to lead to success. Without such a carefully structured, sequenced activity the danger of an *interference factor* is very great.

Unit 4E, Modelling effects on screen

The expectation at the end of Unit 4E is that children should be able to use a LOGO program *to write repeating procedures to produce a desired outcome*.

The children will have been introduced to a floor turtle in Year 2 (two years previously), and will, hopefully, have used it a few times since then in relation to Maths and Geography etc. But it is still not unreasonable to suppose that they have only remembered the simpler elements, and have not remembered about repeats (hence the reason that repeats are re-introduced in Unit 4E).

The integrated task assumes they understand repeats and procedures, and in order to be able to carry out the integrated task the children have to understand:

- that the screen turtle obeys the same language commands as the floor turtle, and that they have to type commands in immediate mode;

- that the screen turtle can be given commands to produce a specific shape on screen, and that the turtle can be moved before it starts drawing (by using the commands *pendown* and *penup* to move the turtle);

- that instructions can be repeated;
- that groups of instructions can be named (procedures); and
- that procedures can call other procedures.

Perhaps the key element here is that the children are learning a new language, and are having to understand the difference between entering commands directly and calling a procedure. Again, this is not something trivial, and it is essentially new to the children (despite using a floor turtle previously). Introducing these elements in a carefully structured, sequential manner is more likely to lead to success.

Familiarity and conceptual complexity

What is common to both these units is that they are introducing elements that are conceptually unfamiliar to the children.

Comparing these units with Unit 3A, Combining text and images, what the children need to learn in order to carry out the integrated task in this unit is how to:

- change the style and size of the font (and perhaps the colour);
- make changes to the wording of the text, by highlighting and using the delete key;
- insert punctuation, including exclamation marks and question marks (which involve using the shift key); and
- insert images and resize them.

A key difference is that this unit (3A) is conceptually much simpler than the other units (3C and 4E).

In setting the scene in Unit 3A, the children are supposed to learn that *text and graphics can be combined to communicate information*. We agree that the kind of activity suggested is a good way to introduce the work to be done, but it is hardly complex conceptually. Indeed, all the short, focused tasks are not only conceptually simple but also conceptually familiar. The children have been working with, and talking about, texts almost daily for the previous two years, and by their third year they will know that writing can be different sizes and colours, that wording can be changed and that punctuation is important.

The concept of an electronic text containing images is familiar to them. Neither are any of the techniques complex, because word processors are used frequently, both in schools and at home. In addition, because they are easy to incorporate into everyday work in schools it is likely that at least some of the children will already be familiar with at least some of the techniques. The children will be able to pick up, fairly quickly and easily, any techniques they do not already know, either from their peers or with very limited help from the teacher. It is not so much learning the *techniques* that causes problems for the children; it is converting these techniques into *routines*.

So the question that needs to be asked is whether it is really necessary to have such a structured 'subskill' approach with this unit. Could not these techniques be introduced seamlessly through a series of interesting, integrated tasks throughout the year, rather than in a medium-term plan, with a series of disembedded short, focused tasks that might not interest the children very much? And what does the teacher do with the children who already know how to (e.g.) change font type, size and colour? Differentiation is a problem with this approach.

We are suggesting that the applications used for the aspect of *Exchanging and sharing information* (with text) are conceptually simple and familiar, and that the limiting factor in their use is the literacy levels of the children, rather than their understanding of ICT.

In contrast, the applications central to *Finding things out* and *Making things happen* are unfamiliar and conceptually complex (in terms of ICT).

It is true that we can offer analogies to help children understand the concepts, such as drawing their attention to the fact that information in a database is structured as a record card or as a table. But, even so, they have to get used to the fact that a database can be thought of *both* as a series of record cards *and* as a table. In the non-ICT world the structure cannot be changed with a simple click!

Programming languages do, of course, have features in common with natural languages, but at the very least it is a new language to be learned, and there are differences – one of the main differences being that we have to be so precise for our instructions to be interpreted by the computer.

We shall be developing this later, and will outline in subsequent chapters how to deliver *Exchanging and sharing information* in a more integrated manner, and not only make it more meaningful but also enable ICT as a subject to be delivered in a more effective manner.

The difference between the key stages

As can be seen, the key characteristic of level 1 is the exploratory use of ICT. This can be illustrated by considering Unit 1C (The information around us), a unit concerned with Finding Things Out.

Unit 1C, The information around us

According to QCA, at the end of this unit *children will know that information exists in a variety of forms and be able to gather it from a variety of sources.*

The learning objectives in setting the scene and in the short, focused tasks are as follows:

- **key idea:** that information can be presented in a variety of forms;
- **key idea:** that information comes from a variety of sources;
- **key idea:** that sounds convey information (this includes using a tape recorder);
- **key idea:** that pictures provide information;
- **key idea:** that information is all around us in a variety of forms;
- **key idea:** that computers use icons to provide information and instructions;
- **key idea:** that certain 'rules' (or conventions) are applied in communicating and presenting information.

Note that they are all key *ideas*; the children are not being taught any *techniques* at all.

If we examine the integrated task, this is not doing anything different from the series of activities that have been done before (in *setting the scene* and the *short, focused tasks*).

Integrated task

to show that information can be presented in a variety of forms and collected from a variety of sources

Ask the children to work in groups to collect information about an agreed topic. Encourage them to think about what they want to find out about the subject (but they should be prepared to find out other things).

Ask the children to think about where and how they will find out the information and how they will collect and present it.

Encourage the children to collect information in a variety of forms, e.g. *representational pictures, interviews, books, photographs*. Ask them to make a simple display of the materials they collect.

In this unit all the activities are of the same sort of nature, whether classified as setting the scene; a short, focused task; or an integrated task. Neither should we be surprised. As no ICT techniques are being taught, there is no interference factor to avoid.

Consequently, this unit lends itself to a series of activities carried out by the teacher and the children, many of which can be integrated seamlessly into the normal course of other classroom activities, some during carpet time, some as activities in which the teacher is using the computer and some as part of normal maths lessons.

Unit 1E, Representing information graphically: pictograms

Here the children use a graphing package to select appropriate icons, recognise quantities and create a pictogram. The expectation at the end of the unit is that children should be able to *use a graphing package to select appropriate icons, recognise quantities and create a pictogram*.

Now it does not require much thought to see that the ICT techniques that need to be taught here are very limited. A pictogram program is almost just a 'point and click' program, requiring little in terms of the teaching of techniques. This is clear when the unit is examined in more detail.

Setting the scene is concerned with ensuring that they understand pictograms. But as this is part of the normal daily mathematics lesson anyway, does it really need a separate ICT session? It is also a bit odd to include as a 'technique' the objective to use (paper-based) *pictograms to answer simple questions*. Is this a technique? If so, it is certainly not an *ICT* technique.

The first and *only* short, focused task is concerned with the key idea (and also the technique) of being able to use a pictogram program to create a pictogram with ICT – knowing which icons to click on to choose the appropriate pictogram and which icons to click on to enter the data.

The integrated task is to use it – but what has been done earlier? Surely there is only really one task, and one lesson. Before introducing ICT to create a pictogram, the teacher ensures that paper-based pictograms have been used in the past in a daily mathematics lesson. Then there are two lessons:

Lesson 1

A lesson where ICT is used to create a pictogram, the lesson having the structure of a QCA unit, but it is a single lesson rather than a medium-term plan (and which takes for its content a planned mathematics activity which uses a pictogram):

- Setting the scene: ICT can be used to create pictograms. Demonstrate to the class how to enter data and show them the icons which will produce a pictogram of data entered.

- A task which combines a short, focused task and an integrated task: ask each child to choose the icons that will create a pictogram (individual children go to the computer one at a time). Print the pictogram and use it to answer the questions relating to the mathematics activity.

Lesson 2

In order to consolidate the learning, another integrated task in which the children create their own pictograms individually (or in pairs, etc.).

The use of pictograms can then be embedded into more mathematics lessons, to consolidate the learning and to ensure that the techniques learnt become routines.

TABLE 7.2 A content analysis of the techniques taught in Year 1 of the QCA Scheme

An introduction to modelling (1A) **technique:** to use a mouse to move and place items accurately on a screen **technique:** to use simple tools in a painting package **technique:** to print out their painting **technique:** to add stamps/motifs or clip art to a scene
Using a word bank (1B) **technique:** keyboard familiarity **technique:** to select, and listen to, text using the mouse
The information around us (1C) *no* techniques taught or used
Labelling and classifying (1D) *no* techniques taught – word bank used (techniques needed not relevant to learning objectives of unit)
Representing information graphically: pictograms (1E) **technique:** to use pictograms to answer simple questions
Understanding instructions and making things happen (1F) *no* ICT techniques taught or used (though use of Roamer is optional)

An overview of units in Year 1

A content analysis of the units in Year 1 shows clearly how very few ICT techniques are being taught (see Table 7.2).

This fact, that few techniques are being taught, is not surprising. We noted earlier that level 1 is characterised by the use of ICT to **explore options** and **make choices** to **communicate meaning**. Children develop **familiarity** with simple ICT tools. The level 1 attainment target states that pupils:

- explore information from various sources, showing they know that information exists in different forms;
- recognise that many everyday devices respond to signals and instructions.

In addition, they:

- use ICT to work with text, images and sound to help them share their ideas;
- make choices when using such devices to produce different outcomes;
- talk about their use of ICT.

The emphasis at level 1 is not about learning many techniques, but more about becoming familiar with different ICT tools and different ICT media.

As the children are not being taught many techniques there is little danger of an interference factor, and consequently, there is no need to adopt the structure and methodology of the QCA Scheme of Work. Rather, the activities can be integrated seamlessly into normal classroom activities. What is important is that the learning objectives are covered.

One advantage of moving away from the mindset of the QCA structure and methodology is that we can then embed more ICT experiences into the year, and more reinforcement and consolidation, more purposeful use of ICT, and higher expectations of what children can achieve.

TABLE 7.3 The expectations of Unit 1B, Using a word bank

EXPECTATIONS At the end of this unit:	
most children will:	enter single words from a keyboard; use a word bank to assemble sentences that communicate meaning
some children will not have made so much progress and will:	enter single words from a keyboard; use a word bank to combine words, with help
some children will have progressed further and will:	use ICT to create sentences that communicate meaning, using the keyboard for the majority of the text

As can be seen from the table above, the expectation in terms of what techniques the children will have learnt by the end of Year 1 is very limited, given the resources now available in schools. For example, consider the expectations of the Unit 1B, Using a word bank (see Table 7.3).

Given that this unit is meant to take place over half a term, the expectations are perhaps realistic if we assume that some children will be completely unfamiliar with a word processor, whether or not it has a word bank. Moreover, the different stages of the children's literacy development will mean that it is not realistic to expect all of them to *use ICT to create sentences that communicate meaning, using the keyboard for the majority of the text*. This is why it is only a reasonable expectation for some of the children, not for all of them.

Yet surely this expectation is one that we would want for *all* children by the end of the year (unless they have specific language-learning difficulties). This higher expectation *is* possible if one envisages progress over the whole of Year 1, and not just during half a term.

So by changing the way these learning objectives are taught, so that they are embedded into literacy work done over the year rather than half a term, we can then have the expectation that:

- all children without specific language learning difficulties will, by the end of Year 1,
  use ICT to create sentences that communicate meaning, using the keyboard for the majority of the text.

The main factor that will determine when the children will be able to achieve this will be their *stage of literacy development*, as the ICT techniques are conceptually simple, and require less motor control than handwriting.

The appropriate teaching approaches for those whose literacy development is less advanced will include the teacher and/or teaching assistant scribing using a word processor, and a teaching assistant helping the children – for example by reading out the difficult words in the word bank, helping them find the letters on the keyboard, etc.

Units in Year 2

In Year 2 the demands begin to change, given that children start using ICT in a purposeful manner. Yet even here there are opportunities for delivering the ICT curriculum in a more integrated manner.

Units 2A, 2B and 2C do not make many demands in terms of techniques, and can be embedded into other work done over the year, so that all children can, whatever their ability, by the end of the year:

- use a word processor to produce sentences that communicate meaning (Writing stories: communicating information using text, 2A);

- use a computer graphics package to create a picture (Creating pictures, 2B);

- navigate a CD-ROM (Finding information, 2C).

The concepts in the remaining two units will be less familiar, and more complex conceptually, so these may benefit from the QCA approach:

- Routes: controlling a floor turtle (2D);
- Questions and answers (2E).

The pedagogical underpinning of the QCA Scheme of Work

The structure of the units in the QCA Scheme of Work for ICT has, as its underlying pedagogical basis, a behaviourist sub-skills approach to teaching, very reminiscent of the principles of instructional design as outlined by Gagné and his co-workers (see Gagné 1975; Gagné and Briggs 1974; and Gagné *et al.* 1992).

We will first outline the similarities, and then discuss an alternative approach, based on a less directed approach, involving scaffolding children's learning, and based on a Vygotskian approach to teaching.

Gagné and Briggs: principles of instructional design

The essence of a 'Gagnérian' approach is:

- to undertake a *Task Analysis* in order to determine the *prerequisite skills* necessary for the learner to successfully complete the task in question;
- to teach those prerequisite skills;
- the learner should then be able to learn the new task without any additional teaching being necessary.

Gagné uses the term *intellectual skill*. An example of an intellectual skill is the ability to multiply, which is knowing a rule. This is different from knowing a fact (verbal information), and also different from a motor skill (like being able to throw a ball).

Gagné and Briggs (1974:101) state that:

> one wants to ensure that prerequisite intellectual skills and verbal information that are necessary for any given topic have been previously learned. For example, the topic of adding fractions is introduced in arithmetic after the student has learned to multiply and divide whole numbers, because the operations required in adding fractions include these simpler operations.

This is because, in order to add, say, $5/6$ and $2/3$ together, one needs to:

- find the lowest common denominator (6);
- multiply the numerator and denominator of $2/3$ by 2 to get $4/6$;
- add $5/6$ and $4/6$ to get $9/6$; and
- divide the numerator by the denominator to get 1 and $3/6$ (i.e. one-and-a-half).

These steps require the prerequisite intellectual skills of addition, multiplication and division. Gagné and Briggs (*ibid.*:108) proceed to explain that:

> The structure of intellectual skills makes it possible to design with considerable precision effective conditions for learning them. When this is done, the learning of intellectual skills becomes a process which is easy for a teacher to manage. In addition, the process of learning becomes highly reinforcing for the learner, because he is frequently realising that with apparent and satisfying suddenness he knows how to do some things that he didn't know before. Thus the activity of learning takes on, for him, an excitement which is at the opposite pole from 'drill' and 'rote recitation'.

The key to the design of conditions for this effective kind of learning is the *learning hierarchy*. 'The learning hierarchy is an arrangement of intellectual skill objectives into a pattern which shows the prerequisite relationships among them' (*ibid.*:109). A *Task Analysis* consists of constructing such a learning hierarchy of prerequisite skills. Figure 7.1 shows an outline of such a learning hierarchy.

In the QCA Scheme of Work a task analysis has been made of the skills needed in order to successfully complete each integrated task. The QCA assumes some of these are already known, because they have been introduced in previous units. These are listed in the section 'Where the unit fits in'. The remainder are taught in the short, focused tasks.

Following Gagné, if the teaching of the short, focused tasks is successful, the children should be able to complete the integrated task without any additional help from the teacher.

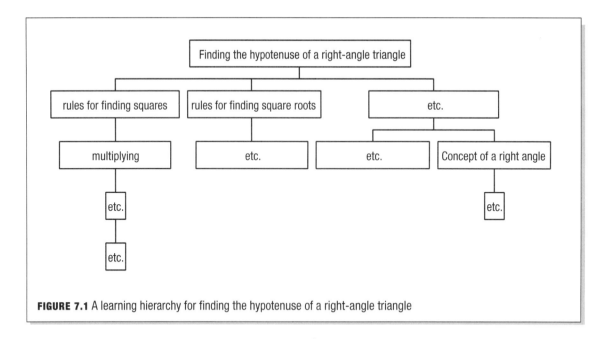

FIGURE 7.1 A learning hierarchy for finding the hypotenuse of a right-angle triangle

Vygotsky and the scaffolding of learning

The Vygotskian approach is, however, very different. Key concepts in this approach are the *Zone of Proximal Development* and *scaffolding*. The Zone of Proximal Development (ZPD) is defined as:

> The distance between the actual development level as determined by independent problem solving and the level of potential development as determined through problem solving under adult guidance or in collaboration with more able peers.

> (Vygotsky 1978: 86)

For Vygotsky, what moves children on in their learning and development is being given challenges that they would be unable to complete on their own, but which they are able to complete with the help of another. But this help has to be of a particular kind, namely *scaffolding*. Maybin *et al.* (1992: 188) explain this as follows:

> 'Scaffolding' is not just any assistance which helps a learner accomplish a task. It is help which will enable a learner to accomplish a task which they would not have been quite able to manage on their own, and it is help which is intended to bring the learner closer to a state of competence which will enable them eventually to complete such a task on their own.

In other words, for teacher intervention to count as scaffolding, there would need to be some evidence that:

- the teacher wished to enable the child to develop a skill or concept, or achieve a particular understanding;
- the learner had accomplished the task with the teacher's help; or
- the learner had achieved some greater level of independent competence as a result of the scaffolding (that is, demonstrating their increased competence or improved level of understanding in dealing independently with some subsequent problem).

Note that this final condition is the one which satisfies one of the conditions for ensuring that children develop ICT capability – namely that the children are able to apply their 'skills' in a new situation.

The Vygotskian principle for 'instructional design' is, therefore, to set a task that is just too difficult for children to complete on their own, and for the teacher to ensure the necessary scaffolding is there for the learning to take place (whether that scaffolding is provided by the teacher or in some other way).

If we accept Vygotskian principles, why have the short, focused tasks? These are disembedded tasks and go against the principles of the ICT National Curriculum in that they do not focus on ICT capability but merely on ICT techniques. Why not just have a series of integrated tasks?

Of course, we do not have a scheme of work along these lines, so we would have to produce one.

Choosing which approach to adopt

The contrast between these two approaches is stark.

Gagné and Briggs/QCA	Vygotsky
Ensure that integrated task *is* achievable by the children on their own, without any help from the teacher.	Ensure that the integrated task is *not* achievable by the children on their own, but is within the children's ZPD, and that the necessary scaffolding is provided.
Short, focused tasks followed by an integrated task.	A series of integrated tasks.

How does the teacher decide between these approaches? There are both principles and practicalities that will determine the choice. First, there is a scheme of work provided (by QCA) following the principles of Gagné and Briggs, but not one following the Vygotskian principles. However, to what extent is the QCA Scheme of Work satisfactory?

As it stands it can be seen that the QCA Scheme of Work does not, the way it is described, take account of individual differences. In any class, some children will already have some or all of the skills necessary to complete the integrated task successfully, whereas others may need to learn all the skills.

One solution to this is for the teacher to conduct a skills audit, and only teach the short, focused tasks to those who need to learn the skill in question. But if the teaching is done in a computer suite, what then do the children do who already have the skills? Do they practise their skills, and if so, will it be a purposeful task? If so, will it turn into an integrated task? Do they learn a new skill? If so, is their integrated task going to be different?

Another factor worth mentioning is the impact of the computer suite on the teaching of the short, focused tasks. Designed as they were to be short and focused, they do not really lend themselves to a lesson delivered in a computer suite.

One alternative is to think of interesting things to do which reinforce the skills still further, and make use of the whole lesson time in the computer suite. Another alternative is to deliver a sequence of integrated tasks, each one building on the previous one in terms of the skills needed.

When we start taking into account individual differences, and the likelihood of access to a computer suite, modifying the QCA Scheme of Work in a meaningful, purposeful way seems to be moving us towards a Vygotskian approach. The reader may like to reflect upon and respond to the following questions: How did you develop your ICT capability? What kind of approach would you favour?

In the following chapters we outline a scheme of work designed to take into account these issues. Earlier on (in Chapter 2) we recommended the article by Atherton (2000). At this point we urge the reader to read her article if they have not already done so.

ICT capability and ICT as a subject

The ICT National Curriculum, and the guidance provided by the QCA Scheme of Work, emphasises ICT capability, as it is concerned that pupils not only learn about ICT but are also able to use ICT to help enhance their work in other subjects. This is, of course, very desirable, and a 'good thing', but we consider that the QCA does not give enough attention to ICT as a subject, and that this has two undesirable consequences. One consequence is that the QCA finds it difficult to give enough prominence to some ICT resources and activities in its Scheme of Work. Key ICT applications, LOGO and object-based programs, are not given enough attention, probably because it is difficult to find many uses for these in other subjects. In addition, the use of spreadsheets and control and monitoring are introduced later than they need be. If the emphasis were on ICT as a subject as well as ICT capability, these ICT applications would be given more prominence and would be introduced earlier. In addition, too much emphasis is given to ICT resources concerned with *Exchanging and sharing information* with text, as opposed to paint, music and sound-recording applications.

Another consequence is that general issues such as file management are not introduced in a carefully sequenced and structured manner, if at all, as Wood and Webb (2002:18) observe:

> We also want to find ways of extending the understanding of some of the key techniques, e.g. one of the techniques at level 2 is being to save a file. We want to extend this understanding as the child progresses through the school. They need to really understand what happens when a file is saved – for example, saving over others' work.
>
> Deleting text on a screen does not mean that you now have a clean file to use for another purpose. Re-typing and clicking save overwrites the previous file. So children need to know what the SAVE AS concept is . . . why does SAVE AS come up the first time you click SAVE? What is the difference between them? By the time they reach upper Key Stage 2 they should be beginning to understand how files are organised on a computer. How do you navigate them? Manipulate them? (copy, delete, move, directory structure . . .)
>
> You can understand why the Programmes of Study left out operating systems, not wanting to favour one or the other, but you surely cannot achieve capability without understanding the concepts around their design. Yet this is nowhere in the curriculum and not covered in the QCA Scheme of Work. It's all hidden and implied.
>
> Cut, copy and paste is another useful key technique – for example knowing how to use this technique within an application is useful but when you understand how it can be used generically across applications then you become more effective in using a variety of software.

In the following chapters we present a way of delivering the ICT National Curriculum in a way that also teaches file management and other general issues. This is done in an integrated way, following a Vygotskian rather than a Gagnérian approach to teaching. This alternative way also offers more opportunities for techniques to become routines.

Activities

1. Choose a QCA unit from Key Stage 1 and demonstrate how, where and when – in the curriculum and everyday planning – the unit objectives could be met rather than adopting a structured medium-term planning approach. For example, it may be the case that all the techniques and key ideas taught in QCA Unit 1F, 'Understanding instructions and making things happen', could be incorporated (introduced and reinforced) into literacy, numeracy and PE lessons.

2. In QCA Unit 6A, 'Multimedia presentations', the only references to an audience are:

   Discuss with the class the difference between a CD-ROM and books and videos, and demonstrate that a CD-ROM includes a range of media and offers the user different options. **Discuss how these options address the needs of different audiences.**

   Divide the class into groups and ask them to create a page which includes a menu of sounds. The page could be a page of sounds recorded from musical instruments, **or an interactive birthday greeting for an infant class**, which includes hot spots linked to sounds.

   Divide the class into small groups and ask each group to choose a subject for their presentation **and to describe their audience**. Ask each group to draw a diagram of their presentation, showing how the pages link. Children should then design their pages on screen and print out their results.

   This assumes that the pupils already have a good understanding of what it means to respond to the needs of an audience. How would you adapt the tasks within this QCA unit or work in order to better prepare pupils for the integrated task of preparing a presentation for an intended audience?

8

What, when, how and why: teaching ICT

Objectives

- To understand why, for some aspects of the ICT National Curriculum, a move away from the QCA structure and methodology would provide a more effective pedagogy
- To understand that when it is sensible to follow the QCA prescribed structure, then improvements to the content may be necessary

In this chapter we will be thinking about the what, when, how and why of teaching the ICT National Curriculum. 'What' to teach and 'when' is provided by a Scheme of Work, and, of course, we have the QCA ICT scheme. However, in Chapter 7, and throughout this book, we have put forward suggestions for what we see as improvements to that scheme; further specific examples will be outlined in this chapter. For the 'how' and 'why', examples will demonstrate how the content within a QCA unit could be taught, and why, in some instances, improvements should be made.

In the first part of the chapter, teaching and learning in Key Stage 1 will be considered. This is followed in the second part by an illustration of how two QCA units can be combined to provide an enriched teaching and learning experience. Finally, because what we are proposing for the teaching of *Exchanging and sharing information* is different from the other aspects, the ideas are presented as a separate chapter.

The structure for the rest of this chapter will therefore be as follows:

1. Teaching and learning in Key Stage 1:

   - Teaching and enhancing the content of a QCA unit – two examples;
   - Examples of how an existing QCA unit may not warrant a medium-term planning approach or specific ICT lessons.

2. Teaching and learning in Key Stage 2:

   - Combining objectives from ICT QCA Unit 5B with History QCA Unit 11, to create an integrated and enhanced ICT experience.

Teaching and learning in Key Stage 1

In order to fulfil the Key Stage 1 Programme of Study, children only need to be introduced to a small number of computer programs and be taught very few techniques. For example, the following only require the children to be able to point and click:

- *My World*;
- a simple adventure program;
- graphing program;
- branching database.

The following only require children to learn a few basic techniques:

- a CD-ROM encyclopaedia;
- a painting program;
- word processor;
- simple flatfile database;
- floor turtle (e.g., Roamer).

What Key Stage 1 work *does* involve is the introduction of some important concepts (key ideas) and these are often best taught with children away from a computer and by whole-class teaching, demonstration and discussion. In addition, analysis of the Key Stage 1 units shows that the integrated tasks are often no different from the short, focused tasks, and that the QCA structure, with its medium-term plan approach, is not always necessary. *Finding things out* and *Exchanging and sharing information* objectives, in particular, are best taught as part of the everyday activities within the classroom, with key opportunities to develop ICT capability being identified within those activities.

A move away from the QCA structure and methodology would mean that more ICT experiences could be embedded into Key Stage 1, thereby facilitating more reinforcement and consolidation, more purposeful use of ICT and higher expectations of what children can achieve. The reason why the two named aspects have the potential for a different teaching and learning approach is their strong cross-curricular links, and the fact that, at times, children are not being taught any ICT techniques at all. For example, as in QCA Unit 1C: The information around us.

If we consider the broad range of topics covered in Key Stage 1, it is clear that there will be opportunities on a regular basis, throughout the year, for children to understand that information is all around us in a variety of forms (Unit 1C), to sort and classify objects using ICT (Unit 1D), to collect and present data as pictograms (Unit 1E), to use a CD-ROM to find things out (Unit 2C), and to ask questions in different ways (Unit 2E). Rather than opt for the short, one-off approach of a QCA unit of work, we are advocating that concepts and techniques are revisited, and processes developed more often, across the curriculum. In this way a teacher would have the whole year for children to achieve the expected outcomes and not just the average six weeks taken to complete a QCA unit. Furthermore, this extended period would provide the opportunity for children to achieve the outcomes defined by QCA as those for *the children who have progressed further.*

However, despite the above points, there are instances where it is sensible to follow the QCA prescribed structure, but with improvements to the content where necessary. These units can be identified as those with specific ICT concepts to teach – concepts that are not generic and therefore do not easily lend themselves to a cross-curricular approach. For example, contrast the key idea that computers can represent real and fantasy situations (QCA Unit 1A), with the learning objective that pictures provide information (QCA Unit 1C). The latter objective could naturally form part of a lesson in a number of subject areas, while the former would warrant a significant amount of teaching and learning time, and be not simply a minor part of a lesson that provided a rather tenuous link to computer simulations.

What follows are two sets of examples. In the first set, the QCA structure is maintained, but details are added to some of the short, focused tasks to illustrate how lessons could be organised and delivered. Suggested improvements to the unit content are also made. In the second set of examples an alternative to the medium-term planning approach, or even specific ICT lessons, is proposed.

Teaching and enhancing the content of a QCA unit

Example 1: QCA Unit 1A: An introduction to modelling

Key idea: computers can represent real or fantasy situations.

Outcome: children understand that the computer can be used to represent real situations.

Classroom organisation and resources: whole-class teaching, electronic whiteboard, *My World* program, a teddy and a selection of teddy clothes.

Component of capability being developed: conceptual understanding.

Setting the scene

The teacher reminds the children that [in mathematics] they have been thinking about daily routines and ordering them in time (National Numeracy Strategy measures objective 78).

One of the things that we have to do in the morning is to get dressed. Is that an easy thing to do? Why / why not? Do you get any help from someone else? What kind of help do you need? Perhaps we need help with zips, buttons or tying laces.

The teacher could ask if anyone has ever dressed a teddy. 'How is dressing your Teddy the same/different from dressing yourself? Is it easier or more difficult? Why?' A demonstration of how to put some of the items of clothing on to the teddy could follow.

Using the interactive whiteboard the teacher could show the children the dressing teddy screen that is part of the *My World* program. The teacher could ask the children which item of clothing they should put on to Ted first. As the teacher 'taps' on the screen to select, and 'drags' the item of clothing, he/she should describe the actions. The children could be asked which item would be next, and a child chosen to come out and 'select' and 'drag' the item into place. The teacher could ask the children if they know how they would 'select' the clothes if they were using the computer in the classroom, confirming that they would use the mouse instead of their hands and that they would click the mouse button rather than tap the screen.

Children should be encouraged to consider how dressing the teddy on screen is different from dressing a real teddy.

The focus of the lesson moves to the use of the *My World* screen called *Find Ted*. The teacher uses a combination of whole-class demonstration and the children using the whiteboard themselves to (a) find Ted and (b) help children think about how this computer representation is similar to, but different from, the real scenario. For example, the teacher could hide the class teddy under a rug and then compare this to hiding Ted under a rug on the screen, i.e. only the real 3D objects distort.

Summarise the main points from the lesson.

Follow-up: Lesson 1

Key idea: a computer representation allows the user to make choices.

Technique: mouse control.

Outcome: children understand that they can make choices and that people make different choices for different reasons; be able to use the mouse to move and place objects with accuracy.

Classroom organisation and resources: whole-class teaching, electronic whiteboard, the big bus website (www.thebigbus.com), follow-up group work.

Component of capability being developed: conceptual understanding and techniques.

The children are reminded that the computer can be used to represent real situations and that in previous lessons they have used the computer to dress Ted. 'Today we are going to dress another bear called Bo, but this time we have to make some decisions about which clothes to put on Bo depending on what he is going to do that day.'

From the Big Bus website (*www.thebigbus.com*) an activity called 'Dress Bo Bear' is accessed and displayed on the electronic whiteboard. Most of the activities on this site require users to subscribe, but this particular activity is available as a demonstration. The Big Bus has produced a CD-ROM containing activities especially for use on an interactive whiteboard. One of the nine activities on 'The Whiteboard Companion' CD-ROM is 'Dressing Bo Bear'.

Bo is going out in the rain, and so the children have to decide which clothes to dress Bo in. This is a multimedia site and the instructions are spoken: 'Dress Bo for going out in the rain.' Also, when you select the words under each item you can hear them spoken. The teacher could ask the children if this is a good idea and point out that when we do this, a pair or ears are shown on screen indicating that there is something to hear. The activity could continue until Bo is dressed appropriately for the rain.

The site is interactive, so choosing an item for Bo to wear will result in a spoken response, in this case, 'Oops! Bo doesn't need a swimming costume in the rain.'

As this was a whole-class lesson using the electronic whiteboard, the second objective of developing mouse techniques will only be achieved if the teacher plans follow-up work on the computer for small groups or pairs. Children could revisit the *My World* screens to develop their mouse control but also to discuss and decide, for example, where to look for / hide Ted, and also dress Bo Bear for themselves. Adult support should help children to reflect on and describe their actions. Also, if this work is done throughout the week, children could be given the opportunity to tell the rest of the class what they have been doing.

If the teacher chose to undertake the follow-up work as a whole-class activity in a computer suite, it might prove difficult to provide the level of adult support needed to use this type of software effectively, as teacher intervention in modelling activities is critical in ensuring that children understand the underlying concepts.

Follow-up: Lesson Two

Key idea: a computer can be used to represent a wide range of environments, and some are more elaborate than others; a computer model is not an exact replica of the original.
Outcome: children understand that a computer can be used to simulate / model an environment where choices can be made; understand that representations of real or fantasy situations do not replicate real life exactly.
Classroom organisation and resources: whole-class teaching, electronic whiteboard, a simple adventure game such as Freddy Teddy's Adventure (see *www.topologika.co.uk/*), follow-up group work.
Component of capability being developed: conceptual understanding, techniques, processes and higher-order skills.

The electronic whiteboard could be used to display the Freddy Teddy's Adventure game. Having reminded the children that the computer can represent real situations, and that they have used it to do things like dress a teddy and play hide-and-seek with Ted, they could be asked to recall in what ways the computer situations have been similar to / different from the real thing. The teacher explains that today they are going to meet another teddy.

This teddy is called Freddy and rather than dress him or decide which clothes he should wear, we are going to join him in an adventure. The adventure takes place in a wood and we will have to make lots of decisions about what to do and where to go in order to solve a puzzle. That's what the adventure will be.

Early on in the program the user has to choose a starting point for the adventure by selecting one of the pictures on screen. The teacher could ask the children if we could jump from one place to another in this way, in real life. Together, the teacher and children complete the first part of the adventure using the electronic whiteboard.

The children are involved in the decision-making relating to the adventure game, discussing the decisions or choices they make and why they make them. They also respond to a number of key questions posed by the teacher to help them to reflect on the computer simulation. For example, 'if they were out in the countryside would they be able to hear anything? What might they hear? Can they hear the same sorts of things when they use the adventure game? What other differences are there? Can we smell the flowers and leaves when we use the adventure game? Do the characters in the simulation ever get tired?'

The adventure could be completed over several days, with the teacher and children working together as a whole class. Or, after a brief whole-class introduction, the children could work in small groups, taking it in turns to operate the mouse and discussing what decisions to make. If this approach is taken, it is essential that children regularly share and discuss what they have done with the whole class and are encouraged to think about the simulated scenario.

The teacher should model and support the process of completing the adventure game, demonstrating some of the higher-order skills that would be needed to 'manage' successful completion. For example, the children could be asked how they could remember where they had already been in the adventure and what were the consequences of a particular decision that was made.

Tell the class about any problems that you had and what you did to solve them. How will this help another group? How might we record the routes we have taken, places visited or things found? The children could agree a strategy and design a recording system with the support and guidance of the teacher.

> **Follow-up: Lesson 3**
>
> *Key idea*: a computer can be used to create representations of various scenarios.
> *Techniques*: use simple tools in a painting package, to print out work, to add stamps or clip art to a scene.
> *Outcome*: children can use a painting program to create a representation of a scenario and print it out. They can select and add stamps or clip art to a scene.
> *Classroom organisation and resources*: whole-class teaching, electronic whiteboard, a painting package such as RM Colour Magic, a printer, a help sheet, follow-up group work.
> *Component of capability being developed*: conceptual understanding and techniques.

The RM Colour Magic painting program could be displayed to the whole class via an electronic whiteboard. The teacher explains to the children that they are going to use RM Colour Magic to create a beach scene (prompted by a recent holiday story in class), and demonstrates the simple tools and how stamps can be used to create a more complex representation. The stamps featured in RM Colour Magic make this application particularly suitable for this activity.

I want to start by painting the sand. Which icon do you think I should click on? Yes that's right the one showing a picture of a paintbrush. Let's click it.

Which size of brush will be the best for painting the sand? The big one. Why? Let's see if you are right. But first I need to choose the right colour. What colour is sand?

Now I'm clicking on the yellow colour at the bottom of the screen to choose the colour. What did you notice? I'll choose a different colour and you watch carefully. Yes that's right. The colour that I choose is shown here. Why is that? ... I've drawn a picture and now I want to add some stamps. Which icon do you think I need to click on so that I can stamp some pictures onto the page?

Children go on to produce their own pictures on the class computers or in a computer suite. They could use a help sheet to remind them about the different tools.

In the above example, techniques have been demonstrated and underpinned by conceptual understanding. It is important that both teacher and children use the correct vocabulary/technical terms when describing their actions. Sufficient opportunities need to be provided for techniques to become routine. So, ideally, ICT needs to be part and parcel of the classroom environment. Any child who is not able to carry out a technique in a confident, fluent manner after a reasonable amount of time, i.e. is not making reasonable progress, should be given targeted support as a priority. Children should be able to learn techniques with minimum support, and the emphasis should be on them acquiring strategies to encourage independence. For example, rather than simply learning where the flood fill tool is in a particular application, they should be thinking about why the flood fill icon is depicted as it is. Learning in this way should promote transferable skills so that children are able to work out how to 'flood fill' in any painting program.

Points to note

QCA Unit 1A says that children should only use the simplest tools of a painting package and that they should not need any more at this stage. However, Jenny had to use several different techniques to produce her picture – the shape tool, straight line tool, brush, pencil, change colour – and was only really happy when the stamps were added.

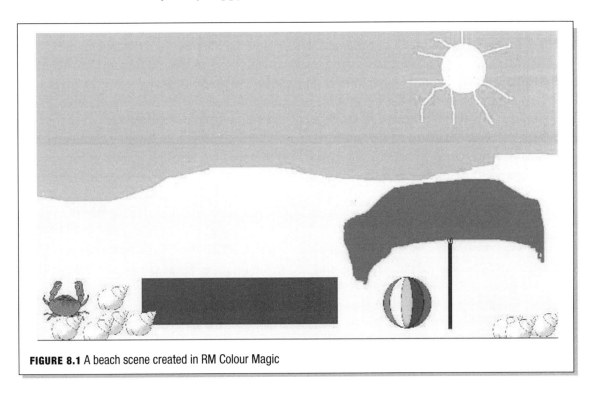

FIGURE 8.1 A beach scene created in RM Colour Magic

Simon was much happier with his outcome, yet he only used two techniques – the stamps and the spray tool.

FIGURE 8.2 A fantasy world created in RM Colour Magic

Children who painted a picture and then looked for stamps were disappointed because they thought they would find a stamp for any item. Some children started by looking at the available stamps and then decided what to paint. As there was only a limited number of stamps this resulted in a limited number of topics drawn. Some children were unable to categorise the stamps into a particular topic by themselves and simply added stamps randomly to their pictures. (This is in no way a criticism of RM Colour Magic, and simply reflects the way in which this particular activity was carried out. See the later teaching point that suggests the children should understand that it would be impossible to have a set of stamps for every scenario that they thought of. The latest version, RM Colour Magic 2.5, features a wide collection of curriculum-relevant pictures in the RM 'Topic Bank' which pupils can turn into image stamps.)

Programs such as Textease could be also be used for this activity. It is not a graphics package, but it does have a picture bank, and adding an image is simply a matter of 'dragging' it onto the page. The dilemma here is that although the techniques to be taught relate to a graphics package, the key idea is not necessarily restricted to learning about 'painting' using ICT.

However, if we do choose to use Textease, then children have not learned any 'painting' techniques, so we need to decide what the main teaching and learning objective is. An analysis of the process involved for the integrated task will help us to decide what the children should be taught.

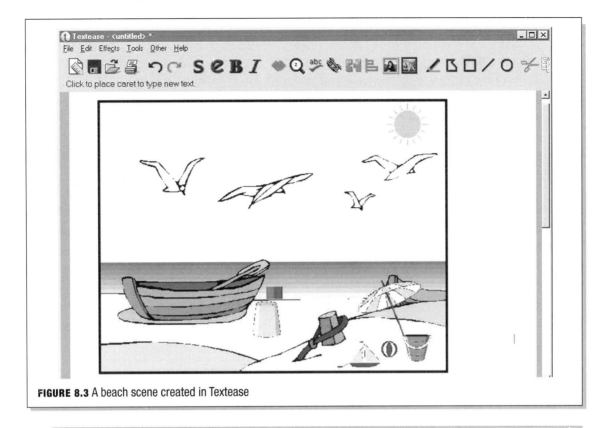

FIGURE 8.3 A beach scene created in Textease

The Integrated task

Objective: to create a representation of a real or a fantasy situation.

Outcome: children should be able to describe their scenario and explain why they made their decisions or choices. They should also explain how their representation differs from real life.

■ Discuss with the children the different ways the computer was used to represent real or fantasy situations. Tell them that they are going to create their own representations and *they can choose* what they would like to represent *and how they will do it using appropriate software*. This might be linked to topic work, e.g. a story or nursery rhyme, designing a new classroom or school, concocting a new set of meals for school dinners, visualising places to go on holiday, fantasy creatures from outer space or new modes of transport for the next century.

■ Children should decide on the environment or representation that they wish to create. *They should think about what it will look like and what sorts of decisions or choices they will have to make*.

■ Some children will be able to use a text tool or a word processor to produce a caption for their representation.

Looking back to the last focused task, it would seem that one way to approach this task would be to extend the work to several lessons, so that the children have a much better understanding of some of the features of different programs. First, the children would be taught some basic techniques to use in the painting program such as RM Colour Magic and would discuss/evaluate their work. Which techniques did they use? What effects did that produce? How did that improve the scenario that they created? The use of stamps could be introduced as a specific teaching point, with a discussion about which stamps are available and why it would be impossible to have an appropriate picture for every scenario that the children thought about.

Next, Textease could be used to create a scenario using the picture bank, and the outcomes could be evaluated. A discussion could centre on how the pictures are sorted into topics and stored in folders. How does that help? What are the differences between Textease and RM Colour Magic? Why are they different? Are they the same kind of program?

The *process* of producing a representation of a real or fantasy situation and the demonstration of *ICT capability* now become much clearer. Children should choose which program, which techniques and which type of images or combinations of images – drawn and clip art – for themselves. They should also be able to justify their choices.

A cross-curricular application

The teacher's guide for the ICT Scheme of Work (QCA / DfES 2003:20) suggests that during their Design &Technology project on 'playgrounds', children could use ICT to create a representation of a playground they have visited, or an imaginary one. They could use clipart, images from the internet or digital images taken during a class visit to a playground. Children should be encouraged to make decisions and choices about which items to include in their representation and where to place them. The enhanced content in QCA Unit 1A would provide a better preparation for the application of capability in the 'playground' project described above, which in turn is a good introduction to the type of graphical modelling that occurs in Year 5, QCA Unit 5A, when pupils use a drawing program to design the layout of a classroom or to plan an improved school site.

Example 2: QCA Unit 2B: Creating pictures

This next example demonstrates how an understanding of the different components of ICT capability is important if the aims of the lessons are to be achieved. Without that knowledge there is always the risk that the work within this Unit could be reduced to simply learning how to use a painting program. Unit 2B is about communicating visually and understanding that with ICT we can try things out, evaluate our work as it progresses by saving different versions, and easily make amendments – and we learn some 'painting' techniques along the way.

It may be the case that working in a computer suite encourages a skills-based (techniques) approach. We feel that we need to make best use of the time when computers are available, and often this equates to 'hands-on', with evaluation and discussion better placed in the classroom. However, time in the classroom is precious, and the opportunities for 'off-computer' work may get lost, especially if we feel that the weekly visit to the suite constitutes the ICT lesson. Also, it might be difficult to collect up the children's ICT work for display and discussion back in the classroom, particularly if 'work in progress' is what we want to review and evaluate, and not a printout of an end-product.

> **Setting the scene**
>
> *Key idea*: ICT can be used to create pictures.
> *Classroom organisation and resources*: whole-class teaching, electronic whiteboard, examples of pictures created using ICT.
> *Component of capability being developed*: conceptual understanding.

Examples of pictures created using ICT are shown to the class. Children are prompted to discuss some of the features of the pictures and how they are different from pictures produced using traditional methods. Presenting computer artwork on a large screen would have the greatest impact, rather than a small, paper copy. Therefore, if at all possible, presentation software and a projector or electronic whiteboard should be used.

If pictures are not readily available in school, then examples may have to be found on the internet or produced specially for the lesson; the discussion should not be hindered by a lack of examples. The children should be encouraged to look for the different techniques that have been used and to suggest which tool has been used. 'How do we know that the pictures have been produced using ICT? How are the colours, lines etc. different from/similar to the pictures produced using non-ICT methods? Are there some things that we can/cannot do using a painting program that can/cannot be done using traditional methods?'

What follows, in the QCA Unit of Work, is a series of lessons where *techniques* are taught. These are:

- to select and use simple mark making tools;
- to use the flood fill tool to create highlights of colour;
- to select and use the straight line, geometric shapes and flood fill tools;
- to select and use the spray tool;
- to use 'save as'.

And the *key idea* that: ICT makes it easy to correct mistakes and explore alternatives.

The *integrated task* is for children to select and use different techniques to communicate ideas through pictures, and the suggested focus is for them to create portraits that visually represent emotions such as anger, sadness, fear and joy. Although the conceptual understanding needed to achieve this outcome is hinted at in the possible teaching activities, it is surprising that there are no key ideas or explicit learning outcomes relating to this visual communication before the integrated task.

Techniques and concepts

Each of the short, focused tasks in the QCA Unit starts by introducing the work of an artist and examining a key feature of their work. For example, the flowing black lines of Jackson

Pollock's 'Yellow Islands' and the use of horizontal and vertical lines plus primary colours of Mondrian. These are useful resources as they provide a very good stimulus for children to learn how to 'flood fill' and use the geometric shape tools, and the styles are easy to recreate. An electronic whiteboard or digital projector would be an ideal way to display artwork to the whole class. The paintings could be shown directly from the internet if a connection is available, or by using presentation software.

The work of Mondrian is also useful as a way of introducing a purposeful use of the 'Save as' technique. A quick search on the internet will yield examples of Mondrian's work where the same image has been altered slightly and then renamed. For example, 'Still Life with Ginger Jar I' and 'Still Life with Ginger Jar II', or 'Composition with Red, Yellow, Blue and Black' and 'Composition with Red, Yellow and Blue'. Children could be asked to do a similar thing – create one image and save it, then experiment with the colours (perhaps warm colours/cool colours) and then save the new image with a different name.

The teaching of techniques has already been described above, with the ideal being a whole-class demonstration via an electronic whiteboard so that children can see what is happening while the teacher articulates what they are doing. Electronic whiteboards also offer the opportunity for children to come to the front of the class and try the techniques for themselves. They, too, could describe what they are doing or, alternatively, provide verbal instructions for someone else to follow.

The short, focused tasks can take place either in the classroom or in a computer suite and decisions might be made according to the 'ICT ethos' of the school. They might also be based on the nature of the tasks. For example, recreating Mondrian's work could be equally successful in an ICT suite or as part of classroom-based art lessons where similar concepts are being developed with traditional materials. In contrast, short, focused tasks that involve the technique of creating a graph on computer take very little time and may be so integrated into another subject that waiting for the weekly ICT lesson is neither practical nor necessary.

Given the nature of the integrated task and the overall aim of Unit 2B, teachers should ensure that adequate time and attention is given to the development of conceptual understanding. So the important teaching points in the QCA unit are:

- Ask the children to use the pen and flood fill tool to create lines and colours **to express themes** such as 'headlights in the city'. Alternatively, children could provide their own **titles which convey how they have used lines and colours**.

- Ask them to **experiment with colour** using the flood fill tool. They could create warm colour pictures, cool colour pictures and pictures in which one colour is made to stand out from the others. **Display the work and discuss the results.**

- **Discuss the differences** between light and colour when viewed on screen and in print, using two examples of the same picture. Introduce the idea of 'painting with light'. Ask them to use the flood fill tool to create a black screen and then to use mark-making tools and various colours to **explore the quality of light and colour on the screen**.

It would help if children were shown a wider range of examples of artwork, examples that demonstrate the use of a particular technique to create an effect. They could be given more opportunities to explore techniques in the painting program in a less directed way but with lots of discussion and evaluation of their own and other children's work.

Processes are best taught by placing children in situations where they have to think for themselves, where it is not obvious what decision they need to make. With a typical QCA unit, they do not really have to think for themselves, as the integrated task is often prescribed, and Unit 2B is no exception. A more effective way to develop capability might be for children to be scaffolded through the integrated task so that the teacher uses it as semi-structured teaching and learning experience, perhaps in the context of Art QCA Unit 1A, Self-portrait. Further opportunities could be identified for children to go through the process of using a graphics program to communicate ideas in a less directed way. For example, the suggested task in the teacher's guide for the ICT Scheme of Work (QCA/DfES 2003:30), where children use the work of artists who used nature as a source of ideas, would provide a stimulus. Alternatively, or as well as, children could design their version of a coat for Joseph (Design &Technology Unit 2D), linked to the story of Joseph's coat of many colours. The graphic design (techniques used) would communicate something about the status of Joseph and his coat.

Examples of how an existing QCA unit may not warrant a medium-term planning approach or specific ICT lessons

> ### Example 1: QCA Unit 1C: The information around us
>
> *Key ideas*: information can be presented in a variety of forms; that sounds convey information; that pictures provide information; information is all around us in a variety of forms; certain 'rules' or conventions are applied in communicating and presenting information.
> *Techniques*: (none using ICT).
> *Integrated task*: to show that information can be presented in a variety of forms and collected from a variety of sources. Children are asked to work in groups to collect information about an agreed topic.
> *Component of capability being developed*: conceptual understanding.

One possible stimulus for thinking about information all around us would be literacy work relating to non-fiction (signs, labels, captions, print in the environment etc.). An effective way to present this work would be a multimedia presentation using a program such as PowerPoint, Textease or Granada Writer, and an electronic whiteboard. The signs and sounds displayed could include digital images taken in the locality.

'What information do the signs and sounds convey? What 'rules' or conventions are used?'

Having taught the basic, initial key idea that *information is all around us in different forms*, teachers should identify one of the numerous opportunities that exist for them to model the process of 'finding things out', by getting the children to think about the different types and sources of information that would be appropriate, and how they would collect, present and interpret what they discovered. Examples of contexts for the *Finding things out* key ideas in QCA Unit 1C include:

- History – how are our toys different from those in the past? (History QCA Unit 1);
- Science – life and living processes. Ourselves (Science QCA Unit 1A);
- History – our local environment in the past. What were homes like a long time ago? (History QCA Unit 2).

Reflection points for teachers planning to model the process of how to find things out:

- What will the context be and how will an interest in finding things out be established?
- What could the children find out? Think about questions to answer.
- Where and how will they find the information? Different sources.
- How will they collect and present the information? Planning the process.
- Will it be possible to collect information in a variety of forms? What will those forms be?
- What questions could be asked of the data? I wonder if...? Is it true that...?
- What might the children find out and what might it mean? Interpreting findings.

This process would be repeated throughout the year, and each time the teacher could withdraw some support, encouraging the children to become more independent in their pursuits to find things out. This is in contrast to retaining the QCA structure which would mean children working through each of the short, focused tasks in Unit 1C, and ending with a group activity where they *collect information about an agreed topic*, in order to achieve the learning objective, *show that information can be presented in a variety of forms and collected from a variety of sources*. Clearly, an improvement would be if the structure was not followed and the key ideas were embedded within another subject and taught as part of an investigative process. This would make effective use of teaching and learning time, have objectives taught within a meaningful, authentic context, and result in higher expectations of what the children could achieve.

Example 2: QCA Unit 1F: Understanding instructions and making things happen

Key ideas: that machines and devices must be controlled; machines and devices can be controlled by a sequence of physical actions; that sequence affects outcome; instructions can be given using a common language, can include measurable units in a common language, recorded for replication and amended and results predicted.

Techniques (none using a computer): to put activities into the correct order; to use directional language to 'control' someone else's actions; use unit lengths and a common language; record a sequence of instructions in a common format; read a set of instructions, predict the results and follow the instructions to test the prediction.

Integrated task: children write sets of instructions, in an agreed format, to get from one place to another. Others read them, predict the outcome and test their prediction.

There are several 'themes' within this Unit. The first is about control in everyday life and how machines and devices are controlled. The second begins with the notion that instructions must be in the correct sequence and then develops into establishing the use of a common language for instructions, including the use of measurable units. Finally, we have the idea that instructions can be recorded in an agreed way, tested and amended.

In the following example, we demonstrate how embedding the key ideas and techniques into other curriculum activities, as and when appropriate, provides an enhanced teaching and learning experience, rather than following the QCA structure as prescribed.

To set the scene, the QCA unit suggests that we:

- Discuss with the class the technology that they see or use, e.g. televisions, video recorders, microwaves, washing machines, toys, traffic lights, supermarket checkouts. Explain how this equipment is operated, e.g. by pressing on/off buttons, turning dials, remote control.
- Show the class some battery-operated toys. Ask the children to draw pictures of the toys and to label the switch and battery compartment. Cut pictures of similar equipment from magazines to make a display and ask the children to group them into categories, e.g. where they are found or how they are controlled.

With the first key idea:

That machines and devices can be controlled by a sequence of physical actions.

Use a tape recorder, with the children, to record sounds. Show the children how the tape recorder buttons are used in the correct sequence to record and play back sound. Divide the class into small groups, give them a simple diagram of a tape recorder and ask them to record some sounds. Ask them to label the buttons on the diagram and write down the order in which they are pressed.

It would be more appropriate to use the first key idea (short, focused task) as a way of setting the scene, when the situation naturally arises. For example, when the children are going to use the tape recorder and need to be shown what to do. Perhaps they are going to listen to a tape, record themselves or interview someone. The importance of learning to use the device will be apparent because it is needed for a 'real' task. Writing a set of instructions, in the correct order, could be part of learning how to operate the device. This could then lead to a discussion about other technology that we can control, as for 'setting the scene'.

Other relevant contexts and starting points might be the literacy work in Year 1 relating to writing instructions, learning to use the class printer or writing a set of instructions in Design & Technology (e.g. to make a fruit salad or to use the microwave when cooking).

The activities suggested above would naturally incorporate the second key idea:

- key idea: that sequence affects outcome.
- technique: to put activities into the correct order.

Unit 1F suggests that we:

Give children a set of cards showing pictures of the stages in a recipe to make sweets. Ask the children to identify the correct sequence by putting the cards in order. Talk about what might happen if the correct order is not followed. Ask them to think of other cases where it is important to carry out instructions in the correct order, e.g. driving a car, building a model. Discuss cases where order is not important, e.g. putting the toppings on a pizza.

It would enhance the activity and conceptual understanding if the children could actually try out their instructions and so appreciate first-hand the importance of getting the sequence correct, rather than thinking about driving a car. For example, the opportunity to work with recipes and food might arise in Design and Technology or when studying festivals in Religious Education.

Children could also think about the different ways to present the instructions for a recipe. For example, a video – why might that help us to understand what to do? Or, use could be made of the wonderful multimedia *Talking Cookery Book 1 – Make Peppermint Creams* from Priory Woods.

Priory Woods is an all age community special school situated in east Middlesbrough. The school caters for pupils with severe learning difficulties and those with profound and multiple needs. *Make Peppermint Creams* is symbol-supported and fully narrated and is the first in a series of simple, easy-to-follow, multimedia recipes.

http://www.priorywoods.middlesbrough.sch.uk/resources/program/programres.htm

The remaining key ideas are also taught without the need for a computer and this would be the best way to develop conceptual understanding. For example, the game of 'people robots' could become part of a Physical Education lesson and is an ideal way to appreciate the need to give instructions in a common format, and that we can record the instructions in an agreed way for replication, testing and amending. It is far better to get to grips with giving and following instructions without the added burden of having to cope with programming a floor turtle such as Roamer.

However, once children are confident and have achieved the learning outcomes from Unit 1F, it would seem sensible to introduce some basic Roamer work, rather than wait until Year 2 (QCA Unit 2D, Routes), especially as the use of a programmable toy is mentioned in the Early Learning Goals and, therefore, Roamers may well have formed part of Foundation Stage activities.

Once again, it is clear that there are advantages to 'letting go' of the rigid structure of a QCA Unit of Work. Objectives can be achieved in a variety of contexts, and there is no need to think in terms of teaching blocks of work, at a single point in the year; it is far better to identify when and where the key ideas, techniques and concepts can be introduced for the first time and then revisited throughout the year.

Teaching and learning in Key Stage 2

The following example illustrates two of the points that have already been made in the discussions relating to teaching and learning in Key Stage 1 above. It demonstrates the need to improve the content of a QCA Unit of Work, if we are to raise our expectations of what children can achieve. In addition, it shows how in some cases the learning objectives from a QCA unit can be more effectively delivered by moving away from the suggested structure and activities, and, instead, incorporating them into a more relevant content.

QCA Unit 5B: Analysing data and asking questions: using complex searches

Chapter 4, 'Progression in *Finding things out*', outlined what we believe constitutes work at a particular National Curriculum level and stressed that judgements are not based solely on the ability to use certain techniques. Another factor would be the level of conceptual understanding that children have of the process of finding things out, which would include the use of higher-order skills.

The *Finding things out* aspect naturally lends itself to the development of higher-order skills. Children can become absorbed in, for example, the history context used to deliver the ICT objectives, and are often keen to plan and carry out a line of enquiry as they learn how to be a history detective. One factor that might inhibit the development of higher-order skills is the amount of time spent on an ICT-based enquiry. If we treat each ICT short, focused task in QCA Unit 5B as an isolated 'skill' lesson, then it is likely that there will not be the opportunity to engage in a sustained research project, where processes can be modelled by the teacher, then practised and demonstrated by the children.

For this reason the following example teaches the short, focused tasks within the same context as the integrated task which, in this instance, seems an appropriate strategy. It is envisaged that this arrangement would provide a richer, more coherent experience that provides opportunities for children to achieve higher levels of ICT attainment than might otherwise be possible.

Combining objectives from ICT QCA Unit 5B with History QCA Unit 11: What was it like for children living in Victorian Britain?

In this History unit, children find out about the lives of Victorian children, how attitudes towards children have changed, and the people who are remembered for their part in these changes. They look at the characteristic features of children's lives in the Victorian period.

QCA History Unit 11 suggests that this topic be introduced by showing pictures of Queen Victoria and her family. Children discuss what they think they can tell from the pictures and also place the Victorian period on a time-line. The discussion extends to Victoria's children and what life would have been like for them. The class also considers whether all children would have had similar experiences. Children then work in groups to share what they already know about the period and feed back to the rest of the class.

Pictures of Queen Victoria and her family are available from the Web and could be displayed to the whole class via an electronic whiteboard. For example, a photograph of Queen Victoria and her family in 1863 is available from *http://learningcurve.pro.gov.uk/snapshots*

Over the coming weeks, children focus on different aspects of Victorian life with a particular emphasis on what it was like for children. They collect information from a range of sources in order to draw conclusions about this period in time. For example:

1. What was life like for a poor child in the 1840s?

Sources include:

- film versions of *Oliver Twist*;

- extracts from contemporary authors (Kingsley, Dickens);
- illustrations of slums and pictures of working children;
- health reports or inspection reports from factories and mines;
- texts about the numbers of hours that children worked, the types of jobs they did and their lack of education;
- CD-ROM encyclopaedia.

2. What was it like going to school at the end of the nineteenth century?

Sources include:

- museum loan services which can provide artefacts, including books and slates;
- illustrations of school life, e.g. uniforms, interiors of classrooms;
- The 1870 Education Act;
- school log books;
- stories;
- diary accounts;
- CD-ROM encyclopaedia.

Having established an interest in the history topic, the teacher could present a database of the 1891 census data for the village of Bourneville. This was the village created by the Cadbury brothers for the people who worked in their factory. The database would allow children to explore the lives of the actual men, women and children who lived in Bourneville and worked in the factory. This provides the context for the ICT work relating to QCA Unit 5B: Analysing data and asking questions using complex searches. The Bourneville database file is available from the Cadbury's History Learning Zone in Black Cat Information Workshop format. (*http://www.cadburylearningzone.co.uk/history/*).

By using a combination of whole-class teaching and group work, the teacher can revise and teach techniques and concepts, and model and scaffold the development of processes and the use of higher-order skills in order to find things out. The children can then be provided with the opportunity to put into practice what they have been taught, with progressively less scaffolding.

It is this supported development of higher-order skills that is missing from the QCA approach, which is unfortunate as we have identified those skills as being key to the achievement of the higher National Curriculum levels.

What follows is an illustration of how the QCA content can be enhanced so that children are better prepared to achieve higher levels of attainment, and a justification for abandoning the QCA suggested activities.

An introductory lesson: Setting the scene for the Bourneville work and revising database concepts and techniques from QCA Unit 3C, Introduction to databases.

An electronic whiteboard or digital projector and screen could be used to show the children the database and explain what the file is about. *How many records are there? How is the data organised?*

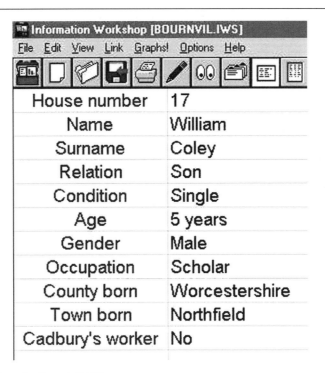

FIGURE 8.4 A record from the Bourneville file

The teacher selects one **record** and asks the children how many **fields** there are and **what information** is held in each one. *What do we mean by* **condition**? *What is a* **scholar**?

There are 116 records in the database, so that means 116 different villagers. How old do you think the oldest/youngest person was at the time of the census? How could we find out if you are right?

If **sort** is not the first suggestion, the teacher could try out some of the initial suggestions, asking if each particular technique would work, or if it was the easiest way to find out if their predictions about age were right. The teacher should establish that sorting the records by age and then looking at the top and bottom records is an efficient way to answer the question.

The children should be encouraged to take an interest in the information about the people of Bourneville, by the teacher having a number of prepared questions that could be answered by using the graphing facility, a simple search or by sorting. Work could either continue with the whole class, with the teacher choosing from the list of questions and selecting a volunteer to use the whiteboard to demonstrate how to find the answer, or with work in a computer suite/use of classroom-based computers, again using the questions as a way of revising basic techniques. If group work is used, other activities in the classroom could involve paper-based tasks relating to the history topic. The Cadbury's Learning Zone has workbooks that can be downloaded in Word format. The activities could provide a starting point for the follow-up work both on and off computer.

What would have been the short, focused tasks in the QCA Unit of Work now becomes whole-class teaching time at the start of the history lessons, and in some cases it may be appropriate for groups to carry out computer activities as follow-up work. However, the main teaching and learning strategy is for children to be provided with an opportunity to apply what they have been taught, including hands-on computer work, later in the project.

Short, focused teaching time

Component of capability being developed: conceptual understanding and techniques.
Technique: search a database using =< and =>.
Classroom organisation and resources: whole-class teaching, electronic whiteboard, Bourneville database.

The teacher reminds the children that in a previous session they found out about the age of the oldest and youngest person in the village (of Bourneville), and explains that today they are going to look at the age distribution. A histogram of ages is displayed and the children are asked what it tells us.

The children should understand that each column represents a range of values, rather than one value.

What can they say about the distribution of ages? What can they not tell from the histogram? The teacher chooses one of the ranges, e.g. 20–30, and asks the children how they can find out which villagers are within that age range.

The children's suggestions and demonstrations are used to establish the technique that they must use to access the correct subset. They need to use > or = to AND < or = to.

Short, focused teaching time

Component of capability being developed: conceptual understanding, techniques and processes.
Key idea: that searches can be carried out using more than one criterion.
Technique: search a database using 'AND'.
Classroom organisation and resources: whole-class teaching, electronic whiteboard, Bourneville database. Sorting/searching/classifying/browsing through the data to find things out.

The Bourneville database file is displayed to the whole class, and the children are told that they are going to browse through the data to see what they can find out. They are reminded that they have been thinking about what it was like for children living in Victorian Britain, and that they have compared the size of families then and now to decide whether homes were more crowded in Victorian times.

Today we are going to see if the village of Bourneville reflects the patterns of family life that we have been finding out about. How could we find out about the size of families in Bourneville?

The records are sorted by 'surname' and the class discuss what that tells them. *How many people are in the Coley family? Who are they? There is William the head of the family, his wife Elizabeth and two daughters and a son. Who is the oldest child?*

We can see from our list view that William Dunn is the only person with that surname. Is he the only person living at number 12? How could we find out? A search for 'House number = 12' shows that Charles Woodall also lives there but as a 'boarder'. What does that mean?

The teacher continues to scroll through the records to see what other questions might be asked and answered. For example, *Does Louisa Fryer live at number 15 by herself? Whose sister-in-law is she? Who does John Grindley lodge with at number 6? Is a lodger the same as a boarder?*

Information Workshop [BOURNVIL.IWS]

File Edit View Link Graphs! Options Help

No.	House number	Name	Surname	Relation	Condition
88	16	Frank	Fowler	Head	Married
92	16	Dora	Fowler	Daughter	Single
94	16	Oliver	Fowler	Son	Single
91	16	Harry	Fowler	Son	Single
89	16	Lydia	Fowler	Wife	Married
93	16	William	Fowler	Son	Single
87	15	Louisa	Fryer	Sister-in-law	Single
62	10	William	Gardiner	Cousin	Single
102	18	Edward	Gough	Head	Married
106	18	Nellie	Gough	Daughter	Single
107	18	Clara	Gough	Daughter	Single
105	18	Emily	Gough	Daughter	Single
104	18	Edward	Gough	Son	Single
108	18	Edward	Gough	Visitor	Married
103	18	Ellen	Gough	Wife	Married
22	3	Emma	Green	Sister-in-law	Single
38	6	John	Grindley	Lodger	Single

FIGURE 8.5 The records sorted by house number

Sorting the records by 'house number' would allow the children to look at how many people occupy a particular address and whether the occupants are always related to one another.

Finally, questions should be posed that would require the use of 'AND' in the search. For example, *how many females worked at the Cadbury's factory?* **Gender is the same as Female AND Cadbury's worker is the same as yes.**

> ### Short, focused teaching time
>
> *Component of capability being developed*: conceptual understanding, techniques and processes.
>
> *Technique*: search a database using 'OR'.
>
> *Classroom organisation and resources*: whole-class teaching, electronic whiteboard, Bourneville database. Sorting/searching/classifying/browsing through the data to find things out.

Is it true that the people who did not work were either children who went to school or married women with families? How could we find out? If children were at school what would their occupation be listed as? **Scholar.** *If people didn't have a job what would their occupation be listed as?* **None.** *So we are looking for people who are either a scholar or have no occupation. We should therefore search for* **Occupation is the same as None OR occupation is the same as Scholar.** *Sorting by 'age' will then help us to answer the question 'What have we found out?'*

The next step

The children now need the opportunity to further develop their ability to answer questions by searching and sorting the data, and the chance to plan and carry out their own lines of enquiry. The teacher has modelled the process for the children but has also involved them in the demonstrations and discussion. Whole-class teaching and access to an electronic whiteboard have been key features of these lessons. The Cadbury's Learning Zone website has another Information Workshop database file. This one is called 'Knorton', and contains the census data for both Bourneville and the neighbourhood village of Stirchley Street. Many Cadbury workers lived in this village but it also contained people who worked for other Midlands industries. The data provide the opportunity for wider exploration of the impact of the new factory and contains the data of nearly 500 people. Given the focus of the QCA History Unit of Work, the class could be asked to concentrate on finding out about the children in the village and their families.

The revised lesson content for QCA Unit 5B has ensured that children have developed a good understanding of databases by addressing the common misconceptions outlined in Chapter 4, and has prepared them to carry out activities that reflect a true level 3 – following lines of enquiry. By incorporating this type of database work into other curriculum areas throughout the year, children would have the opportunity to become more efficient at following lines of enquiry and developing their higher-order skills. As a result of their enriched experiences, the children would be better prepared to work towards higher National Curriculum levels, including creating their own databases in order to test a hypothesis.

Essential elements of the work outlined above were:

- ICT techniques underpinned by conceptual understanding and reflecting common misconceptions;
- a stimulating context for ICT work, one that encouraged an investigative approach;

- having enough time to follow lines of enquiry as the investigative work developed through the topic;
- opportunities to see the process of planning and carrying out a line of enquiry modelled by the teacher;
- opportunities to be scaffolded through the process of carrying out a line of enquiry;
- opportunities for children to carry out a line of enquiry in a new situation.

Activities

1. Select one or more of the following Key Stage 1 QCA units and demonstrate how the learning objectives can be achieved as part of the everyday activities within a Year 1 /Year 2 class:

    Unit 1D: Labelling and classifying

    Unit 1E: Representing information graphically using pictograms

    Unit 1F: Understanding instructions and making things happen

    Unit 2C: Finding information

    Unit 2D: Controlling a floor turtle

    Unit 2E: Questions and answers

2. Reflect on the Key Stage 2 example in this chapter, and the different decisions that could be made about how to organise the teaching and learning. Here are two possible options:

    - ICT objectives integrated into a history topic and delivered through a combination of whole-class, interactive teaching and classroom-based workshops. The workshops would include History & ICT activities, both on and off computer, using a bank of desktop or laptop computers. A fully integrated approach with an emphasis on group work.

    - ICT objectives integrated into a history topic and delivered through a combination of whole-class interactive teaching and a weekly lesson in an ICT suite. An integrated approach but with all hands-on ICT activities taking place once a week, as a whole class, in a computer suite.

    What might be the arguments for and against each option? What might a single lesson be like for each option? Would this unit be as successful without access to whole-class demonstration facilities?

Exchanging and sharing information: an alternative scheme of work

Objectives

- To understand that the structure and teaching methodology of the QCA Scheme of Work may not be the most appropriate way to deliver all aspects of the ICT National Curriculum, in particular Exchanging and Sharing Information
- To understand that there is a lack of balance in the Exchanging and Sharing Information units, with a lot of emphasis on work relating to text, as opposed to text, images and sound

In this chapter we are going to consider the planning and delivery of the *Exchanging and sharing information* Programme of Study. Particular attention will be paid to the way in which the QCA Scheme of Work (QCA/DfES 2000) translates this aspect of the ICT National Curriculum into a set of plans (units of work), and the improvements that could be made.

These proposed improvements are based on two important points that have already been made in this book. Firstly, the recognition that the structure and teaching methodology of the QCA Scheme of Work for ICT is not necessarily the most appropriate way to deliver *all* the aspects. We should not assume that 'one size fits all'. The applications that are used for Exchanging and Sharing Information are conceptually simple and familiar, and the limiting factor in their use is the literacy understanding of the children rather than their understanding of ICT. This opens up the possibilities for an alternative scheme to be devised, one that makes regular use of ICT and mirrors progression in literacy work. Secondly, there is a lack of balance in the Exchanging and Sharing Information QCA units, with a lot of emphasis on work relating to text, as opposed to text, graphics and sound. Furthermore, the work that does take place in relation to sound does nothing to prepare children for their multimedia work in QCA Unit 6A. Therefore any alterative scheme should ensure a more coherent thread of progression from Year 1 to Year 6 for text, graphics and sound.

Other key issues that an alternative scheme should address are the difficulties in providing differentiation, and the need to build the teaching of file management into ICT work throughout the primary years.

In the next section of this chapter, we present an overview of the rationale for an alternative to the QCA Scheme of Work. This is followed by the exemplification of the alternatives for both Key Stage 1 and Key Stage 2.

An alternative approach

One way to think about a different model of delivery is the notion of 'small', 'medium' and 'large' teaching and learning experiences, where a small experience is about learning a new technique, a medium experience provides the opportunity for a technique to become routine and a large experience is similar to a QCA integrated task in that it involves an extended piece of ICT work, but these experiences take place more than once a year and are much less prescriptive.

Small experiences

The sole aim of a small experience is the acquisition of a new technique in the shortest possible time. Children would be introduced to techniques by teacher demonstration and modelling, ideally using an electronic whiteboard. This would be in the context of everyday classroom activities. Lists of techniques would be identified for a particular key stage or year group, and would be based on the nature of work carried out by that particular set of children. For example, a Year 1 child would typically be producing simple sentences, using capital letters and full stops, and beginning to use question marks. Writing simple instructions in the correct order would also be a feature of work at this early stage of writing.

This approach allows for differentiation in that the teacher or classroom assistant can concentrate on teaching a technique to those who might need extra help, while those who have mastered it can go on to apply the technique across the curriculum to support their learning (a medium experience). There will be some pupils who, perhaps because of access to computers at home, will not need to be taught particular techniques, and they can make immediate use of these in a medium experience. Such an approach would require some baseline information about which techniques children could already carry out. This would have to be established if the information were not available from a previous teacher, or if the class were in their first year of schooling. It would also require the ongoing tracking, monitoring and assessment of techniques. This and other assessment issues are discussed in Chapter 10.

A short, intensive teaching of techniques would enable pupils to use them competently enough in a meaningful way as soon as possible, without impeding the achievement of the learning objectives in other subjects. Regular use would then help techniques to become routine.

This is in contrast to the short, focused tasks in a QCA unit that do not offer any obvious differentiation, with some pupils unable to do any of the tasks and others already able to do all the techniques before a unit of work is taught. Also, the reinforcement of techniques as often as possible across the curriculum, but at different times, for different groups, can help to relieve the pressure on resources and curriculum time. For example, if we need to teach the technique of copying and resizing an image, teachers may find that it is not effective use of teaching and learning time for the whole class to produce pictures of tropical fish as per the short, focused task in QCA Unit 4B. Some may never master this in one session, yet others may be capable of producing shoals of extremely elaborate fish without much teacher input. If the lessons are taught in a computer suite it may be difficult for a teacher to find further time to help those who did not master the technique sufficiently well for it to be useful, and provide work that fulfils genuine learning objectives for the rest of the class.

What we are arguing for is the teaching of techniques followed by meaningful application on a daily, weekly and termly basis, throughout the year. As a result of this increased access one would hope that the expected outcomes at the end of a QCA unit for *some* pupils become the expected outcomes for *most* pupils, by the end of the year.

For example, QCA Unit 4A states that at the end of the unit:

- most children will **use the more advanced features** of a word processor to help them match their work to their audience;

and that

- some children will have progressed further and will **choose** and use the **appropriate advanced features** of a word processor to increase their efficiency when matching their work to their audience.

Why not raise expectations and expect *most* children to be able to choose and use appropriate advanced features of a word processor, but *by the end of the year*. By working in this extended timescale a teacher might feel that it is a reasonable expectation for most pupils to achieve this, rather than accept that only a few could do this in the time it takes to complete a QCA unit.

The *Exchanging and sharing information* aspect fits easily into virtually all topics across both key stages. Consequently, the proposed scheme will demonstrate that there are many opportunities for the medium and large experiences.

What we have outlined so far seems to place great emphasis and value on children learning techniques. This is the case to the extent that pupils *need* to be able to carry out a range of techniques competently in order to do interesting and challenging project work. But we should stress that the techniques are only a means to an end and that the overall intention is the 'large' experience, which will develop capability and is what is described in the level descriptors, not the techniques. What we are trying to move away from is the use of large portions of curriculum time to teach undifferentiated techniques that can be decontextualised and too contrived.

Suggested technique lists for each year group are provided within the scheme that follows. A summary of all these small experiences throughout Key Stages 1 and 2 appears at the end of the chapter.

Medium experiences

Medium experiences provide the opportunity for techniques to become routines. In these experiences, children should use the techniques confidently, to the extent that activities are purposeful and support learning in other subjects. Furthermore, the level of confidence should be such that children do not make unreasonable demands on teacher support. As an example, in Year 2 a medium experience could be something as simple as producing a caption for a display, with a child choosing an appropriate font style, size and colour. Or it could be something more demanding, such as a small group taking their turn to access and open the correct program, in order to produce a few simple sentences, correctly punctuated, to write about seaside holidays in the past, with words relating to the passing of time available in a word bank.

One of the important points to note about medium experiences is that not all children carry out the same tasks. So, for example, if during a topic about 'Ourselves', producing a few simple sentences had been identified as a medium experience, then it is likely that only one group will complete the task using ICT. The rest of the class would use non-ICT methods. This makes class organisation and management realistic, and because there are so many ongoing opportunities for medium experiences, all children will have regular access to ICT throughout the year.

Conceptual development

Once again, the reader should be reassured that the alternative scheme goes beyond the teaching of skills, and that the development of conceptual understanding (key ideas in the QCA Scheme of Work) has not been lost. As mentioned previously, one of the *key* reasons why the *Exchanging and sharing information* aspect should be taught differently is its inextricable links with children's literacy understanding. After all, it is within the literacy curriculum that children learn how to, for example:

- select the appropriate style and form to suit a specific purpose and audience;
- plan, compose, edit and refine short non-chronological reports;
- evaluate advertisements for their impact, appeal and honesty, focusing in particular on how information about the produce is presented, e.g. tactics for grabbing attention;
- use appropriate layout conventions for non-fiction.

And it is these concepts that underpin the ICT work relating to *Exchanging and sharing information*.

So, in order to justify not teaching concepts and techniques within the confines of a QCA unit, we should be able to demonstrate that the learning would take place in other ways. The following examples support that argument.

In QCA Unit 1B two of the key ideas are that *words are all around us and convey information* and that *text can be entered into a computer and printed out*. The range of non-fiction work outlined in Year 1, Term 1 of the National Literacy Strategy would ensure that children met the first idea in their literacy work, and the second could be introduced and modelled during any number of lessons in a Year 1 class. In other words, these two ideas do not really warrant any specific ICT lesson time, pupils can simply get on with using the keyboard and a word bank to produce labels and simple sentences whenever the opportunities arise, without the formality of a QCA unit of work.

Similarly, Year 2 literacy work will develop pupils' understanding of the features that distinguish texts such as narrative, information and poetry. A teacher could use an electronic whiteboard to model the editing process in context, thereby developing pupils' understanding of the idea that *ICT lets you correct and improve your work, as you are working or at a later date*. Teachers modelling techniques and processes as often as possible, while at the same time describing their actions, will be supporting conceptual development and the possible transfer of techniques to new situations. Other opportunities to develop conceptual understanding will form part of the 'large' experiences.

Large experiences

These are similar to a QCA integrated task in that they are an extended piece of ICT work. However, key differences are that they are less prescriptive in terms of children being cued into using certain techniques – although this more independent approach is a process that is developed over time, and initially requires some teacher scaffolding – and these ICT 'projects' occur more than once in a year.

This move away from the prescriptive QCA structure is replaced with an emphasis on the development and use of higher-order skills. Working in this less-directed way is a real test of capability and, as mentioned above, children will initially need to be scaffolded in their attempts to plan, organise and manage an ICT project. This should be reflected in the way the large experiences are carried out. Teachers could think about this progression in terms of their own class, and throughout the school.

An example of a large experience in Year 3 would be combined geography and ICT work relating to Geography QCA Unit 16: What's in the news? In geography children would:

- investigate a local issue, for example a new housing estate; closing down of a corner shop.

In literacy work children would have:

- experimented with recounting the same event in a variety of ways, such as in the form of a story, letter, or news report;
- identified and considered audience and how this affects writing;
- improved their own writing and corrected errors;
- considered how ICT can be used to polish and present.

To develop ICT capability children would:

- be supported in their decisions about how best to use ICT to communicate information about the local issue;
- produce letters, posters and newspaper articles (with the support of writing frames, templates and word banks, as appropriate);
- use a variety of word-processing and desktop publishing techniques, including combining text and images taken with a digital camera;

■ review, modify and evaluate work as it progresses;

■ investigate and compare the uses made of ICT by the community and developers to communicate information about the local issue.

A source of ideas for large experiences would be the suggested activities in the teacher's guide for the ICT Scheme of Work (QCA/DfES 2003).

Implementing a new approach

The success of a new scheme would be dependent on the principles being adopted by the whole school. So before outlining the nature of the *Exchanging and sharing information* work that would take place in each key stage, we have summarised the steps that would have to be taken in order to implement the scheme:

■ introducing extra objectives into all year groups to ensure a cohesive thread of progression for work relating to text, graphics and sound;

■ defining the small experiences (a techniques list) for key stages / year groups;

■ outlining a range of opportunities for the meaningful application of techniques (medium experiences);

■ identifying opportunities (mainly in Literacy work) to develop concepts relating to Exchanging and Sharing Information;

■ identifying opportunities for large experiences in order to develop processes and to promote higher-order skills.

The following exemplifications of the planning process for *Exchanging and sharing information* work at Key Stages 1 and 2 will use existing QCA units as a starting point, and identify where additional objectives need to be added. Learning objectives are taken out of the QCA unit structure and 'unravelled' to form a long thread of activity that continues throughout the year. This thread of activity consists of a combination of small, medium and large experiences.

Key Stage 1

For Key Stage 1 it would be appropriate to treat each area of *Exchanging and sharing information* separately. Our exemplification will therefore deal with text, then graphics and then sound.

Text

What will pupils learn?
In accordance with our proposals described above, we need to unpack the techniques and key ideas from the Key Stage 1 QCA units relating to text, and integrate them into the everyday teaching throughout the year, in the form of small and medium experiences. Extended ICT work (large experiences) should also be identified.

In Year 1 that would involve ensuring that the following key ideas are taught, either during literacy work or demonstrated/modelled as part of another area of the curriculum:

- words convey information;
- text can be entered into a computer and printed out;
- text can be selected from a word bank.

In Year 2 it would be:
- there are differences between handwritten and word-processed text;
- text can be entered and corrected;
- the importance of spaces between (typed) words;
- the difference between running text and text with line breaks;
- ICT can be used to rearrange text to make it easier to read;
- ICT can be used to improve text and make a message clearer.

By the *end of Year 1* the majority of children should be able to use the computer to produce simple sentences, in a variety of contexts, that are clear and error-free. The keyboard should be used for the majority of the text.

It is highly unlikely that at the beginning of Year 1 children will have either the keyboard skills or literacy skills to create clear, error-free sentences in a variety of different contexts. Therefore, the early work includes children selecting words from a word bank to support the writing process, learning how to use the delete/backspace key to correct mistakes, and also using the speech facility (if available) to help them to select the correct words (from those available in the word bank), and to listen to their sentences to see (hear) if they make sense. They will also need to use the space bar and recognise the print icon.

By the *end of Year 2* the majority of children should be able to use a word processor to produce sentences that communicate meaning; refine sentences by adding words and making corrections; and alter sentences in the light of comments.

The main difference between this and the Year 1 target is that children are introduced to the idea that *ICT can be used to improve text and make a message clearer.* In other words, they not only generate sentences that communicate meaning but also edit their work (amend it). Children are encouraged to create their text directly on screen and then edit it. This can help them to appreciate that ICT not only ensures that their text is well presented but it can also support them in the editing process, i.e. improving text and making a message clearer.

We can appreciate that as children extend their use of a word processor from the creation of a label to several sentences, they will inevitably need to learn new techniques. For example, they will need to use the shift key to produce a capital letter and the return/'enter' key to insert a line break. For this reason it is unhelpful to produce a definitive list of techniques to be taught in each year group as this might imply that progression in the type of texts that can be produced is defined by the specified techniques. It would be preferable to think of a list of possible end-of-Key-Stage 1 targets from which a teacher can select.

Defining the small learning experiences: a possible Key Stage 1 techniques list

TEXT

Click to select letters, words and pictures (e.g. in Clicker)

Select words and pictures from a word bank to make a simple sentence

Use 'Drag' and 'Drop' (e.g. to move words and pictures in Textease or *My World*)

Type name to make a label

Use the speech facility to check work

Use the delete key

Use the backspace key

Use the space bar

Use shift key to make capital letters

Use enter/return to start a new line

Change font size

Change font style

Change the colour of text

Use full stops

Use the shift key to add speech marks

FILE MANAGEMENT

Click to load applications

Open files (to load own work)

Save work

Print work

Understand the different drives (floppy disk drive, hard drive, CD-ROM drive)

Having established what relevant concepts children would learn, outlined end-of-year expectations and suggested a list of techniques, we can now start to identify the teaching and learning opportunities for the application (further practice and automation) of techniques through medium and large experiences. The sources of information we can use to help with the process are: the National Literacy Strategy (NLS); QCA schemes for National Curriculum subjects; and the teacher's guide for the ICT Scheme of Work (QCA/DfES 2003).

These sources will help us to plan activities that could make use of ICT, by providing a focus for the work and by signalling what the appropriate demands on literacy would be. For example, in Year 2 we might use ICT to write a recount (NLS Term 3:T20), knowing that the expectation that capital letters and full stops will be used is in line with literacy expectations. Support could be provided by having connectives that signal time, e.g. *then, next, meanwhile and later*, available in a word bank.

The NLS writing objectives also show how the different text types and writing targets will provide opportunities for teachers to model ICT techniques and teach relevant concepts through whole-class interactive teaching, ideally using an electronic whiteboard.

Using NLS writing targets and Strand Trackers to plan ICT work

Outlined below is an example of how NLS objectives and targets can be used to plan the nature of ICT work in a particular year group.

By the end of Year 1, in writing, most children will have learned to:

Style: sentence construction:

■ Write simple sentences independently (which could include use of ICT)

Punctuation:

■ Use capital letters and full stops when punctuating a single simple sentence
■ Begin to use question marks (helps with planning which techniques to teach)

Purpose and organisation:

■ Write to communicate meaning – simple recounts, stories that can be re-read, with basic beginning, middle and ending
■ Write simple instructions in correct order

Process:

■ Begin to rehearse sentences before writing and re-read during and after writing (could include the use of the speech facility in a word processor)

And examples of the range of different text types would include:

■ Recounts (Term 3: T20 to write simple recounts linked to topics of interest/study or to personal experience. Make group/class books, e.g. *our day at school, our trip to...*)
■ Non-chronological reports (Term 1:T14 to write captions for their own work)
■ Instructions (Term 1:T16 to write and draw simple instructions and labels for everyday classroom use)
■ Stories (Term 1:T11 to make simple picture storybooks with sentences, modelling them on basic text conventions, e.g. cover, author's name, title, layout)

Opportunities for medium and large experiences

As demonstrated above, there will be numerous opportunities for teachers to plan for children to use a word processor. These opportunities will range from typing a simple caption for a display to a poem that requires use of the return key to start a new line, the addition of a clipart picture (perhaps with help), and the changing of font colour and style before the finished product is printed out for display.

Having modelled the use of a number of techniques in relevant contexts, teachers will have planned opportunities for pupils to apply the techniques on a regular basis. Further demonstrations and teacher input could be targeted at those who have not mastered a technique sufficiently well to use it purposefully. So in any one week a group of pupils may have used a word processor to create labels or lists, another group may have ordered some simple instructions correctly and printed them out, while at other times a few individuals may be having extra help in learning how to type their names. The aim is for pupils to have regular access with activities at an appropriate level. This model lends itself to a style of organisation where there is a small cluster of classroom-based computers and access to an electronic whiteboard.

Outlined below are just a few of the possible opportunities for the purposeful use of techniques (medium experiences) with a word processor. All the contexts are taken from the QCA Schemes of Work across the curriculum. However, even if schools do not use all of the schemes, they will recognise the type of activities as being those that regularly take place in a Key Stage 1 environment.

- Science Unit 1A: Ourselves (Producing simple sentences about each other. Images of the children (use a digital camera) and key words could be available in a picture/word bank)

- D&T Unit 1C: Eat more fruit and vegetables (Examine a range of fruit and vegetables. Develop a sensory vocabulary. Classify fruit and vegetables according to their sensory and other properties. Create labels and word lists. Design and make a product for a particular occasion or group to encourage them to eat more fruit and vegetables. Record in words how the finished product looks and tastes)

- D&T Unit 2A: Vehicles (Make a wheeled vehicle that moves and matches the original design proposal. As a finishing technique, produce text on the computer, print out and stick onto vehicle)

- Geography Unit 5: Where in the world is Barnaby Bear? (Write a short diary or a weather report about the place that Barnaby has visited)

At Key Stage 1, a combination of pupils' knowledge, skills and understanding of literacy and the fairly limited number of ICT techniques learned may limit the scope for large teaching experiences. However, we should not dismiss the possibilities for pupils to participate in an extended piece of text work that allows them to start to make decisions/choices about how to approach a particular task. Furthermore, these mini-projects will be more demanding than the QCA integrated tasks, because they will not follow on from a series of specific technique lessons. Therefore, one of the first steps would be for the children to reflect on what they know, and for them to think about how they would go about addressing the project.

Also, these large experiences offer the chance for the development of ICT capability in that teachers will specifically plan for pupils to review, modify and evaluate what they have done on the computer, which might not always be appropriate or possible with the medium experiences.

These larger experiences could take place in the classroom or a computer suite.

Decisions about how and where to carry out these extended pieces of ICT work will depend to some extent on a teacher's preferred teaching style. Some will prefer to organise and teach the ICT elements of a project once a week, in a computer suite, while others will prefer a more classroom-based, integrated approach where ICT is very much part of the other related activities within a lesson.

Outlined below is just a small sample of the suggested integrated tasks from the teacher's guide for the ICT Scheme of Work (QCA/DfES 2003), and some of our own suggestions.

- Geography Unit 4: Going to the seaside (Design a holiday poster for the seaside in earlier times, using knowledge gained so far. As with most of the extended ICT work, there are opportunities to think about design and layout and to learn how to import clip art with help)

- RE Unit 2C: Celebrations (Draw together what has been learnt about the festival under different headings. What? Who? When? Why? How? Present what has been learnt as a class book or wall display labelled by the children. Incorporate images with help)

- History Unit 4: Why do we remember Florence Nightingale? (Use ICT to write about Florence Nightingale. Give the children a very simple version of the story. Work with the children to make the chapters more interesting (editing) by using words from a word bank as well as their own ideas. Create the final chapter of the story. Produce a class book about Florence Nightingale to include the chapters produced by the children and imported images (with help). These could be taken from the internet by the teacher and put into a picture/word bank for easy access, or be scanned images of the children's own art work)

Graphics

There is one QCA unit relating to graphics in Key Stage 1 and that is Unit 2B: Creating pictures. However, we should note that Unit 1A: An introduction to modelling, does have a short, focused task that introduces pupils to a painting program.

The techniques introduced in Unit 1A are:

- use simple tools in a painting package;
- add stamps/motifs or clip art to a scene;
- print out painting work.

Unit 2B: Creating pictures is about using a computer graphics package to communicate visually. Pupils are expected to select the most appropriate tools to match their purposes. A key aim is that pupils will also appreciate that their work can easily be amended and that ideas can be tried out without spoiling earlier versions, and also that sometimes a screen version is the final version.

What our alternative scheme needs is the opportunity for Year 1 children to spend more time learning how to use the basic tools in a painting program than is planned during Unit 1A. This would equate to SCAA's (1996) exploratory phase, while the learning objectives in Year 2 would provide for purposeful use. In this way pupils would be more confident with a painting package and could use it more often across the curriculum because we would anticipate less demand on teacher support for the basic techniques.

Defining the small learning experiences: A possible Key Stage 1 techniques list

Different applications may have slightly different tools but most would allow the following techniques to be used:

Use the brush tool

Select colours

Use stamps/motifs

Draw geometric shapes

Flood fill

Use the straight line drawing tool

Change brush style and size

Use the spray tool

Use the symmetry tool

Zoom in to add minute detail

Copy and paste sections

Use Undo

Although not strictly related to a graphics program, this is the most appropriate place to record that pupils in Key Stage 1 would enjoy the opportunity to use a digital camera.

Having established the need for more graphics work in Year 1, and suggested a list of techniques for Key Stage 1, we can now start to identify the teaching and learning opportunities. Again, the sources of information we will use to help with the process are: QCA schemes for National Curriculum subjects and the teacher's guide for the ICT Scheme of Work (QCA/DfES 2003).

Medium and large experiences

As with 'text', the aim is for pupils to have *regular* access to activities at an appropriate level. At Key Stage 1 the ICT techniques used in a graphics package may be so straightforward that there is no need to distinguish between 'small' and 'medium' teaching and learning experiences. It may be possible for pupils to grasp the techniques fairly quickly and therefore participate in a number of extended pieces of work that allow them to start to make decisions/choices about how to approach a particular task.

Outlined below are just some of the examples of opportunities for graphics work.

- Science Unit 1D: Light and dark (Produce a picture that makes a clear distinction between night/day or dark/light)
- Art Unit 1A: Self-portrait (Year 1 pupils could investigate mark-making using ICT tools, reinforcing vocabulary such as thin, wavy, bold, broken (lines). Year 2 pupils could explore different types of marks to communicate ideas about themselves and how they would like to be seen by others)

- Art Unit 2B: Mother Nature, designer (Collect examples of designers who used nature as a source of ideas, e.g. William Morris, and designs based on natural forms, animals and birds, e.g. Arabic carpet designs, Polynesian fabrics. Use a display of natural objects created in the art and design lessons. Examine these, using a viewfinder to select a small area).

Take this as a starting point for own design on the computer, using a variety of drawing and painting tools. Pupils might draw and fill in the shapes they have identified in their observational drawings. Print the work, discuss the designs and give reasons for choosing the particular tools. Describe the effects produced. There will be opportunities to investigate use of the symmetry tool, as some of the shapes studied for this unit will be symmetrical.

- Art Unit 2C: Can buildings speak? (Exploring patterns: make rubbings and prints based on different surfaces found in and around buildings, e.g. brickwork, tiles, wood grain. Use a variety of objects and tools to print regular patterns in straight lines and rows and irregular patterns. Explore ways of rotating shapes, e.g. printing an irregular shape and turning it through the points of the compass. Create similar patterns using a graphics program. Use a digital camera to photograph shapes and patterns in buildings)

- History Unit 5: How do we know about the Great Fire of London? (Ask the children to draw or paint a picture showing something important they have learned about the fire. Can the children use colours and techniques in a graphics program to depict a roaring fire, sparks, charred items and smoke?)

- RE Unit 2C: Celebrations (Present what has been learned about festivals as a class book or wall display. Children could use a graphics program to produce artwork for the class book and display (see text work))

- D&T Unit 1A: Moving pictures (Pupils design and make a moving picture for the teacher to use when telling a story)

- D&T Unit 2D: Joseph's Coat (Pupils design and make a colourful fabric coat for Joseph. They could use a graphics program to draw the T-shaped template and to try out different patterns)

- Geography Unit 1: Around our school – the local area (Ask children to photograph: a range of attractive and unattractive places; different uses of land and types of buildings; any changes taking place in the area.

- Geography Unit 17: Global eye (Use a graphics program to create artwork for a persuasive poster asking people to recycle their spectacles. Pupils could copy and paste an image to, for example, create a border)

- Geography Unit 22: A contrasting locality overseas – Tocuaro (Angelica's father is a mask-maker. Design a colourful mask, drawing on the traditional Mexican and earlier Aztec designs. Pupils could use a graphics program to design their mask. Some might find it helpful to use a template that the teacher has created and saved).

Sound

There are no ICT QCA units that directly relate to 'sound' in Key Stage 1, so *we* can decide on a number of appropriate learning objectives and specify some end-of-key-stage targets. Finally, we can map out the opportunities for sound work across the curriculum.

What would we want pupils to know, understand and be able to do?

Pupils should understand that sounds can be recorded, stored and retrieved (played back) using a tape recorder and be able to use a tape recorder themselves. They should also understand how useful this might be. For example, we can record someone talking and then replay it later to remind us what was said. Understanding that we can record sounds outside and then listen to them back in the classroom would also be important, as would the idea that pupils could use a tape recorder to communicate to others what they have done. For example, what they found out in a science experiment.

Sound Recorder in Windows could also be used to record and play back. Children could compare and contrast it with a tape recorder.

In addition, children in Key Stage 1 should have opportunities to explore music composing software, so they can explore the effects of changing musical elements such as tempo and pitch and start to use these expressively.

A possible Key Stage 1 techniques list could therefore be:

- Use 'play', 'rewind' and 'stop' to listen to a story or poem using a tape recorder
- Use 'record', 'rewind' and 'play' to record and listen to speech and sounds
- Record and play back using Sound Recorder
- 'Click' to select sounds in a music program
- Record and play back a short tune in a music program
- Select 'high', 'medium' and 'low' sounds in a music program
- Make the music play faster or slower in a music program.

Teaching and learning opportunities

As with graphics work, the learning objectives for 'sound' are fairly straightforward and therefore the main aim is for pupils to have regular access to the software and equipment so that they become confident users who can apply their capability across the curriculum. Outlined below are some of the possible opportunities for ICT and sound work in Key Stage 1.

- Literacy: Storytelling (Confidently use a tape recorder to listen to taped stories. Retell stories orally; record them onto a tape recorder)
- History Unit 3: What were seaside holidays like in the past? (Arrange for a parent/carer/grandparent to visit the class and tell the children about their childhood seaside holiday. Encourage children to ask questions. Record the event using a tape recorder. Discuss with the children the answers the visitor gave to their questions and highlight the benefits of being able to record and play back the presentation)

- Science Unit 1C: Sorting and using materials (Ask children to compare how waterproof different materials are. Children could describe what they did and tell others what they found out by recording their verbal reports on a tape recorder)

- Music Unit 2: Sounds interesting – Exploring sounds (Pupils develop their ability to identify different sounds and to change and use sounds expressively in response to a stimulus. Go on a 'sound trail', recording sounds and listening carefully to what is heard. Listen to the sounds back in the classroom. Make a sound map)

- Music Unit 5: Taking off – Exploring pitch (What is pitch? Talk about high and low sounds in the environment and imitate them with voices. Tape and play back the children's high, middle and low voices so that they can hear themselves using these different voices. Record a high, medium and low sequence using music composing software)

Activity

Map out an overview of the *Exchanging and sharing information* ICT work for one term in either a Year 1 or Year 2 class. Outline the text, graphics and sound work that will take place, including a context for the work. What will the small, medium and large experiences be? What concepts will be developed? When (in the curriculum) and how (whole class or groups) will this conceptual development take place?

Key Stage 2

The following schemes relating to Key Stage 2 assume that the reader has read the introductory section at the beginning of the chapter. The rationale for an alternative approach is outlined there, along with an explanation of 'small', 'medium' and 'large' experiences, and the steps needed to implement a new approach.

An *Exchanging and sharing information* scheme for Year 3

In Year 3 there are three QCA units of work:

- Combining text and graphics;
- e-mail;
- Manipulating sound.

In accordance with the principles of our alternative scheme, we would suggest that work using a graphics program should be included and also some targets for understanding file management. These additional objectives could be:

- Reinforce, extend and apply work done in Year 2 with a graphics program;

- Reinforce and apply – print, save, open an application, open a file, understanding the different drives;

- Learn how to use 'Save As'.

What follows is a scheme and suggested expected pupil outcomes for the end of Year 3. We will consider work with text, then e-mail, sound and finally graphics work.

Text

In QCA Unit 3A children learn how to use ICT to present information to others; the children understand that there is an audience. The key ideas are that *text and graphics can be combined to communicate information,* and that *ICT can be used to improve text.* For the integrated task, children work in pairs to produce a page for a class magazine. They also think about the advantages of using ICT. These learning objectives help us to plan the focus for work throughout the year.

Earlier in this chapter, it was suggested that development of conceptual understanding (key ideas in the QCA Scheme of Work) can take place in different ways and it is highly likely that children will meet these key ideas in their literacy work. This idea was put forward as one of the main reasons for not retaining the QCA structure and, instead, incorporating ICT objectives into everyday activities. To reinforce this argument, and to demonstrate that the key ideas from Unit 3A do not really warrant any specific ICT lesson time and are better taught in a meaningful context, we would direct the reader to the Year 3 video clip on the National Literacy Strategy CD-ROM, 'Whole class teaching with ICT'. In this teaching extract the children are thinking about story openings using the language of traditional stories. The teacher uses a laptop computer, data projector and the Textease program to enter text (a story opening) and then, in discussion with the children, amends it by selecting words and phrases until the whole class is satisfied with the start of their story. The relevant NLS objective would be:

Year 3 Term 2

T1 to investigate the styles and voices of traditional story language – collect examples, e.g. story openings and endings, scene openings, for example, *Now when...*, *A long time ago...*, list, compare and use in own writing

In Chapter 3 we suggested that a better title for Unit 3A might be 'Using ICT to present work, including inserting graphics to improve presentation'. The key process of producing an effective presentation, which is the focus of this unit, closely matches some of the Year 3 literacy aims. For example, a Term 3 objective (T21) is *to use IT to bring to a published form, discuss the relevance of layout, font, etc.* and, in addition, a Year 3 target statement for writing is *to use IT to 'polish and present'.* This is further evidence that pupils will often have already been taught the key ideas from ICT units of work as part of their literacy lessons.

The techniques that are taught in Unit 3A are:

- alter font type, size and colour for emphasis and effect;

- amend text and save changes;

- combine graphics and text (insert a picture);
- use the shift key to type characters such as question marks.

We could therefore add these to the list from Key Stage 1, to compile a suggested list of techniques as end-of-Year 3 targets.

Defining the small learning experiences: a possible Year 3 techniques list

TEXT
Ongoing techniques from Key Stage 1
Change font size, style and colour (for emphasis and effect)
Highlight text and over-type to amend text
Insert a picture (from a CD-ROM, scanner, digital camera)
Re-size a graphic to fit the page
Use the shift key to type question marks

FILE MANAGEMENT
Ongoing techniques from Key Stage 1
Use 'Save As'
Use 'print preview'
Maximise and minimise windows.

Teaching and learning

Throughout Year 3 there will be numerous opportunities for teachers to plan for pupils to use a word processor/desktop publisher. As with our Key Stage 1 scheme, NLS writing objectives will provide us with a good way to track the opportunities for development of conceptual understanding relating to *Exchanging and sharing information*, to demonstrate and model techniques, and to help with planning a range of ICT work that makes appropriate demands on the literacy understanding of the children.

Examples of the relevant literacy objectives are shown below.

- Recounts (T3:T22 experiment with recounting the same event in a variety of ways, such as in the form of a story, a letter, a news report)
- Non-chronological report (T1:T22 to write simple non-chronological reports from known information)
- Instructions (T2:T13 to discuss the merits and limitations of particular instructional texts, including IT and other media texts, and to compare these with others, where appropriate, to give an overall evaluation)
- Note-making (T2:T17 exploring ways of writing ideas, messages, in shortened forms (could be an email))
- Story structure (T1:T15 to begin to organise stories into paragraphs)
- Poetry (T1:T14 invent calligrams and a range of shape poems, selecting appropriate words and careful presentation. Build up class collections)

- Punctuation (Demarcate sentences, using full stops, capital letters, question and exclamation marks, begin to use speech marks and capital letters for a range of purposes, secure the use of commas in a list)

- Process (Identify and consider audience and how this affects writing. Be able to improve own writing and correct errors. Use IT to polish and present).

Medium experiences

Having established some of the ways in which techniques and concepts can be taught, we can think about the opportunities for medium experiences. Outlined below are a few of the possible opportunities for this type of ICT work.

- Geography Unit 7: Weather around the world (What will the weather be like? How will it affect what we do? Write a postcard describing the range of weather conditions and leisure activities that depend on the weather experienced on holiday, e.g. going to the beach on a hot day, staying in the shade by a hotel pool on a very hot day. Some children could use a postcard template saved in a desktop publisher to write their postcard. This work could also include inserting a picture to create the front view of their postcard)

- Geography Unit 16: What's in the news? Years 3–6 (What is in the local, national or international news today? Use images of geographical events, e.g. flooding, as a stimulus for report writing. Some children could use ICT to write their news report)

- History Unit 6A: Why have people invaded and settled in Britain in the past? A Roman case study in Years 3/4 (Who was Boudicca? Ask the children to draw a picture of Boudicca and write a short description of what they think she was really like. Some children could use ICT to write about Boudicca, including scanning in their pictures of her)

- History Unit 7: Why did Henry VIII marry six times? Years 3/4 (What was Henry VIII like as a person? Write a brief description of Henry or annotate a picture to show his character. Some children could use ICT to combine text and graphics when writing about Henry VIII's character)

- History Unit 9: What was it like for children in the Second World War? Years 3/4 (What was it like to be an evacuee? Ask the children to imagine they are evacuees and to write a letter home or diary extracts. Some children could use ICT to write their letters or diary extracts.)

- RE Unit 3B: How and why do Hindus celebrate Diwali? (How do Hindus prepare for Diwali? Discuss what captions, illustrations and messages are appropriate for New Year and Diwali cards. Ask the children to make a Diwali card for a Hindu friend. Children could use a word processor to produce the words for the card. They could experiment with font style, size and colour. Children could use ICT to combine text and graphics to produce their card. Their own artwork could be scanned or they could use images produced in a graphics package (see the later section on graphics work))

In Year 3 pupils will use ICT purposefully (level 2). However, their use of new techniques such as inserting graphics, and their literacy work relating to audience and using ICT to publish work, will provide pupils with the opportunities to work towards level 3. Not only do pupils learn the technique of combining text and graphics (by inserting an image into a document), they should also appreciate that the combination of an appropriate picture and words helps us to communicate more effectively.

Large experiences

Outlined below are the suggested large learning experiences that offer opportunities for extended ICT work. It is hoped that as a consequence of pupils making more regular use of techniques, the teaching and learning focus can be on conceptual understanding, processes and development of higher-order skills, rather than on basic routines. Also there would be planned opportunities for pupils to review, modify and evaluate their work and to develop an awareness of the uses of ICT inside and outside of school.

The examples are taken from the teacher's guide for the ICT Scheme of Work (QCA/DfES 2003) and some of our own suggestions. These larger experiences would be appropriate for work in the classroom or a computer suite. Decisions about how and where to carry out these extended pieces of ICT work will depend to some extent on a teacher's preferred teaching style. Some will prefer to organise and teach the ICT elements of a project once a week, in a computer suite, while others will prefer a more classroom-based, integrated approach, where ICT is very much part of the other related activities within a lesson.

- Science Unit 3B: Helping plants grow well (Ask the children to produce a leaflet giving advice on how to look after plants in the classroom or at home. Children could consider these intended audiences and discuss why the images and text might be different for each)

- Linked to Year 3: Literacy work (Children work in pairs or small groups to write a short play script for a traditional story or fable using ICT. They follow this up by combining text and graphics to produce either a programme or flyer for their play)

- Science Unit 3A: Teeth and eating (Combine text and graphics to produce a poster identifying different food types and their effects on the body. Talk about the possible audience for such a poster. Encourage children to select and insert appropriate pictures and to choose appropriate font sizes, colours and styles to convey their message. Ask children to explain their choices)

- D&T Unit 3A: Packaging (Use ICT to produce the pictures and text for a package design. The package is for a specific purpose, e.g. a packet for a healthy eating bar or cereal, a box for a magic spell. The text and graphics should reflect the product)

E-mail

In QCA Unit 3E, children learn how to use electronic mail to send and receive messages. They learn about communicating over distances and consider and compare different methods of communication. Several QCA units in other subject areas provide authentic tasks for this form of exchanging and sharing of information. For example, in their geography work children e-mail for a real purpose when they find out about contrasting locations or holiday destinations.

The techniques that are taught in this unit are to:

- read e-mail;

- read, annotate and reply to e-mail;

- send e-mails using an address book;

- add an attachment to an e-mail.

Different techniques will lend themselves to different types of activity. For example, reading, annotating and replying to an e-mail implies some kind of ongoing work and, in fact, the suggested QCA short, focused task for this technique is to develop a short piece of written work by e-mailing it between a couple of schools. However, the techniques of sending, reading and replying to an e-mail may be used to simply request some information, read the response and reply with a thank you message.

The nature of a task undertaken when using e-mail may lead us to make a judgement about the National Curriculum level at which a child is working. For example, developing a story over a period of time by collaborating with another school via e-mail attachments is more demanding than simply establishing a link with a school in a contrasting locality to exchange basic information. But it is the literacy element of the first task that is more demanding, and not the ICT. What is more important is that children understand the concept of electronic communication and appreciate when and why it is appropriate to use this particular form of exchange.

Teaching and learning opportunities

Throughout Year 3 there will be a number of opportunities for teachers to incorporate the use of e-mail into their lessons. Outlined below are a few suggestions:

- Geography Unit 18: Connecting ourselves to the world Years 3–6 (Finding out about the locality of a twinned school via e-mail. Children could send letters via e-mail, attach a guide about the area around their school and ask questions about the twinned school by attaching a questionnaire)

- Geography Unit 24: Passport to the world Years 1–6 (Find out about favourite holiday locations. Ask pairs of children to 'adopt' a city and research it. Children could e-mail tourist information centres in order to gather information)

- Literacy work Year 3 (e-mailing a partner school to share and exchange book reviews)

- Literacy term 2: T17 (Make clear notes through exploring ways of writing ideas and messages, in shortened forms such as notes, lists, headlines, telegrams, to understand that some words are more essential to meaning than others. Children could look at the different uses of e-mail and the difference between an official request for information and a brief, shortened message to a friend via e-mail to perhaps update them with some news)

Sound

In QCA Unit 3B children learn how to use music composing software to communicate their musical ideas. Other suggested activities are for children to:

- select and play musical sounds on an electronic keyboard;
- search a CD-ROM to find and listen to a particular musical instrument;
- use a tape recorder to record a sound sample.

It would also be appropriate for children in Year 3 to record and play back using Sound Recorder.

The unit appears to do two different things. Pupils select, locate and record sounds, and they also use music composing software to organise and reorganise sounds.

Teaching and learning opportunities

Throughout Year 3 there will be opportunities for children to achieve both sets of objectives. Searching a CD-ROM to find and listen to a particular musical instrument, and using a tape recorder to record a sound sample, are straightforward activities. So the first set of examples below focus on children understanding that sounds can be recorded, stored and retrieved and why this might be useful.

- History Unit 18: What was it like to live here in the past? Years 3/4 (How can oral sources help us to find out about how people lived? Invite a visitor to school who is able to talk about changes over time in the local area. Before the visitor comes into school, ask the children to practise interviewing teachers, family and friends. Collect information during the interview by taking notes and recording on tape. Help the children to identify the facts from the visitor's opinions)

- Geography Unit 16: What's in the news? Years 3–6 (What will the weather be like today or tomorrow? Use regional, national or international television weather forecasts to develop children's understanding of weather symbols and variations in weather across different counties, countries and continents. Ask the children to produce and present their own weather forecasts. Listen to a radio weather forecast. How is it the same as/different from a television forecast? Children to record their own radio forecast using a tape recorder)

This second set of examples focus on opportunities to use music composing software:

- Music Unit 9: Animal magic Years 3/4 (Exploring descriptive sounds. Children think about how different musical elements can be used and combined to describe different animals. For example, listen to *The Carnival of the Animals* by Saint-Saëns and compare the animals with the sounds used. How does the music help us to imagine their size or how they move? Children use music composing software to create their own animal music. Experiment with loud, quiet, fast, slow, high, low or a mixture, staying on the same note or moving in small steps/big jumps – high to low, low to high. They could also change the type of instrument used. Children develop an understanding of the ways in which musical elements can be combined expressively)

- Music Unit 13: Painting with sound Years 3/4 (Exploring sound colours. How can music describe images and moods? How can we use sounds to create a picture or mood? Children listen to music that describes an event, scene, person or animal. They talk about how the music makes them feel, and the kinds of pictures it makes in their heads. They analyse and comment on how sounds are used to create different moods. The children go on to explore the use of sounds to create a picture or mood. Music composing software can be used to compliment this work)

Graphics

There are no QCA units relating to graphics work in Year 3, so, as proposed earlier, we suggest that teachers specifically plan for pupils to reinforce the techniques taught in Year 2. This regular use will help techniques to become routines.

The end-of-Year 3 targets could therefore be for most children to confidently use a range of techniques in a graphics program to support work across the curriculum. A suggested techniques list is given below.

With minimum support they will be able to open applications, use 'save as' to save, retrieve, and print out their work. An appropriate target for children in Year 3 would also be for them to be able to use a digital camera and a scanner to provide relevant images for work across the curriculum.

Suggested graphics techniques list for the end of Year 3:

Ongoing techniques from Key Stage 1
Use the brush tool
Select colours
Use stamps/motifs
Draw geometric shapes
Flood fill
Use the straight line drawing tool
Change brush style and size
Use the spray tool
Use the symmetry tool
Zoom in to add minute detail
Copy and paste sections
Use Undo

The list could be adapted to reflect the minor differences between the various graphics programs.

Suggested opportunities for graphics work

Some of the activities outlined below would make good use of classroom computers/laptops because they form only a small part of some other work. For example, making a monster's face in Design and Technology. Other examples would lend themselves to more extended ICT work, for example the Hindu patterns and Diwali cards, and might benefit from access to a computer suite or cluster of computers.

■ RE Unit 3B: How and why do Hindus celebrate Diwali? (How do Hindus prepare for Diwali? Ask children to produce a Diwali card for a Hindu friend. Use a graphics program to create suitable images for the card. Show children designs of colourful geometric rangoli patterns and ask them to recreate some of the patterns using a graphics program)

■ D&T Unit 3A: Packaging (Children could use a graphics program to help them to design and produce a packet for a specific purpose, e.g. for sweets or a healthy snack bar. The graphics and text on the packet should compliment the contents)

■ D&T Unit 3C: Moving mechanisms (Children investigate simple pneumatic systems and design and make a model of a monster that has moving parts controlled by pneumatics. This could be linked to stories of poems. Children could use a graphics program to help create the finished product – for example the monster's face)

■ History Years 3/4 (Children could use a graphics program to produce computer artwork relating to the study of Romans, Vikings and ancient Egypt)

Year 3 and National Curriculum levels

The activities outlined in this Year 3 scheme would allow children to confidently work at level 2 as defined by the NC Attainment Target level descriptors; generating, recording and amending their work – using ICT purposefully.

However, there are clearly opportunities to go beyond this and to start to move children towards level 3. What distinguishes level 3 work is that it involves pupils revising their work, rather than making minor changes, in order to present their work more effectively to an audience. This would include revising/redrafting work, making more substantial changes, including changes to the organisation and structure of their work.

In order to achieve level 3, children will need to learn and use certain techniques (e.g. incorporating images, using 'save as' in order to evaluate successive drafts) and understand the relevant concepts.

In order to know what revisions to make, children need to be able to evaluate their work and know whether or not the proposed changes will enhance communication (of what is being presented). The ability to do this is a higher-order skill, and (for text work) is associated with children's literacy development. See Chapter 3, 'Progression in Exchanging and Sharing Information', for a fuller discussion.

So, in the above Year 3 scheme, children will sometimes be working at level 2 (purposeful use of ICT):

■ use a graphics program to create a monster's face for a D&T project;

■ use a graphics program to create artwork relating to the study of ancient Egypt;

■ send an e-mail to a tourist information centre to find out about a particular city;

■ imagine you are an evacuee. Use a word processor to write a letter home or a diary extract.

At other times the children will be learning some of the new techniques needed to work at level 3:

■ insert an image into a text document to combine text and graphics. The image could be scanned, be from a clipart CD-ROM, or taken with a digital camera;

- learn how and when to use 'save as' rather than 'save';
- highlight and change font style, size and colour.

At other times the children will be developing the conceptual understanding needed to work at level 3:

- understand that font style, size and colour can be changed for emphasis and effect;
- understand that a particular style of font and choice of image can communicate something about a product (packaging);
- identify and consider audience and how this affects writing (literacy work);
- ICT can be used to improve text.

At other times the children will be working at level 3 (use ICT to generate, develop, organise and present their work):

- using sounds to create a picture or a mood. Children use a music composing program to explore the effect of changing pitch, tempo etc. They compose a tune that creates a particular mood. As part of the process they evaluate and revise their work as it progresses.

The work undertaken in Year 4 will provide opportunities for children to achieve level 3 in the other elements of *Exchanging and sharing information,* namely text and graphics.

Activity

Map out an overview of the *Exchanging and sharing information* ICT work for one term in Year 3. Outline the text, graphics, e-mail and sound work that will take place, including a context for the work. What will the small, medium and large experiences be? What concepts will be developed? When (in the curriculum) and how (whole-class or groups) will this conceptual development take place?

An *Exchanging and sharing information* scheme for Year 4

In Year 4 there are two QCA units of work:

- writing for different audiences;
- developing images using repeating patterns.

In addition, we have suggested that work relating to e-mail and sound should be included and also some targets for understanding file management. Those additional objectives could be:

- reinforce, extend and apply the Year 3 work with e-mails;
- learn how to insert sounds from a CD-ROM of sound clips or from a folder on the hard drive. Insert sounds from a sound bank such as Textease or Granada Writer (which is straightforward and may have been covered previously);

- reinforce and apply the Year 3 targets: save as, print, save, open an application, open a file, understanding the different drives and, in addition, learn about the different file types (text, picture, sound).

Text

QCA Unit 4A, Writing for different audiences, is about children using ICT to organise, reorganise, develop and explore ideas, and that working with information in this way can aid understanding. They learn how to use the more advanced features of a word processor to help them match their work to their audience.

The key technique is learning to cut and paste and the key process is learning to develop ideas, to revise/redraft work. As stated in Chapter 3, 'Progression in *Exchanging and sharing information*', we feel that the unit title is very misleading and gives the idea that children are writing for different audiences, when in fact what they learn to do is present their work more effectively to an audience. Hence our suggestion that the unit could be better named 'Using ICT to develop written language'.

The key ideas within the unit are:

- newspapers use a variety of presentation techniques and written effects to communicate messages;
- ICT can be used to reorganise text to make its meaning clearer;
- ICT can be used to amend text and to correct mistakes;
- ICT can be used to automate the amendment of text.

For the integrated task children are asked to use ICT to create a newspaper article. For this to be work at level 3 the children should be developing their ideas by reflecting on and amending their articles over a period of time. They will use techniques such as amending font style, size and colour to identify headlines, sub-headings and key pieces of text, as well as using cut and paste to develop the written work that should be factually accurate, clear, lively and interesting.

We have already argued that the development of conceptual understanding, and the demonstration and modelling of ICT techniques can take place in different ways, and it is highly likely that children will have met the above objectives in their literacy work. Year 4 is no exception. We can clearly see from the sample NLS objectives below that the key ideas from the QCA ICT units do not really warrant any specific ICT lesson time and are better taught in a meaningful context. The literacy lessons provide opportunities for whole-class interactive teaching, where children could be supported in their developing ideas about how to present effectively their work to an audience. For example:

T3:T19 to evaluate advertisements for their impact, appeal and honesty, focusing in particular on how information about the product is presented e.g. tactics for grabbing attention;

T1:T17 identify features of non-fiction texts in print and IT, e.g. headings, lists, bullet points, captions which support the reader in gaining information effectively;

T1:T24 write newspaper style reports including using IT to draft and layout reports

- Style: language effects (Use adjectives and adverbs selectively to create variety and add interest)
- Purpose and organisation (Use appropriate layout conventions for non-fiction)
- Process (Edit in relation to audience and purpose, enhancing or deleting, justifying choices)

The techniques from Unit 4A that need to be taught and applied throughout the year are:

- alter font size and use effects to indicate relative importance;
- use cut and paste to re-order a piece of text;
- delete, insert and replace text to improve clarity and create mood;
- use spell checker (IT spell-checks as a spelling strategy only start to appear in Year 5 of the NLS);
- amend text using find and replace.

Defining the small learning experiences: a possible Year 4 techniques list

Ongoing techniques from Year 3:

- Use 'Cut' and 'Paste'
- Use 'spell check'
- Amend text using 'find and replace'.

FILE MANAGEMENT
Reinforce and apply the Year 3 techniques
Copy and paste from one application to another
Learn about the different file types (text, picture, sound).

Medium experiences

Because we are advocating a model where not everyone will be doing the same task at the same time, and the activities are differentiated, a small cluster of classroom-based computers (or laptops) and access to an electronic whiteboard is probably the best way to organise the ICT resources for our small and medium teaching and learning experiences.

Outlined below are some of the possible opportunities for the medium experiences including cutting and pasting to develop a piece of work. Some QCA units state that all the groups (the whole class) use ICT to produce a report (e.g. Geography Unit 8). However, unless the teacher has decided to make the activity one of the large experiences, we would suggest that only one group be assigned to the ICT resources. Throughout the year there will be enough opportunities for every group to use ICT on a regular basis, and by limiting the small and medium experiences to groups rather than the whole class, the children can be given the appropriate time and support needed to progress.

- Science Unit 4B: Habitats (Think about the effect on plants and animals of changing conditions in a particular habitat in various ways e.g. draining the pond, removing the pondweed, removing the shade, ground cover. Prepare a presentation to an audience to explain why the organisms could no longer live in a changed habitat or write a letter opposing a change that would alter a habitat. Some children could use ICT to produce their presentation or letter)

- Geography Unit 8: Improving the environment (How much do we throw away in the school grounds? How could it be reduced? Groups to investigate litter in different parts of the school grounds, with a view to finding out if people use rubbish bins properly. For each area, weigh the rubbish in the bins and the rubbish not in the bins. Compare the results. Each group to present their findings using spreadsheets and simple graphing software. Examine the findings and think how improvements could be made. Submit proposals to the head teacher. Some groups could use ICT to present their findings. They could insert tables and graphs into their word-processed document)

- RE Unit 4A: How and why do Hindus worship at home and in the mandir? (What are the main activities in an act of worship in the home? Ask the children to draw objects involved in puja and write about how each is used. Create a set of labels for the artefacts on the puja tray. Use ICT to make a zigzag book for younger children showing some of the main activities in Hindu puja)

In Year 4 pupils will use ICT purposefully (level 2) and to develop their ideas (level 3). Their use of new techniques such as 'copy and paste', and their literacy work relating to drafting and redrafting, will provide pupils with the opportunities to work at Level 3. Not only do they learn the technique of copying and pasting, pupils should also use the technique to revise their work, making substantial changes, including changes to the organisation and structure in order to communicate effectively.

Large experiences

Suggested large learning experiences that offer opportunities for extended ICT work are detailed below. The examples are taken from the integrated tasks in the teacher's guide for the ICT Scheme of Work (QCA/DfES 2003), and some of our own suggestions. These larger experiences would be appropriate for work in the classroom or a computer suite. However, as much of the work is done collaboratively in groups and is very much embedded within other subjects, working on classroom-based computers or laptops may be conducive to a richer learning experience. See the section in Chapter 7, 'Pedagogical underpinning of the QCA Scheme of Work', and the recommendation in Chapter 2 to read the article by Atherton (2000). Although the article relates to multimedia work, it gives a very clear picture of how to integrate the use of ICT, whatever the focus might be.

- D&T Units 4A & 4D (At the end of a D&T unit of work, children work in pairs to produce a clear set of instructions so that someone else could carry out the same (D&T) task. They think about the target audience, key features of instructional texts and the use of illustrations (such as images taken with a digital camera). Reviewing and modifying work in progress is part of the process)

- Citizenship Unit 7: Children's rights-human rights (Based on work carried out in circle time, children consider needs, wants and rights and the difference between them. In pairs they develop a charter for children's rights. They use ICT to present their charter, which should be developed into a logical and persuasive argument. Reviewing and modifying work in progress is part of the process)

- RE Unit 4D: What religions are represented in our neighbourhood? (How can people find out about religion in our neighbourhood? As a class children compile a directory documenting the religious traditions in the neighbourhood for people to access who have just moved here. Children present their work in progress to the rest of the class, giving time for critical comments and feedback. Ask the groups to edit their materials in light of their peers' comments and then make a whole-class presentation. Within this project there are opportunities for children to use word processors, desktop publishers, digital cameras and scanners and to select from the range of techniques that they have been taught. For example, changing font style, size and colour for effect, inserting graphics and cutting and pasting to develop their text work. They will be saving different versions and evaluating work as it progresses)

End-of-Year 4 targets for text work

Most children will be able to confidently draw on a range of ICT techniques to communicate information effectively to an audience. In the process of creating the final product, children would have developed their ideas by evaluating and revising their work. Work at this level goes beyond simply editing text and would require the use of higher-order skills.

With minimum support they will be able to open applications, use 'save as' and save, retrieve their work and print it out. They will be able to insert a graphic or a chart into a document and move and re-size it as necessary. The graphic could be a scanned image, an image from a clipart CD-ROM or an image taken with a digital camera. In order to do this, children would need to have some understanding of the different drives. For example, floppy disk drive, hard drive and CD-ROM drive. In order to draft and redraft their work children would need to be able to use 'cut/copy and paste'.

Graphics

In QCA Unit 4B children learn how to use a graphics package to develop an image using a variety of tools and techniques. In the Year 4 unit relating to 'text', children learned how to 'cut/copy and paste' to develop their work with a word processor. In this graphics unit they learn how to 'cut/copy and paste' to develop their work with a graphics program. The short, focused task designed to teach this technique uses the context of designing a wrapping paper with a repeating pattern; hence the title of the unit, 'Developing images using repeating patterns'.

However, as outlined in Chapter 3, 'Progression in *Exchanging and sharing information*', we feel that this title is misleading in that children do much more than the implied pattern of repeating images. What the children actually do (for the integrated task) is produce a mixed-media collage using a variety of materials created on, and away from, the computer. They use scanned images, images created in the graphics program, techniques including copying and re-sizing an image and visual effects such as reflection and symmetry. The emphasis is as much on the process of reviewing and developing the work over a number of weeks as it is on learning new techniques. We have suggested that 'Developing images and digital art' might be a better title because children explore the use of a paint program as an artistic tool in its own right.

Suggested techniques list for the end of Year 4

Ongoing techniques from Year 3
Select, copy, paste and re-size areas of the screen
Import graphics from a scanner
Import graphics from a digital camera.

Teaching and learning

Creating a mixed-media collage would be considered a 'large' learning experience and would take several weeks to complete. Hopefully, the planned regular access to a graphics program from Year 1 onwards would produce pupils who were confident with the basic skills, and therefore any major project, such as that in Unit 4B, would not need to be delivered in such a structured way, with its series of unrelated tasks. Instead, teachers could approach the production of a collage in a more holistic way.

Even though there is this graphics focus in Year 4, children would benefit from the opportunity to have further small and medium experiences throughout the year.

Suggested opportunities for additional graphics work in Year 4

- History Unit 6A: A Roman case study (Children are introduced to the idea that, throughout history, pattern has been used to increase the value of objects and to display the skill of the craftsman. Use a variety of media to produce a Roman mosaic, including scanned images to make a composite image. Review work in progress and amend the designs, saving draft versions)

- Art Unit 4A: Viewpoints (Explore how to convey the atmosphere and story of a dream. Explore different viewpoints in the school environment as a setting for their dream. Collect visual and other information from different viewpoints; investigate a variety of methods and techniques, using shape, tone and texture in drawing, photography and print-making; compare ideas, methods and approaches used in their own and others' work. Modify and improve work to realise own intentions. Extend this work by using ICT to create a mixed-media collage to convey their dream. Examples of surrealist artists who have used the theme of dreams and nightmares in their work would provide a good stimulus, particularly the abstract style of artists such as Miro. See 'Women and Bird in the Moonlight'

- Art Unit 3B: Investigating pattern (Investigate patterns in textiles from different times and cultures. Use ideas from these as starting points for developing their own designs. The unit suggests that children use ICT to explore: how paint software can be used to explore symmetry, how a shape can be copied, re-sized and multiple copies made, how to flood-fill shapes with different colours etc.)

- History (Topics such as the Romans, Vikings, Tudors and ancient Egypt will provide a meaningful context for small and medium graphics experiences)

E-mail

There are no QCA units relating to e-mail in Year 4, so, as proposed earlier, we suggest that teachers specifically plan for pupils to reinforce the techniques taught in Year 3 so that they become routines:

read e-mail;
read, annotate and reply to e-mail;
send e-mails using an address book;
add an attachment to an e-mail.

In our Year 3 scheme we suggested that a number of geography units could provide a context for e-mailing. As these are 'continuous' units they will provide ongoing opportunities.

In addition, the Year 4 Term 2 literacy objective to 'collaborate with others to work stories in chapters, using plans with particular audiences in mind' could make use of e-mail to write collaboratively with a partner school.

Sound

There are no QCA units relating to sound in Year 4, so we suggest that teachers specifically plan for pupils to develop their knowledge and understanding of sound beyond that of music composing software, in order to prepare them for their multimedia work in Year 6. For example, they could learn how to:

- insert sounds from a folder on the hard drive, or from a CD-ROM of sound clips; and
- insert sounds from a sound bank such as Textease or Granada Writer.

Incorporating a sound file into a Textease or Granada Writer file is straightforward; it is no more difficult than dragging an image from the picture bank onto the page. For this reason, it may be that children will have made use of this facility before they reach Year 4. However, we should not make the mistake of assuming that simply dragging pictures and sounds onto a page and adding text constitutes a multimedia presentation as expected in QCA Unit 6A.

Perhaps what is more important is for children in Year 4 to appreciate that we can create and store sound as a file, just as we can pictures and text. So a Year 4 target would be for children to insert a sound file from a sound clip CD-ROM or from a folder on the hard drive. This is no more difficult than the technique of inserting a picture that was taught in Year 3.

A possible context for this work might be for children to write stories and poems on screen and insert an appropriate sound clip from CD-ROM. For example, animal poems with animal sounds, sci-fi stories with alien sounds.

Year 4 and National Curriculum levels

In our suggested Year 4 scheme children will sometimes be working at level 2 (purposeful use of ICT):

- copy type and print out a poem for a display;
- create labels and captions for the classroom and for displays.

At other times the children will be learning some of the new techniques needed to work at level 3:

- cut/copy and paste text;
- select, copy, paste and resize part of the screen in a graphics program;
- use 'save as'.

At other times the children will be developing the conceptual understanding needed to work at level 3:

- identify and consider audience and how this affects writing (literacy work);
- ICT can be used to improve text and graphics.

The work undertaken in Year 4 has provided opportunities for children to achieve level 3 in two elements of exchanging and sharing information, i.e. text and graphics.

Activity

Map out an overview of the *Exchanging and sharing information* ICT work for one term in Year 4. Outline the text, graphics, e-mail and sound work that will take place, including a context for the work. What will the small, medium and large experiences be? What concepts will be developed? When (in the curriculum) and how (whole class or groups) will this conceptual development take place?

An *Exchanging and sharing information* scheme for Year 5

There are no QCA units relating to *Exchanging and sharing information* in Year 5, so we suggest that teachers specifically plan for pupils to reinforce the techniques taught in Years 3 and 4, and also to develop children's knowledge and understanding of sound, and file types and file size, in preparation for the multimedia work in Year 6.

Text and graphics

Throughout Year 5 there will be numerous opportunities for children to use word processing and desktop publishing programs. Therefore, teachers should ensure that children continue to have small and medium learning experiences as often as is possible. It is probably the case that the time needed to deliver other ICT aspects in Year 5 (e.g. controlling devices, sensing equipment, graphical modelling), dominates the timetable. However, it would be unfortunate if this excluded Year 5 from the opportunity to experience one large experience with text and graphics.

Perhaps a simple target that also helps to develop understanding of file management might be to ensure that children have inserted a saved graphic into a word processor or desktop publisher. The difference here is that the graphic is one produced and saved by the children, rather than a commercially produced clip on CD-ROM or from the internet.

A Technique checklist for Year 5

Ongoing text and file management techniques from Year 4:

- to be able to insert the following into a word-processed or desktop published document:
  - clipart from within a program (picture bank);
  - an image from a digital camera;
  - a scanned image;
  - clipart from a CD-ROM;
  - images created in a graphics program.

File management

Learn about file types and sizes. For example, will a file fit onto a floppy disc? How much space does a sound file take up?

Learn to recognise the following file types – text, images and sound, (.txt, .bmp, .jpg, .wmf, .wav).

Have an understanding of the differences between image files. For example, bitmaps and jpegs.

Understand directory structure.

Listed below are just a few of the many opportunities to work with text and graphics in Year 5. Again we suggest that the NLS objectives provide opportunities to model the use of ICT techniques in context and to develop conceptual understanding. A sample of relevant literacy objectives is listed below, followed by cross-curricular opportunities for text and graphics.

- Non-chronological report (T2:T22 to plan, compose, edit and refine short non-chronological reports using reading as a source, focusing on clarity, conciseness and impersonal style)

- Persuasion (T3: T18 to write a commentary on an issue on paper or screen (e.g. as a news editorial or leaflet), setting out and justifying a personal view; to use structures from reading to set out and link points, e.g. numbered lists, bullet points; T3: T17 to draft and write individual, group or class letters for real purposes, e.g. put a point of view, comment on an emotive issue, protest; to edit and present to finished state)

- Fiction (T2: T13 review and edit writing to produce a final form, matched to the needs of an identified reader)

Cross-curricular opportunities for combining text and graphics in Year 5

- Science Unit 5A: Keeping healthy (Make posters to inform other children of the effects of drugs, alcohol and tobacco. Some children could use ICT to create their posters)

- D&T Unit 5B: Bread (Writing and illustrating a class book of bread recipes. Each group could be responsible for one recipe. Children could use ICT to create the book)

- Geography Unit 13: A contrasting UK locality – Llandudno (Produce a class book (using ICT) about Llandudno that can be shared with other classes in the school)

- History Unit 14: Who were the ancient Greeks? Years 5/6) (Complete a written account of the Battle of Marathon showing understanding of the perspective of either an Athenian or a Spartan on the battle. Some children could use ICT)

Graphics

Teachers should find opportunities to reinforce, extend and apply the graphics work from Years 3 and 4. For example, producing illustrations in the style of a painting on Greek pottery. However, the main focus in Year 5 will be on object-based drawing programs (as introduced in Unit 5A: Graphical modelling), and work could include communicating designs in D&T or to drawing plans in geography.

E-mail

Teachers should find opportunities to reinforce, extend and apply work with e-mails.

- read e-mail;
- read, annotate and reply to e-mail;
- send e-mails using an address book;
- add an attachment to an e-mail.

Sound

Having learned how to insert a sound file into a document in Year 4, children in Year 5 could learn how to use Sound Recorder or Audacity to create and save their own sound files and insert them into a document. Audacity is similar to Sound Recorder but offers more advanced features. It is freely available from the internet. (See *http://audacity.sourceforge.net/*).

Music QCA Unit 18: Journey into space – Exploring sound sources – offers a possible context for work with Audacity or Sound Recorder. Children record their voices and explore the effects available when playing back. For example, echo and reverse.

Activity

Map out an overview of the *Exchanging and sharing information* ICT work for one term in Year 5. Outline the text, graphics, e-mail and sound work that will take place, including a context for the work. What will the small, medium and large experiences be? What concepts will be developed? When (in the curriculum) and how (whole class or groups) will this conceptual development take place?

An *Exchanging and sharing information* scheme for Year 6

In Year 6 there is only one QCA unit relating to *Exchanging and sharing information* but it has the potential to draw on all the *Exchanging and sharing information* QCA units taught in Years 3–5, and would be a major project. Children combine text, graphics, sounds and possibly animations and video clips. Pages are linked together by creating hyperlinks in a multimedia authoring program.

In preparing for their presentation, children could be taught how to create folders to collect and organise different types of media – text, graphics and sound. They could then select resources from those saved and organised in their folders.

Text: created by the children and/or copied from sources such as CD-ROMs or the internet (acknowledging sources). Text files could be saved in a folder and developed later.

Graphics: inserting pictures from clip art CD-ROMs, digital cameras, scanners, own images created in a graphics program and images from the internet.

Sound: inserting sounds from CD-ROMs, those produced using Audacity or Sound Recorder and sounds accessed from the internet, e.g. *www.a1freesoundeffects.com*.

Video: inserting video clips created using, for example, Movie Creator from TAG Learning.

There will be a number of appropriate contexts for this multimedia work. However, one influence might be the ability to define the intended audience because the key process in Unit 6A is learning which forms to combine to take into consideration the needs of the audience. Level 4 work would, typically, be authoring for their peers; level 5 for other audiences (e.g. younger children). See Chapter 3, 'Progression in *Exchanging and sharing information*', for a fuller discussion.

As with all our suggested activities, from Year 1 to Year 6, we advocate that teachers move away from the prescribed QCA structure and follow a more integrated approach. For those who intend to undertake a multimedia project in school, we would recommend reading the article by Atherton (2000). This article would provide a stimulus for discussion about planning, teaching and classroom organisation for this type of work, and ideas about how best to help children to understand the needs of an audience.

Teachers may still find the time for regular word-processing work throughout Year 6 so we have included a few sample literacy objectives that would provide opportunities for appropriate Year 6 tasks.

- Recount (T1: T14 to develop the skills of biographical and autobiographical writing in role, adapting distinctive voices, e.g. of historical characters, through:

  - preparing a CV

  - composing a biographical account based on research

  - describing a person from different perspectives, e.g. police description, school report, newspaper obituary)

- Instructions (T3:T22 to select the appropriate style and form to suit a specific purpose and audience, drawing on knowledge of different non-fiction text types)

- Discussion (T2:T19 to write a balanced report of a controversial issue:

- summarising fairly the competing views
- analysing strengths and weaknesses of different positions)

- Organisational features (T1:T18 use IT to bring to a publication standard, e.g. compiling a class newspaper, paying attention to layout and presentation)

- Fiction and poetry (T1: T9 prepare a short section of a story as a script, e.g. using stage directions, location/setting; T3:T13 write a sequence of poems linked by theme or form, e.g. a haiku calendar)

- Process (Use IT to plan, revise and edit writing for publication. Discuss and select appropriate style and form to suit specific purpose and audience, drawing on knowledge of different texts)

Activity

Map out an overview of the *Exchanging and sharing information* ICT work for one term in Year 6. Outline the text, graphics, e-mail and sound work that will take place, including a context for the work. What will the small, medium and large experiences be? What concepts will be developed? When (in the curriculum) and how (whole class or groups), will this conceptual development take place?

Summary

In this chapter, it has been possible to demonstrate that for the *Exchanging and sharing information* aspect of the ICT National Curriculum, progression can be achieved in a more cohesive way if additional learning objectives for text, graphics, e-mail and sound are incorporated into each year group. Furthermore, development of ICT capability is closely tied to a child's literacy understanding, and this provides a clear rationale for an alternative scheme of work.

A summary of the small experiences throughout Key Stages 1 and 2

Small learning experiences: A possible Key Stage 1 techniques list

Text

Click to select letters, words and pictures (e.g. in Clicker)

Select words and pictures from a word bank to make a simple sentence

Use 'Drag' and 'Drop' (e.g. to move words and pictures in Textease or *MyWorld*)

Type name to make a label

Use the speech facility to check work

Use the delete key

Use the backspace key

Use the space bar

Use shift key to make capital letters

Use enter/return to start a new line

Change font size

Change font style

Change the colour of text

Use full stops

Use the shift key to add speech marks

Graphics

(Different applications may have slightly different tools but most would allow the following techniques to be used.)

Use the brush tool

Select colours

Use stamps/motifs

Draw geometric shapes

Flood fill

Use the straight line drawing tool

Change brush style and size

Use the spray tool

Use the symmetry tool

Zoom in to add minute detail

Copy and paste sections

Use Undo

Sound

Use 'play', 'rewind' and 'stop' to listen to a story or poem using a tape recorder

Use 'record', 'rewind' and 'play' to record and listen to speech and sounds

Record and play back using Sound Recorder

'Click' to select sounds in a music program

Record and play back a short tune in a music program

Select 'high', 'medium' and 'low' sounds in a music program

Make the music play faster or slower in a music program

File management

Click to load applications

Open files (to load own work)

Save work

Print work

Understand the different drives (floppy disk drive, hard drive, CD-ROM drive)

Small learning experiences: a possible Year 3 techniques list

Text

Ongoing techniques from Key Stage 1

Change font size, style and colour (for emphasis and effect)

Highlight text and over-type to amend text

Insert a picture (from a CD-ROM, scanner, digital camera)

Re-size a graphic to fit the page

Use the shift key to type question marks

E-mail

Read e-mail

Read, annotate and reply to e-mail

Send e-mail using an address book

Add an attachment to an e-mail

Graphics

Ongoing techniques from Key Stage 1

Use the brush tool

Select colours

Use stamps/motifs

Draw geometric shapes

Flood fill

Use the straight line drawing tool

Change brush style and size

Use the spray tool

Use the symmetry tool

Zoom in to add minute detail

Copy and paste sections

Use Undo

Sound

Use music composing software to communicate musical ideas
Select and play musical sounds on an electronic keyboard
Search a CD-ROM to find and listen to a particular musical instrument
Use a tape recorder to record a sound sample
Record and play back using Sound Recorder

File management

Ongoing techniques from Key Stage 1
Use 'Save as'
Use 'print preview'
Maximise & minimise windows

Small learning experiences: a possible Year 4 techniques list

Text

The ongoing techniques from Year 3
Use 'Cut' and 'Paste'
Use 'spell check'
Amend text using 'find and replace'

E-mail

Reinforce, extend and apply the Year 3 work with e-mails
Read e-mail
Read, annotate and reply to e-mail
Send e-mail using an address book
Add an attachment to an e-mail

Graphics

Ongoing techniques from Year 3
Select, copy, paste and re-size areas of the screen
Import graphics from a scanner
Import graphics from a digital camera

Sound

Insert sounds from a CD-ROM of sound clips or from a folder on the hard drive
Insert sounds from a sound bank such as Textease or Granada Writer (which is straightforward and may have been covered previously)

File management

Reinforce and apply the techniques taught in Year 3
Copy and paste from one application to another
Learn about the different file types (text, picture, sound)

Small learning experiences: a possible Year 5 techniques list

Text

Ongoing techniques from Year 4

Be able to insert the following into a word-processed or desktop published document:

- clipart from within a program (picture bank);
- an image from a digital camera;
- a scanned image;
- clipart from a CD-ROM;
- images created in a graphics program

E-mail

Reinforce the techniques taught in Year 3 so that they become routines

Read e-mail

Read, annotate and reply to e-mail

Send e-mail using an address book

Add an attachment to an e-mail

Graphics

Ongoing techniques from Year 4

Work relating to object-based drawing programs (as introduced in Unit 5A, Graphical modelling)

Sound

Use Sound Recorder or Audacity to create and save own sound files and insert them into a document

File management

Ongoing techniques from Year 4

Learn about file types and sizes. For example, will a file fit onto a floppy disc? How much space does a sound file take up?

Learn to recognise the following file types – text, images and sound (.txt, .bmp, .jpg, .wmf, .wav)

Have an understanding of the differences between image files. For example, bitmaps and jpegs

Understand directory structure

Small learning experiences: a possible Year 6 techniques list

Multimedia

Combine text, graphics, sounds and possibly animations and video clips

Link pages together by creating hyperlinks in a multimedia authoring program.

File management

Create folders to collect and organise different types of media – text, graphics, and sound
Select resources from those saved and organised in folders

Text

Ongoing techniques from Year 5
Create and/or copy text from sources such as CD-ROMs or the internet (acknowledging sources)
Save text files in a folder and develop later

Graphics

Ongoing techniques from Year 5
Insert pictures from clip art CD-ROMs, digital cameras, scanners, own images created in a graphics program and images from the internet

Sound

Ongoing techniques from Year 5
Insert sounds from CD-ROMs, those produced using Audacity or Sound Recorder and sounds accessed from the internet, e.g. *www.a1freesoundeffects.com*

Video

Insert video clips created using, for example, Digital Blue Digital Movie Creator from TAG Learning

10

Assessing ICT capability

Objectives

- To understand that a good knowledge and understanding of the ICT National Curriculum Programme of Study is crucial when carrying out an assessment of ICT capability
- To understand the key issues to consider when assessing ICT capability
- To be able to evaluate the available guidance relating to assessment

In principle, assessing ICT is not so different from assessing any other National Curriculum subject. The process will be the same in that teachers will plan a lesson or series of lessons, with learning objectives that can be stated as learning outcomes against which to assess a child. Teachers will then use a range of assessment strategies to make judgements about pupils. Those strategies will be the same for ICT. For example, techniques such as questioning, observation, discussion, monitoring work in progress and assessing a finished product will all be used as and when appropriate.

If this is true then why do teachers express more concerns about how to assess ICT than any other subject? The reason is that ICT is the least well-understood subject. Many teachers are uncertain about what the ICT National Curriculum Programmes of Study really mean. It is hardly surprising that if someone does not fully understand the curriculum, they will have concerns about how to assess it. Conversely, once the ICT National Curriculum is understood, the teacher should, in principle, have no difficulty in knowing how to assess progress in ICT capability in general terms.

The previous chapters of this book set out to explicate this subject knowledge. Some further advice relating to assessment is provided in the two sections of this chapter entitled 'Issues to consider when assessing ICT capability' and 'Assessing capability: different strategies for each component'.

There is a lot of guidance to be found on the internet about assessing ICT capability, as can be demonstrated by carrying out a Google search for 'Primary ICT and assessment'. The problem is that the information available seems to be designed to attempt to provide guidance for teachers who do *not* have the relevant subject knowledge, rather than trying to provide them *with* the subject knowledge. Later in this chapter, in the section entitled 'Problems with the guidance available' it will be argued that this approach cannot succeed.

So to summarise: if a teacher understands what constitutes progression in ICT capability, they will not need the guidance. If a teacher does not have this subject knowledge, the guidance available will not help – indeed, it is unlikely that any guidance could really help a teacher without the necessary subject knowledge. If you do not know what you are looking for, the only guidance that really helps is that which provides this prerequisite knowledge and understanding.

There are two sections in the remainder of this chapter. In the first, we present an overview of key issues to consider when assessing ICT capability; in the second, we explain why the guidance available is not really very helpful.

Issues to consider when assessing ICT capability

As will be clear by now, ICT capability is far more than a set of techniques, yet in some cases, techniques are the only things that are assessed. Furthermore, there is sometimes an attempt to assign a National Curriculum level to a particular technique/set of techniques. This does not make sense. There is no mention of techniques in the attainment targets; they are phrased at the level of *processes*, as can be seen, for example, in the attainment target for level 3:

> Pupils use ICT to save information and to find and use appropriate stored information, following straightforward lines of enquiry. They use ICT to generate, develop, organise and present their work. They share and exchange their ideas with others. They use sequences of instructions to control devices and achieve specific outcomes. They make appropriate choices when using ICT-based models or simulations to help them find things out and solve problems. They describe their use of ICT and its use outside school.

McLean (1997) has offered a useful way of thinking about level expectations. Previously he had been asked what level the setting of TABS on a word processor was. In order to drive the point home about how ICT is not just about assessing techniques such as these, he suggested that a level expectation is something about which one can say that 'The nation expects every child to be able to...' without laughing. Compare the two following statements:

> The nation expects every nine-year-old child to know how to set TABS.

> The nation expects every nine-year-old child to know how to develop their writing (cf. the statement from AT level 3, *They use ICT to generate, develop, organise and present their work*.)

> While the former statement is laughable, the latter is laudable.

Assessment purposes

Before we continue, it is best to consider why a teacher should want to assess pupils' ICT capability. There is no statutory responsibility to assign a level to pupils at Key Stages 1 and 2, only at Key Stage 3. There is, however, a reporting requirement and, of course, a need for formative assessment, assessment geared to ensuring that teaching is pitched appropriately.

Given the importance of *Reviewing, modifying and evaluating work as it progresses*, there is also a need for the pupils to reflect on what they have learned. Teachers, therefore, need to keep records that enable them to:

(a) pitch their teaching appropriately (this is formative assessment, or assessment for learning);

(b) pass on appropriate information about the pupils' ICT capability to other teachers; and

(c) report to parents on how their children are progressing.

We need to consider what sort of information is needed for each of these purposes.

(a) Assessment for learning

In relation to the first purpose, it is clearly necessary for teachers to keep a reasonable amount of information of various kinds in order to be able to plan appropriate learning experiences. As ICT capability is composed of *routines, techniques, concepts, processes* and *higher-order skills*, teachers therefore need to assess all these in some way. Neither should we forget that there are four aspects, including *Reviewing, modifying and evaluating work as it progresses*, and also the fifth element, *Breadth of study*.

Because a *process*, as defined by Kennewell *et al.* (2000), subsumes all the other elements, it might be thought that simply making a judgement in terms of what processes a pupil can undertake is all that is needed, i.e. all we need to do is to assign a level. If the aim were solely summative assessment, this might be true (but see the comments below with respect to the second purpose, passing on appropriate information about the pupils' ICT capability to other teachers). However, just knowing a level, or even a description of the pupil's ICT capability in terms of processes, would not really help in designing appropriate learning experiences. For example, a teacher would normally want to keep track of the pupils' knowledge of techniques.

While assessment solely in terms of processes is not sufficient, it is certainly necessary, and one reason for this is that the teacher needs to have some idea of the pupil's position in relation to progression in ICT capability in the primary phase of schooling. As is discussed in more detail in earlier chapters, progression in the different elements takes the form shown in the table below.

The above are key assessment points in the assessment of ICT capability – milestones in the pupil's development of ICT capability – but the information needed at each assessment point differs significantly.

At level 1 it is very easy to make an assessment about a pupil's ability to explore ICT resources. In one sense it is also fairly easy to make an assessment in terms of their purposeful use of ICT (level 2). Usually, pupils will be placed in a setting where purposeful use is required because of the very instructions given by the teacher – for example, the teacher might explain to the class 'that they will be using the techniques they have learnt to produce their own books' (QCA Unit 2A: Writing stories: communicating information using text). Strictly speaking, however, the teacher should assess whether the pupils could, independently, make the choice of using ICT to undertake some purposeful task. In other words, the pupils should be placed in what can be termed an *independent assessment setting*, where pupils are able to

TABLE 10.1 Progression in ICT

	Level 1	Level 2	Level 3	Level 4
Exchanging and sharing information	Exploratory	Purposeful	Developing ideas – reorganising, redrafting	Multimedia authoring with a sense of audience
Making things happen	Exploratory	Purposeful	Developing ideas – creating, testing, improving and refining their instructions	Creating a model of a system, with inputs and outputs
Finding things out	Exploratory	Purposeful	Following a line of enquiry	Evaluating the accuracy and plausibility of information
Developing ideas	Exploratory	Exploratory	Developing ideas (solving problems)	Developing ideas (exploring patterns and relationships)
Reviewing, modifying and evaluating work as it progresses		Review what they have done to help them develop their ideas (describe the effects of their actions, and talk about what they might change in future work)		Review what they and others have done to help them develop their ideas (describe and talk about the effectiveness of their work with ICT, comparing it with other methods and considering the effect it has on others [for example, the impact made by a desktop-published newsletter or poster] and talk about how they could improve future work)
Breadth of study		Work with a range of information to investigate the different ways it can be presented, explore a variety of ICT tools, and talk about the uses of ICT inside and outside school		Work with a range of information to consider its characteristics and purposes, work with others to explore a variety of information sources and ICT tools, and investigate and compare the uses of ICT inside and outside school

make a choice as to whether or not they use ICT, and to choose which features of a particular ICT application to use etc.

The assessment points for levels 3 and 4 are more complex, and it is even more important for the teacher to place the pupils in independent assessment settings, where the pupils can make choices and the teacher can observe their behaviour. This is not always very realistic, as it presupposes that there are a fair number of opportunities for pupils to apply their ICT capability. It is most realistic with tasks relating to *Exchanging and sharing information* with text, and least realistic with such activities relating to *Making things happen*, where opportunities tend only to arise when delivering the QCA units, or similar structured teaching situations.

Following the QCA Scheme of Work also militates against such independent assessment settings, as the very nature and position of the short, focused tasks cue the pupil into what techniques are relevant, as can be seen, for example, by the wording of the integrated task for Unit 2A, namely:

> Explain to the class that *they will be using the techniques they have learnt* to produce their own books. Ask the class to *recall what they have learnt so far* [our italics].

The QCA recognise this in their comments about 'making a judgement' (2003:7):

> In planning for units of work and classroom approaches, you will need to provide opportunities for children to display their achievements in different ways, and to work in a range of situations. As they make progress it will be necessary to provide them with opportunities to engage in open-ended tasks that allow them to apply their ICT capability independently.

This comment at first seems to contradict what is said on the previous page (QCA 2003:6):

> Any assessment of a formal nature is likely to take place towards the end of each unit, where the integrated tasks in this scheme of work provide good opportunities for children to demonstrate their capabilities.

However, the latter comment is meant to emphasise that the short, focused tasks are not the place to attempt to assess ICT capability being, as they are, devoted to the teaching of techniques and key ideas (concepts) which constitute part of what is meant by ICT capability. It is, however, misleading if it is taken to mean that ICT capability can be assessed purely in the integrated task. What the integrated task can do is to:

- provide opportunities to apply the techniques learned;
- provide opportunities for the teacher to note misconceptions, in relation to the pupils' conceptual knowledge;
- provide opportunities for pupils to review what they and others have done to help them develop their ideas, describe and talk about the effectiveness of their work with ICT, comparing it with other methods and considering the effect it has on others, and talk about how they could improve future work (*Reviewing, modifying and evaluating work as it progresses*);

- provide opportunities for pupils to investigate and compare the uses of ICT inside and outside school (*Breadth of study*);
- provide opportunities for the teacher to scaffold the use of higher-order skills;
- provide an opportunity for the teacher to have a *tentative idea* about the pupils' ICT capability – it can only be a tentative idea, as the integrated tasks are not truly independent assessment settings.

The ideal is, therefore, that there would be a number of independent assessment settings, corresponding at least to the three key assessment points at Year 2, Year 4 and Year 6, for all the aspects.

In reality, however, this is perhaps unrealistic. The opportunities for independent assessment settings for control and LOGO are few and far between, as they also are for spreadsheet modelling, graphical modelling and simulations. In other words it is probably unrealistic to expect independent assessment settings for the aspect of *Developing ideas* and *Making things happen*.

Exchanging and sharing information and *Finding things out* can, however, be incorporated into the other curriculum areas, thus creating opportunities for independent assessment settings.

(b) Information for other teachers

In relation to the second purpose, it would not be very helpful for the teacher to simply report that a pupil was functioning at level 3 (say), as this information simply states that level 3 is the 'best fit', and that particular pupil might be functioning above or below that level in relation to one of the aspects. More information would be needed, and more than would be provided even by reference to AT level descriptions. For example, a teacher would need to know more than just that a pupil could *use ICT to generate, develop, organise and present their work;* they would need to know in which media they had experience in doing this. Was it with text as in a word processor, with text and graphics as with a DTP package, with an image manipulation program (and if so with a painting and/or drawing program)? It would also be helpful to know which programs they had used.

(c) Reports to parents

In relation to the third purpose, it would not be very meaningful for the parents if the teacher simply stated that a pupil was functioning at a particular level. Neither would statements in the form of AT level descriptions be very helpful. Again, more information would be needed, as for teachers, but phrased in a way that was most meaningful for the parents, who do not have the same, shared vocabulary as teachers.

The above means that teachers, in practice, do have to keep information about the pupils' ICT capability, in some sense related to the Attainment Target level descriptions, even if they do not actually assign a level to a pupil.

Assessing capability: different strategies for each component

In this book we have acknowledged the usefulness of Kennewell *et al.'s* (2000) definition of capability in helping teachers to understand what they are trying to achieve and to make decisions about the most appropriate teaching and learning strategy. It is equally useful when it comes to thinking about assessment, as each component will require a different assessment strategy.

What do we need to know about pupils and why?

Techniques

We would want to know if a child could perform a technique after having seen a whole-class or small-group demonstration. Initially, they might need some support in the form of a reminder or by using a help sheet. However, if the child continued to need this kind of support, then our assessment would be that they were not making adequate progress and we would need to find out why.

Techniques should be relatively easy to assess, and can be recorded using the type of check-lists that are commonplace when tracking skills. There are numerous coding systems (see examples in Tables 10.2 and 10.3) that can be adopted to identify three different stages of acquisition. For example, I can do X with some help; I can do X without help; I can help some-one else to do X. The use of the phrase 'I can do...' reminds teachers that assessment of techniques can be by self-assessment. Our sample scheme for *Exchanging and sharing information* in Chapter 9 provided example lists of techniques for a particular year group. This could be done for all aspects of the ICT National Curriculum, thereby creating end-of-year targets for each class.

In addition to the summative end of unit/end-of-year assessments, some teachers will assess and record the outcomes for the short, focused tasks, i.e. techniques and key ideas. The types of skills tracks that are used in other subjects could be adopted, along with the recording codes that are often used. For example, being able to do something with help, would be recorded as a/and would become an X when it could be carried out unaided. Colour coding systems are also popular, where red, amber and green can represent the developing ability to do something. Allowing children to record their own achievements using 'I can do...' sheets can be motivating and can encourage them to take some responsibility for their progress.

TABLE 10.2 An ICT skills track

Name	Use the flood fill tool	Select and use the spray tool	Select and use different brush sizes
Jane A.			
Peter W.			

TABLE 10.3 An example of an 'I can do' record sheet

I can...	Name:	
I can use the forward, backward, left and right keys to make the Roamer move	Date:	☺
I can enter a sequence of instructions to control the floor turtle	Date:	☺

Routines

We would want to know, and be able to describe, how techniques were being executed. For example, a child might be hesitant, steady or fluent. This type of assessment information would help teachers to plan opportunities for a child to, say, move from inserting a picture hesitantly to doing it fluently. Teachers could make a judgement based on observation.

Concepts

We would want to know if a child had any misconceptions. Concepts can be assessed by an error analysis technique. Teachers will find out whether children have the concepts by noting mistakes and misconceptions. Children's conceptual understandings can also be assessed by the use of effective questioning and discussion; hence the importance of *Reviewing, modifying and evaluating work as it progresses*.

Processes and higher-order skills

Whether a child can be said to be able to carry out a process can only really be judged by whether they can make decisions. Higher-order skills are assessed by the extent to which scaffolding is necessary. So we would want to know if a child was able to make decisions about, for example:

- which media to combine, and in what way, in order to present some particular information to a specific audience;
- which series of techniques to use in order to follow a line of enquiry to prove or disprove an hypothesis;
- which techniques to use in a graphics program in order to produce a portrait that visually represents feelings.

Using the example of a multimedia presentation, we could say that this type of assessment information would help teachers to ensure that children understood the concept of 'audience' and not just the mechanics of adding text, graphics and sound to a page.

Processes cannot be assessed using a tick-box approach or by making judgements based on a printout, although printouts can be collated and annotated after assessment has taken place as evidence of achievement. What teachers need to judge are the decisions children made in order to create the finished product. However, this poses a couple of problems. The first is related to the use of a QCA Integrated Task for assessment purposes and has been discussed above. The second relates to the issue of planning for assessment.

Planning for the assessment of process, rather than techniques, has time implications. Teachers will need to focus on a group and observe how they plan and carry out a task, intervening when appropriate and asking key questions. The fact that children will probably be working in a group situation for extended ICT work can also pose a problem.

Careful observations will need to be made to establish the contribution and progress of the individual members. Discussion could take place after the group has completed the task, with the teacher asking children to explain the decisions they made and why they made them. This self-evaluation is, of course, part of the learning experience – *reviewing, modifying and evaluating work as it progresses* – and creates a diagnostic teaching experience.

Higher-order skills

As with processes, higher-order skills can only really be assessed if children carry out a task other than a highly structured QCA integrated task. Here again, questioning and discussion about how and why children did something will play a vital role in any assessment decisions.

This key aspect of assessing ICT capability is reflected in the National Curriculum as:

4. **Pupils should be taught to:**

   a) review what they and others have done to help them develop their ideas

   b) describe and talk about the effectiveness of their work with ICT, comparing it with other methods and considering the effect it has on others [for example, the impact made by a desk-top-published newsletter or poster]

   c) talk about how they could improve future work

Other information that could contribute to the assessment of a child's ICT capability would be:

- whether or not they had access to a computer at home. This type of information would help teachers to gauge the impact that home use might be having on capability and the possible need to set more challenging work in school. Also, it would help teachers to ensure that those who are less fortunate do not fall behind because of a lack of regular access to ICT outside of school;

- their attitude to ICT. Are they confident? Do they dominate group activities or are they reticent? Do they persevere or give up easily? This type of information might help when we are considering the make up of groups for an ICT activity or extended piece of work;

- their use of the correct technical vocabulary. This type of information would help teachers to ensure that they are introducing and using the correct technical terms in lessons;

- their level of awareness of the uses of ICT inside and outside of school. This type of information would help teachers to identify the need to plan more opportunities for pupils to reflect on what it means to live and work in a technological society.

Problems with the guidance available

Guidance can be found in three main forms. The revised and updated QCA ICT Teacher's Guide (2003: 6–9) provides some guidance on assessment and ICT, some of which is discussed in the previous section.

1. The QCA ICT Teacher's Guide highlights the National Curriculum in Action website – an on-line portfolio of pupils' work – as a resource to help teachers to understand national expectations in ICT by providing exemplifications.

2. The QCA guidance together with the actual structure of a QCA unit of work has prompted a fairly universal response to recording progress and attainment in ICT. This

response can be seen in the large numbers of assessment proformas produced by LEAs and schools that are readily available from the internet (cf. a Google search for 'Primary ICT and assessment').

The assessment proformas produced by LEAs and schools

Often these proformas collate information taken from the National Curriculum Programme of Study for ICT, relevant QCA units, level descriptors, national expectations for ICT and the key characteristics of progression in ICT capability, and present them in a variety of ways, usually in the form of a grid. Extracts from some of these recording sheets will be presented and discussed below. Having all this relevant assessment information together on one page of A4 paper is, without doubt, useful when it comes to recording achievement. However, in the majority of cases the focus tends to be on recording, and there appears to be a lack of the specific support and detailed guidance that is needed to carry out accurate and consistent assessment in a way that is easy to manage.

End-of-year/key stage assessment record sheets

A number of examples of recording sheets that are designed to record end-of-year or end-of-key-stage assessments can be found on the internet. Two examples are presented and discussed below.

TABLE 10.4 An end-of-key-stage assessment record sheet

Level	*Finding things out*	*Exchanging and sharing information*	*Developing ideas and Making things happen*
1	Pupils explore information from various sources, and know that information exists in different forms.	Pupils use ICT to work with text, images and sound to help them share their ideas. Pupils talk about their use of ICT.	Pupils recognise that many everyday devices respond to signals and instructions. Pupils make choices when using such devices to produce different outcomes.
2	Pupils use ICT to organise and classify information and to present their findings. They enter, save and retrieve work.	Pupils use ICT to help them generate, amend and record their work and share ideas in different forms, including, text, tables, images and sound. Pupils talk about their experiences of ICT both inside and outside school.	Pupils plan and give instructions to make things happen and describe the effects. Pupils use ICT to explore what happens in real or imaginary situations.

Comment

This recording sheet simply reorganises the attainment target level descriptions. It can hardly be classified as 'guidance'.

TABLE 10.5 An end-of year assessment record for a Year 1 pupil

YEAR 1					
1A An introduction to modelling	1B Using a word bank	1C Information around us	1D Labelling and classifying	1E Representing information graphically: pictograms	1F Understanding instructions and making things happen

Level 1

Level 1 is characterised by the use of ICT to **explore options** and **make choices** to **communicate meaning**. Pupils develop **familiarity** with simple ICT tools.

Typically, pupils:

- explore information from various sources, showing they know that it exists in different forms;
- present and share ideas using text, images and sounds – they talk about using ICT;
- recognise that everyday devices respond to signals and make simple choices when using devices.

EXAMPLE: As part of a project about life and living things pupils look at information on wild animals. They use books, magazines, photographs and a CD-ROM. They talk about where different wild animals live. They use an art package to create a jungle scene, choosing appropriate animals and placing them onto a background. They make a class display and talk about the similarities and differences between printouts, photographs and other media.

Comment

The first part of this record sheet simply represents the information in the attainment targets. The example only really helps if the teacher understands progression in ICT capability. If the teacher does not, what sort of use of a CD-ROM is being referred to?

The expected outcomes in the QCA units

The Teacher's Guide encourages teachers to allocate children to one of the three expected outcomes shown on each QCA unit, but more specifically, to note those who made 'more' or 'less' progress than was expected within the QCA unit. Sample assessment proformas show that in some cases there is also an attempt to assign a National Curriculum level to each of the three statements about expected outcomes (QCA 2003:6).

In this scheme of work, the learning outcomes identify what each child is expected to learn within each unit. The expectations described in each unit broadly correspond to levels in the National Curriculum for ICT as follows:

Year 2, level 2

Year 4, level 3

Year 6, level 4

Teachers may wish to make a note of when a child's progress differs markedly from that which is expected within the units. This provides the basis for more focused support. It is also a straightforward method for passing on information about children to the next teacher or school without creating an overly bureaucratic system of record-keeping.

This method of recording assessment is very popular, and is certainly better than simply keeping a checklist of techniques learned.

TABLE 10.6 An example of an 'end of unit', whole-class recording sheet

	Unit 2B: Creating pictures	
Most children will have: used a computer graphics package to create a picture; selected the most appropriate tools to match their purposes. (Level 2)	Some children will not have made so much progress and will have…; used a computer graphics package to create a picture. (Level 1)	Some children will have progressed further and will have… used a computer graphics package to create a picture; selected the most appropriate tools to match their purposes; developed an image and modified and corrected their work as they went along. (Level 3)
Names	Names	Names

Comment

First, how is the judgement made as to whether the pupil has *developed an image and modified and corrected their work as they went along*? To be level 3 it has to go beyond correcting (amending) to revising (reorganising).

Secondly, the classification for level 1 is oversimplified. The difference in the descriptions for levels 1 and 2 is whether or not the pupil has *selected the most appropriate tools to match their purposes*. But a pupil may fail to select the most appropriate tools for one of three reasons:

1. because they are not trying to make choices to match any purposes, i.e. they are not using the program purposefully, but only exploring;
2. they are trying to make choices, but they are not good at making the right choices;
3. they are trying to make choices, but they do not have enough knowledge of the techniques available.

There is a great deal of difference between the first case and the other two. Only in the first case are we likely to want to place the pupil clearly at level 1.

TABLE 10.7 Extract from an end-of-year assessment record for a Year 6 pupil

Name	(Level 3)	(Level 4)	(Level 5)
6A – Multimedia presentation	Use a multimedia authoring package to assemble images, sound and text on a multimedia page	Use a multimedia authoring program to organise, refine and present a set of linked multimedia pages, which incorporated images, sounds and text	Use a multimedia package to organise, refine and present a set of linked multimedia pages, which incorporated images, sound and text; created pages that offered users a variety of options; presented information that matched the needs of the audience
6B – Spreadsheet Modelling	Use a spreadsheet to calculate totals	Explore the effects of changing data in a spreadsheet	Explore the effects of changing data; make predictions and use a spreadsheet to test them

Comments

Concerning the multimedia unit of work:

The expectations are taken from the QCA unit, but are not correctly aligned with the level descriptions:

■ *Use a multimedia authoring package to assemble images, sound and text on a multimedia page* is classified as level 3, but, in fact, is level 2 – simply purposeful use (*They enter, save and retrieve work. They use ICT to help them generate, amend and record their work and share their ideas in different forms, including text, tables, images and sound*).

■ *Use a multimedia authoring program to organise, refine and present a set of linked multimedia pages, which incorporated images, sounds and text* is classified as level 4, but in fact is level 3 (*They use ICT to generate, develop, organise and present their work*).

■ *Use a multimedia package to organise, refine and present a set of linked multimedia pages, which incorporated images, sound and text; created pages that offered users a variety of options; presented information that matched the needs of the audience* is classified as level 5, but in fact is level 4 (*They use ICT to present information in different forms and show they are aware of the intended audience and the need for quality in their presentations*).

This is not a criticism of the QCA scheme, as the QCA did not assign these levels.

Concerning the spreadsheet modelling unit of work

The expectations are taken from the QCA unit, but are not correctly aligned with the level descriptions:

- *Use a spreadsheet to calculate totals* is classified as level 3, but given that this describes a technique should not really be given a level at all. If it had to be given a level it is difficult to see how it could be classed as anything beyond purposeful use (level 2).

- *Explored the effects of changing data in a spreadsheet* is classified as level 4, but is it really anything beyond level 3? *(They make appropriate choices when using ICT-based models or simulations to help them find things out and solve problems)*.

- *Explored the effects of changing data; make predictions and use a spreadsheet to test them* is classified at level 5, but is actually level 4 *(They use ICT-based models and simulations to explore patterns and relationships, and make predictions about the consequences of their decisions)*.

This is not a criticism of the QCA scheme, as the QCA did not assign these levels.

What has been demonstrated with the above examples is that although there is a wide range of assessment documentation easily available via the internet, as with all information it should be evaluated before use.

National Curriculum in Action website

The National Curriculum in Action website uses pupils' work and case study material to show what the National Curriculum in ICT looks like in practice: *http://www.ncaction.org.uk/subjects/ict/judgements.htm*

The examples given show:

- the standard of pupils' work at different ages and key stages;
- how the Programmes of Study translate into real activities; and
- the effective use of ICT across the curriculum.

These examples come from different pupils, schools and contexts.
They include:

- pupils' responses to structured tasks and questions;
- results of open-ended investigations.

For each piece of work there are:

Activity objectives: these set out the purpose, teaching and learning objectives of the work.

Activity descriptions: these provide details of what the pupil actually did. They also describe the context, the level of support provided and the extent to which the activity was structured.

Commentary: this explains why the piece of work:

- shows a pupil's performance in relation to particular aspects of the level description; and/or
- is a good example of the Programme of Study in practice.

The first thing to bear in mind is that one cannot judge the level of performance of a pupil by examining just one example of their work, as the QCA would be the first to point out. They state (QCA 2003: 7):

> End-of-year or end-of-key-stage assessments are made by taking into account strengths and weaknesses in performance across a range of contexts and over a period of time, rather than by focusing on a single piece of work. A single piece of work is unlikely to cover all the expectations set out in a level description. It will probably provide partial evidence of attainment in one or two aspects of a level description. If you look at it alongside other pieces of work covering a range of contexts, you will be able to make a judgement about which level best fits a child's overall performance.

The second thing to bear in mind is that one needs more detailed information than is usually provided in order to make any judgement, and that one needs information about the process as well as the end-product.

In Chapter 4 we described one of the scenarios to illustrate what it means for a pupil to work at level 4 in *Finding things out*.

In general terms we find that the scenarios are more helpful in providing concrete examples of the kinds of activities relating to the aspects than in providing guidance concerning assessment. This is because the commentaries are not unambiguously interpreted by teachers. Hence their usefulness is limited.

Below we examine an example from the National Curriculum in Action site and add comments to demonstrate how judgements are difficult to make without having a detailed level of information.

Web Challenge

Activity Description

The pupils used the web to find information and answer a series of questions set by the teacher. They presented their findings using desktop publishing software.

Working in pairs, the pupils had 70 minutes in an ICT suite to complete the task. They used the search features of a number of different search engines, having identified key words in the 'challenge' questions. They then investigated likely hits to find their answers.

They copied pictures from the web and composed their own text from information found on websites.

Activity Objectives

To use web search engines to answer a range of questions.
To present findings on a single side of A4, combining text and graphics.

Commentary

In this example, James and David have used a search engine to locate information on the web, following straightforward lines of enquiry.

They have combined text and images from a variety of sources, organising information using desktop publishing software. They have copied images from the web and imported them into a page.

James and David have made effective use of ICT techniques to complete *the short, focused task [our italics – see our comments below]* defined by the teacher.

This example illustrates aspects of work at level 3. James and David are able to find information following straightforward lines of enquiry. They use ICT to organise and present their work.

To make further progress, James and David could be given opportunities to investigate information from a variety of sources, checking for plausibility and accuracy. Their findings could be organised for a specific purpose or audience. Opportunities could be provided for them to reflect critically and refine their work.

Subject: ICT

- Year: 6

- Evidence for: level 3

- This work shows evidence of: Developing ideas and making things happen, Finding things out

- NC programme of study: p1a, p2a

- Scheme of work: 6D:Teachers using the internet to search large databases and to interpret information

Comments

It is quite difficult to think about justifying this work in terms of a National Curriculum level because it seems to be just a short, focused task, as is mentioned in their own commentary (see our italics above), and would presumably form part of some wider plan to develop capability. However, we can still make some observations to demonstrate the difficulties of providing work that exemplifies a particular aspect and level, without having more detailed information.

First, one of the reasons for justifying the *Finding things out* work as showing evidence of level 3 seems to be that they 'followed straightforward lines of enquiry'. But this is tautological, as this is precisely the wording of the attainment target (*Level 3: Pupils use ICT to save information and to find and use appropriate stored information, following straightforward lines of enquiry*). This is equivalent to saying that it shows evidence of pupils as functioning at level 3 because they are functioning at level 3.

Without a fuller description of the process used to find the answers to their 'challenge' questions it would seem that the boys did the following:

They were given a set of 'challenge' questions set by the teacher and asked to use the internet to find the answers. They identified key words from within the questions and typed them into a search engine. Information that would provide the answers was located by investigating likely hits resulting from the key word search.

In effect, it would seem that the boys only used a simple search (key words from given questions) to filter out information about such things as Henri Matisse. The characteristic of level 3 is that pupils use ICT to develop their ideas and it is difficult from the task description to decide in what way the children did this. They certainly used ICT purposefully to find the answers to their 'challenge' questions, but there is no evidence of their following a straightforward line of enquiry (level 3), only evidence of searching purposefully (level 2).

Secondly, the justification for the *Developing ideas* work showing evidence of level 3 seems to be that they organised text and images using a desktop publisher so that the findings could be presented on a single side of A4.

The boys have demonstrated some technical ability in that they would probably have had to re-size the pictures they copied from the web to make them fit onto the page. However, organising text and images so that they fit onto a single side of A4 can be done at a superficial level or at a rather more thoughtful level. If the attitude was simply to 'get it to fit' (e.g. by making the picture smaller, or by deleting a sentence somewhat at random) one would be reluctant to credit them with developing their ideas, and only really credit them with purposeful use of ICT. If, however, they had given the matter serious consideration, before deciding to revise their writing to make it more succinct, leaving out minor details, or deciding that the communication would be just as effective if the picture was smaller, then this would constitute 'developing their ideas', and hence be evidence of working at level 3.

This highlights the importance of having enough information about the process at which the pupils arrived at the end-product, which the National Curriculum in Action site does not usually provide. The end-result is that the reader is left to puzzle out what the guidance is meant to illustrate, which rather defeats the object of this as guidance.

Other on-line portfolios

The following sites also have examples of pupils' ICT work presented in the form of an electronic portfolio:

Northern Grid (*http://www.northerngrid.org/ngflwebsite/ict.htm*)

ICT assessment has often relied heavily on teachers' intuition. Not confident in their own ICT abilities, many teachers have been even less confident in assessing pupils' ICT work. As a result, there have been large discrepancies in levelling of ICT work in both primary and secondary schools. This project aims to provide guidance and practical solutions in the area of ICT Assessment.

Oxfordshire LEA – Sharing good practice (*http://www.ict.oxon-lea.gov.uk/*)

http://www.west-borough.kent.sch.uk/ictportfolio.htm

http://www.kented.org.uk/ngfl/assessment/

http://www.ict.oxon-lea.gov.uk/portfolio/portfolio_main.html

Surrey LEA

http://www.fours.co.uk/default.asp?V_DOC_ID=3873

The following Becta site has guidance about how to carry out a teacher assessment of primary ICT: *http://www.ictadvice.org.uk*

Activity

To what extent do the on-line portfolios assist when assessing pupils' ICT work? On each site, find an example of the outcome of a particular QCA unit of work and compare the judgements made about a child's attainment.

Reflect on the assessment records that have been discussed in this chapter. Which method of recording would you prefer and why?

References

Atherton, T. (2002) 'Developing ideas with multimedia in the primary classroom', in Loveless, A. and Dore, B. (eds) *ICT in the Primary School*. Buckingham: Open University Press, pp. 125–45.

Bazalgette, C. (1989) *Primary Media Education: A Curriculum Statement*. London: BFI.

Bazalgette, C. (1990) 'New developments in media education', in Potter, F. (ed.) *Reading, Learning and Media Education*. Oxford: Basil Blackwell.

DfEE (1999) *National Numeracy Strategy*. Sudbury: DfEE.

Finlayson, H. and Cook, D. (1998) 'The value of passive software in young children's collaborative work', in Monteith, M. (ed.) *IT for Learning Enhancement*. Exeter: Intellect.

Fitts, P.M. and Posner, M.J. (1967) *Human Performance*. Belmont, CA: Brooks/Cole.

Frankland, J., Wiggins, C., Belson, D. and Aynsley, C. (2003) *Internet Proficiency Scheme for Key Stage 2 Pupils: Teachers' Pack*. Annesley: DfES.

Gagné, R.M. (1975) *Essentials of Learning for Instruction*. New York: Holt, Rinehart & Winston.

Gagné, R.M. and Briggs, L.J. (1974) *Principles of Instructional Design*. New York: Holt, Rinehart & Winston.

Gagné, R.M. , Briggs, L.J. and Wager, W.W. (1992) *Principles of Instructional Design* (4th edn). Belmont: Wadsworth/Thomson Learning.

Gifford, C. (ed.) (1995) *Making Sense of Information*. Coventry: NCET.

Jones, A. and Mercer, N. (1993) 'Theories of learning and information technology', in Scrimshaw, P. (ed.) *Language, Classrooms and Computers*. London: Routledge.

Kennewell, S., Parkinson, J. and Tanner, H. (2000) *Developing the ICT Capable School*. London: Routledge.

Lachs, V. (2000) *Making Multimedia in the Classroom: A Teachers' Guide*. London: Routledge.

Lodge, J. (1992) 'Information skills, databases and primary project work', in Lodge, J. (ed.) *Computer Data Handling in the Primary School*. London: David Fulton Publishers.

Loveless, A. (1997) 'Working with images, developing ideas', in McFarlane, A. (ed.) *Information Technology and Authentic Learning*. London: Routledge.

Maybin, J., Mercer, N. and Stierer, B. (1992) 'Scaffolding in the classroom', in K. Norman (ed.) *Thinking Voices: The Work of the National Oracy Project*. London: Hodder & Stoughton, pp. 165–95.

Miller, G. A. (1956) 'The magical number seven, plus or minus two: some limits on our capacity for processing information'. *Psychological Review*, **63**, 81–92.

Papert, S. (1980) *Mindstorms: Children, Computers, and Powerful Ideas*. Brighton: Harvester Press.

Postman, N. (1983) *The Disappearance of Childhood*. New York: Delacorte Press.

QCA (1998) *Information Technology: A Scheme of Work for Key Stages 1 and 2*. London: Qualifications and Curriculum Authority.

QCA (2003) *Information and Communication Technology (ICT): Teacher's Guide*. London: QCA, pp. 8–9.

Ross, A. (1989) 'Fossils, conkers, and parachutes: children's data from scientific experiments'. *Primary Teaching Studies*, **4**, (2), 106–30. See also: Ross, A. *Promoting Scientific Thinking with Information Handling Programs* (http://www.mape.org.uk/curriculum/science/science1.htm)

Salomon, G. and Globerson, T. (1987) 'Skill may not be enough: the role of the mindfulness in learning and transfer'. *International Journal of Educational Research*, **11** (6): 623–37.

SCAA (1996) *Information Technology Exemplification of Standards: Consistency in Teacher Assessment*: Key Stage 3. Hayes: School Curriculum and Assessment Authority.

SCAA (1997) *Expectations in Information Technology at Key Stages 1 and 2*. Hayes: School Curriculum and Assessment Authority.

Smith, H. (1997) 'Do electronic databases enable children to engage in information processing?' in Somekh, B. and Davis, N. (eds) *Using Information Technology Effectively in Teaching and Learning*. London: Routledge.

Smith, H. (1999) *Opportunities for Information and Communication Technology in the Primary School*. Stoke-on-Trent: Trentham Books.

Spavold (1989) 'Children and databases: an analysis of data entry and query formulation'. *Journal of Computer Assisted Learning*, **5**, 145–60.

Thompson, B. and Mackay, D. (1979) *Breakthrough to Literacy: Teacher's Manual*. Harlow: Longman for School Council.

Underwood, J. and Underwood, G. (1990) *Computers and Learning: Helping Children Acquire Thinking Skills*. Oxford: Blackwells.

Vygotsky, L. (1978) *Mind in Society*. Cambridge, MA: Harvard University Press.

Weizenbaum, J. (1984) *Computer Power and Human Reason*. Harmondsworth: Penguin.

Wood, C. and Webb, A. (2002) 'A new model for teaching ICT'. *Teaching ICT*, **1**, (3), 2–20.

Wood, J. (2003) *A Report on the Use of Information and Communications Technology (ICT) in Art and Design*. Coventry: Becta.

Websites

Cadbury Learning Zone: www.cadburylearningzone.co.uk/

Clairol: www.clairol.co.uk/

Dulux : www.dulux.co.uk/

National Curriculum in Action: http://www.ncaction.org.uk/

The Big Bus www.thebigbus.com

Treacletart.net http://www.treacletart.net/

ICT resources

Audacity (http://audacity.sourceforge.net/)

Black Cat Designer. Granada Learning (http://www.granada-learning.com)

Clicker4. Crick Software (http://www.cricksoft.com/)

Digital Blue Digital Movie Creator. TAG Learning (http://www.taglearning.com/index.php)

Ecolog. Data Harvest Group Ltd (http://www.data-harvest.co.uk/index.html)

Flowol2. Data Harvest Group Ltd (http://www.data-harvest.co.uk/index.html)

Freddy Teddy's Adventures. Topologika Software Ltd (http://www.topologika.co.uk)

Granada Writer. Granada Learning (http://www.granada-learning.com)

Information Workshop. Granada Learning (http://www.granada-learning.com)

MSWLogo. (http://www.softronix.com)

My World (Dress Teddy, Find Ted) Dial Solutions (http://www.dialsolutions.com/welcome.html)

RM Colour Magic RM PLC (http://www.rm.com/)

Roamer Valiant Technology Ltd (http://www.valiant-technology.com/)

SPEX+ AspexSoftware. (http://www.aspexsoftware.com/spex.htm)

SuperLogo. Logotron (http://www.logo.com/)

Textease. Softease Ltd (http://www.softease.com/)

The Model Shop. Sherston Publishing Group (http://www.sherston.com/)

WriteAway. Granada Learning (http://www.granada-learning.com)

Index

Numbers, Words and Pictures 2

Age 5-8

BlackCat

Building on the success of the original *Numbers, Words and Pictures*, this new release has been designed to give a better and brighter introduction to ICT in the early years. This fully integrated suite of tools can be run from a simple menu, exchange data between programs and configured to suit the needs of individual pupils. *Numbers, Words and Pictures 2* is the perfect introductory toolkit to ICT for Key Stage 1 and Early Years and brings together data-handling, graphs, painting, turtle graphics and word processing tools in a package that will save you time and money.

Curriculum Match
QCA Quick Guide: 1B, 1C, 1D, 1E, 1F, 2A, 2B, 2E, 3A, 3C, 4B
Key Stage 1 & Lower Key Stage 2, Levels A-B of the Scottish 5-14 Curriculum

ORDER FORM

			Qty	Value
Single User	1844410994/B0009	£89	.....	....
3 User Pack	1406005908/B0009	£139	.....	....
5 User Pack	1406005916/B0009	£179	.....	....
10 User Pack	1406005924/B0009	£269	.....	....
20 Licences Only	1406005932/B0009	£359	.....	....
Site Pack	1844411753/B0009	£449	.....	....
5 Licences Only	1406005940/B0009	£100	.....	....

Subtotal ....
P & P ....
VAT (17.5%)* ....
TOTAL ....

P & P

P & P charges will be added to your invoice at the following rates + VAT. The rates below are for UK delivery. If you have any questions about International postage rates please call us on

0845 602 1937.

£1.00 minimum charge for licences
£3.50 for orders under the value of £100
£7.00 for orders over the value of £100

To see our full terms and conditions of sale log-on to:
www.granada-learning.com/ts&cs

Please complete delivery details:

NAME: ....
ADDRESS:..
....
....
POSTCODE: ....
TEL: ....
FAX: ....
EMAIL:..

How to order:

☐ If you wish to be contacted via email please opt in by ticking this box

SEND TO: **Granada Learning Orders**
Granada Learning Distribution Services
FREEPOST LON 16517
Swindon SN2 8BR

BY FAX: **0845 601 5358**
BY PHONE: **0845 602 1937**

☐ Please invoice me. My purchase order reference is ....

☐ I enclose a cheque payable to Granada Learning Limited (include postage and packing)

☐ Please charge to my credit card (we accept all major credit cards including switch).

Credit Card No: ☐☐☐☐ ☐☐☐☐ ☐☐☐☐ ☐☐☐☐ ☐☐☐☐

Issue number (Switch only): ☐☐ **Exp. Date:** ☐☐

*VAT is applicable for software

SuperTools

Age 5-11

BlackCat

SuperTools is the complete primary toolbox. It includes updated versions of old favourites, such as *Information Workshop 2000*, and innovative products like *Fresco*. *SuperTools* has been designed to bring together a complete set of tools that cover all the key areas of ICT in the classroom. Pupils can use this package to create presentations, web pages and artwork whilst gaining their first experience of using a word-processor and spreadsheets.

All of the programs within *SuperTools* are suitable for a range of ages through the use of four built-in levels. New levels can be created by the teacher, to suit individuals or groups of pupils.

Curriculum Match
QCA Quick Guide: 1B, 1C, 1F, 2A, 2B, 2D, 2E, 3A, 3C, 4A-4E, 5B-5D, 6A, 6B
Key Stage 1-2, Levels A-C of the Scottish 5-14 Curriculum

ORDER FORM

English Version			Qty	Value
Single User	1842359649/B0009	£199	.....	....
5 User Pack	1406006033/B0009	£425	.....	....
10 User Pack	1406006041/B0009	£625	.....	....
20 User Pack	140600605X/B0009	£899	.....	....
5 Licences Only	1406006068/B0009	£250	.....	....
Welsh Version				
Single Version	1842356623/B0009	£199	.....	....
5 User Pack	1406007730/B0009	£425	.....	....
10 User Pack	1406007749/B0009	£625	.....	....
20 User Pack	1406007757/B0009	£899	.....	....
5 Licences Only	1406007765/B0009	£250	.....	....

Subtotal ....
P & P ....
VAT (17.5%)* ....
TOTAL ....

P & P

P & P charges will be added to your invoice at the following rates + VAT. The rates below are for UK delivery. If you have any questions about International postage rates please call us on

0845 602 1937

£1.00 minimum charge for licences
£3.50 for orders under the value of £100
£7.00 for orders over the value of £100

To see our full terms and conditions of sale log-on to:
www.granada-learning.com/ts&cs

Please complete delivery details:

NAME: ....
ADDRESS:..
....
....
POSTCODE: ....
TEL: ....
FAX: ....
EMAIL:...

How to order:

☐ If you wish to be contacted via email please opt in by ticking this box

SEND TO: **Granada Learning Orders**
Granada Learning Distribution Services
FREEPOST LON 16517
Swindon SN2 8BR

BY FAX: **0845 601 5358**

BY PHONE: **0845 602 1937**

☐ Please invoice me. My purchase order reference is ....

☐ I enclose a cheque payable to Granada Learning Limited (include postage and packing)

☐ Please charge to my credit card (we accept all major credit cards including switch).

Credit Card No: ☐☐☐☐ ☐☐☐☐ ☐☐☐☐ ☐☐☐☐

Issue number (Switch only): ☐☐   Exp. Date: ☐☐   *VAT is applicable for software